Kardelen has become a special ministry p nanted to reach Turkey with the love of C ... ave an aligned heart for those with special needs and disabilities. It is a perfect fit for our church to be on there on the ground with this ministry of Christ to the least of these.

--Pastor Bruce
First Baptist Church of Geneva

This compassion-based ministry has touched hundreds with the tangible love of Christ here in a primarily Muslim nation through their practical works of help. I am proud of this ministry, and have seen first-hand how their heart of service, years of experience, and passion for things which break the Lord's heart, are worthy of support.

--Pastor John
Salvation Church-Ankara, Turkey
Member of the Foursquare International Fellowship: Middle East, North Africa, and Central Asia

Kardelen Mercy Teams

Whether you were born into a wealthy family in Istanbul or an impoverished one in Delhi, it makes little difference if you were born with special needs. Chances are that both you and your family will be stigmatized and rejected. In Turkey, if your family has connections, they might abandon you to a state-run orphanage where you will die a slow death from neglect. If you are poor then you will likely be doomed to living tied-up in your bed in the back room of a brick and mortar slum dwelling. The appalling lack of care, hygiene and medical attention will mean an early death.

For a few children in 1998, this glum reality began to change when God called Kardelen Mercy Teams to work in an orphanage in Ankara. Kardelen worked to change cultural attitudes toward persons with disabilities, and increase societal help to meet the needs of those with disabilities. Their work continues to reveal Christ by empowering people and families struggling with disabilities.

Mental and/or physical disability affects nearly 17 percent of the 73 million people living in Turkey. Kardelen passionately works to seek out and reach families and individuals affected by special needs: one child at a time.

We are always finding new ways to assist in the physical, emotional and spiritual care and support of the disabled. This includes training family members, institutional staff and volunteers, improving nutrition, and offering physical therapy and respectful treatment for disabled persons. We also focus on strengthening and equipping families with disabled children to provide some or all of the essential care for their children.

Kardelen also serves as an advocacy group: promoting the belief that all people, regardless of race, religion, gender, gifting or circumstances are made in the image of God. And as such, are precious in the sight of God and the worthy of His love.

Mission Statement

Kardelen Mercy Teams is the Turkey-based outreach of the Friends of Kardelen Foundation, a 501(c)(3) U.S. charity incorporated to support the care of the disabled and their families in Turkey.

Friends of Kardelen Foundation 501(c)3
4215 Tierra Rejada Road #191
Moorpark, California 93021 U.S.A.

www.KardelenMercyTeams.com
thesnowdrop.wordpress.com

cry out

Norita Erickson

CRY OUT

by Norita Erickson

Friends of Kardelen Foundation 501(c)3
4215 Tierra Rejada Road #191
Moorpark, California 93021 U.S.A.

www.KardelenMercyTeams.com
thesnowdrop.wordpress.com

Designer: Anneli Anderson, www.DesignAnneli.com

This book is available for purchase at www.amazon.com

This book is dedicated to Ken who, for over the 45 years that we've known each other, has been the one who believed that the Creator of the universe was at work in us to change the world we live in.

You have been my coach, my champion, my teammate, my inspiration.

Thank you.

CONTENTS

FORWARD

The digital clock above the bus driver reads 4:30 a.m. A cobalt sky turns aqua as we travel up the steep highway on our way to the newly-built international airport. We still have another ten miles to go when familiar landmarks cause my heart to beat faster.

The broken-down signboard advertising "Husain's Quality Meat and Barbeque" flies past just as I catch a glimpse of the sparkling new stone minaret and mosque next to the gas station and mini-market. Green neon lights encircle the parapet where decades ago the muezzin would call the faithful to prayer. I can just make out the loud speakers from which the recorded wake-up call had sounded not fifteen minutes previous. Street lamps continue to light the way, one illuminating the yellow and black sign announcing the presence of The Castle (Saray): Rehabilitation and Care Center.

I sit up and peer in the dim light; for a couple of seconds I can just make out the walls and guard room, the gate and parking lot where three buses are parked and some unfamiliar buildings beyond. The next moment we enter an underpass only to emerge about fifty yards past the campus. If you hadn't known it was there and what it was you'd never have known that you drove past an institution housing nearly 800 children and young adults with disabilities.

I sit back and let a tear fall before praying, as I always do, when passing those closed gates. Memories flood my mind—twelve years of relationship. How much has changed? What has changed? What has happened to the older ones I knew and loved? In danger of breaking into sobs, I quickly finger my passport and ticket and try to focus on the upcoming trip to Los Angeles, my hometown. There I will speak about God's passion for those who, because of their physical or mental disabilities, have become the *forgotten abused.* There I will give testimony to His wonderful and powerful plan for redemption and rescue.

Ken and I left the States in 1979 with a sense that the LORD was calling us to share the Gospel of Jesus Christ, the love of God, with people who would not likely be in a place to hear or learn about it.

After leading a language and culture acquisition experimental project in Paris, we moved to The Netherlands for seven years, where we lived among and made friendships with people from Iran, Morocco, Afghanistan, India and Turkey. Our journey of faith finally brought us to move to Ankara, the capital of Turkey in 1987.

With our two small children we lived as ex-pats in this city that has grown from 4.5 million when we arrived to more than 6 million inhabitants. Ken began his career teaching English at a local university in Ankara while I stayed very busy in the local Turkish church. I taught an inter-denominational women's Bible study for more than twelve years. My greatest joy was serving as a volunteer translator and project researcher for a local charity.

We raised money to purchase needed items for schools or hospitals. Since most of the members came from the diplomatic or international business community who were only in town for a few years, they were grateful to have someone like me on board. My previous years of speaking the language while working as a social worker and deacon in Amsterdam served us well.

Within a short time, however, I had to face the fact that modern Turkey, while officially resisting being called "Third World," was rife with social inequities and poverty. This became heartbreakingly obvious to those of us on the committee whenever we walked through the doors of a state-sponsored school or hospital. In comparison to the privately owned institutions, these places were overflowing with desperately poor people trying to get some semblance of health care or a chance at an education.

Our committee received countless requests for books, wall paint, desks, blackboards and chalk, uniforms, school supplies, or basic sports equipment from schools both within and outside the city. Hospitals made requests for blood analyzers, incubators, nebulizers, and X-ray processors, as well as pajamas, hospital gowns, and sheets. Many times, I found myself comparing the places we visited to the ghettos of East Los Angeles, where I had taught English in the public schools twelve years before. Materially speaking, those inner-city schools and hospitals were so much better and well supplied. I enjoyed the job immensely. We visited every requesting institution in order to see for ourselves what was necessary and what we could reasonably donate. Gala balls, fashion shows, and other smaller fundraising activities meant that we usually raised just under $25,000 a year. Over the eighteen years I belonged to this group, I learned how to scour the backstreets of the city in order to find items from local medical suppliers, how to bargain, and how to determine whether some things could only be found overseas.

In 1995 I was asked to arrange a visit to a state-run institution outside the city gates.

Saray (Turkish for "Palace" or "Castle"), is a very big institution built on the road heading to the airport. We hoped that we could contribute in some small way to the well-being of the children housed there. But the people in charge at Saray were not helpful. Twice they left us standing and waiting after failing to send the promised transportation to pick us up and bring us to the institution.

This was my first experience with administrators and politicians. It turned out that the political party, to which the director belonged at the time, did not want to have any "charity" from foreigners so we were "blown off." With that new information on the table, we set any potential Saray project on the shelf.

Two years later, though, for some strange reason I couldn't get Saray out of my mind. And a new chapter of ministry opened. But even after more than eighteen years of ministry in different countries, cultures and forms, I never could have imagined that our shepherd, Jesus, would lead us into in a battleground of compassion and justice for which we were totally untrained.

What you are about to read comes from my experiences and those I have worked with from 1998 to the present in 2013. At times, I have changed the names of people or places to protect those involved, but the account and events are true—no matter how disturbing and unfathomable they may sometimes seem to our modern, "civilized" minds. I have chosen to arrange them in a fashion that I believe best represents the overall story I am telling, so the material is not always presented in chronological order. Additionally, I sometimes narrate portions as an author looking back (mostly in the beginning), but for the most part I offer you snippets of notes and journal entries. In writing this I referred often to the descriptions of events that I've recorded over the years but I also interviewed many of those who served alongside me. I tried to translate their narratives as best I could, fully aware that much inevitably gets lost in translation. My apologies to these wonderful people who deserve to have their stories heard, who are the heroines and heroes living unappreciated and sometimes reviled for their activism.

More than anything, I hope your heart beats with our Kardelen hearts as you read about those whom the world has too often forgotten or neglected and abused, but whom Father God loves as His own sons and daughters—those precious ones who need someone to cry out to the Lord on their behalf.

CHAPTER 1

Day and Night, Night and Day

The Spirit of the Sovereign Lord is on me, because the Lord has anointed me to proclaim good news to the poor.... To bestow on them a crown of beauty instead of ashes, the oil of joy instead of mourning, a garment of praise instead of a spirit of despair. They will be called oaks of righteousness, a planting of the Lord, for the display of his splendor.

Isaiah 61:1, 3

/////

"Norita, I want you to meet Jane." Harriet, my Dutch friend, came up to me after church on Sunday in February 1998. Actually I already knew Jane, having met her the fall before at a women's conference in a city on the south coast. This twenty-four year old English teacher hailed from the U.K. but was living at the time in the beautiful Aegean Sea city of Izmir, about an hour's drive away from the famous and fascinating open-air archeological museum of Ephesus. Making the nine-hour bus trip, Jane had come to Ankara for a purpose. She and Harriet had gone out to a state-run orphanage the day before so that Jane could visit a child. Imagine my surprise when I heard that they'd visited Saray.

Besides teaching in Izmir, Jane had volunteered as a "Visitor Auntie" at the local orphanage there. While there she had befriended a four-year-old boy who was profoundly sight-impaired, Ali-John. They became special friends and she would go to the residential facility once a week to see him. He would grow excited and giggle when he heard her voice calling him, and their few hours together were his lifeline to joy.

One day when she went to visit, she was told that he had been transferred to Ankara. Devastated by the loss of her little friend, she had asked the powers-that-be if she could see him again and they apparently saw no problem in it. Concerned for his welfare, Jane phoned Harriet that she was coming to make a visit to the Saray Orphanage and Rehabilitation Centre. They decided to go out and visit the place together.

They found Ali-John living in a group-housing situation that obviously frightened him. Upon seeing him, Jane and Harriet knew he was not being cared for. He'd cried out in recognition when Jane had first called out to him. He clung to her with all his strength before being pulled off her by the staff and shuttled back into the room he shared with twenty other boys who appeared to be much older than him. Upset, Harriet and Jane walked out of the institution's front gates, collapsed in tears against the brick wall across the street, and began doing the only thing they knew to do at that moment: pray aloud and cry out to God, "Lord, have mercy. Help. Don't let these children suffer anymore! You are the Father of the fatherless. Show Your power and save Your children here."

////

I had to get out there and see for myself. So I decided to bring it up at the committee meeting: "I'll just take the bus out to the neighboring village tomorrow and walk in," I said. "What can they do to me? I'll check it out and write a proposal for the committee. Surely there must be some things they could use."

The next day, after nearly two hours traveling on local transportation, I was let off at the front gate. A chill wind was blowing in from the north. The sky was overcast. Not a soul in sight.

Saray had been built on acreage eleven miles from the city center and, for all intents and purposes, was far away from the bustle of Ankara. Large concrete-gray and faded-green two-story structures dotted the barren winter landscape. A set of broken swings and a rusted slide stood on a weedy hill near the front gate, just behind what turned out to be an unmanned guard's room. A few cars and an old blue bus sat parked in the gravel lot that separated the gate from the outdoor steps. These fronted two of the largest buildings in sight. Looking out over the cars, seeming to keep vigilant watch, was the ubiquitous gold-painted bust of Mustafa Kemal Ataturk—the charismatic and prolific founder of the modern republic of Turkey.

I walked into what I hoped would be the administrative offices. Dimly lit by blue-white fluorescent lights, the concrete floors and white-washed plastered walls resonated with the sound of my footsteps. A crudely drawn arrow pointed me in the direction of what I hoped was the main office. Above the arrow, a poster warned: "In the event of a nuclear attack …"

Stomping heavily out of one door, a stoop-shouldered teenage boy carrying a tray of empty tea glasses nearly collided with me. He jumped back, and keeping his eyes averted, he tried to scoot past me. I tried to look into the room he'd just exited.

"Excuse me," I said to the boy. "Could you tell me where the director's office is?"

He jumped back again, clearly spooked, and with lowered eyes, he gestured with his chin and nodded dumbly. Without ever making eye contact, he turned his head and pointed with his elbow to the door at the end of the corridor.

I walked into a tiny front office and took a seat to wait for the secretary to finish speaking on the phone before asking if it would be possible to see the person in charge. I explained that I had come from a charitable-giving organization that was interested in helping out. She immediately grew flustered: "Ummm, great, this is very unusual. I will have to see if our director has any time." Then she picked up the receiver again to phone her boss, who sat five feet away behind a closed wooden door.

After a few moments, she motioned for me to go through the door behind her. I soon found myself in a typical Turkish director's ostentatiously decorated and spacious room. Behind his "banker's chic" leather chair and finely polished mahogany desk sat the portrait of Mustafa Kemal Ataturk. Next to two black leather-upholstered armchairs, a large aquarium hosted several yellow, orange, black, and turquoise tropical fish, adding some color to the room. I tried to ignore the only really irritating feature in this room: the coils of neon lighting. (They are everywhere in Turkey, particularly in institutions like schools or hospitals—and I hate them.)

I introduced myself and came right to the point: "Will you please give me a tour of Saray?" As I had countless times in the past at schools and hospitals, I went on to explain, "We want to help out with clothes or toys or whatever might be possible for us to do. We're not a big group, but we're dedicated volunteers."

Expecting to be stonewalled, I was overjoyed when he responded, "Why, of course. I'd be happy to do that. I've only been here as director for a few months now, but we welcome any help." He said that since his political party garnered so many seats in the newly formed coalition government, more socially savvy people had been put in administrative places. Clearly he intended to give me a "political science in Turkey" lesson. I tried to understand but, in the end, found it all too complicated and so different from our two-party American system.

The Saray facility was spread out over several acres. After putting on our coats, he directed me outside. There, he pointed out staff housing, an administrative and classroom structure, several dormitory buildings, a small clinic, and, two hundred yards up a gravel pathway, a large three-story building. To the left of the front gate stood a separate two-story structure: "This is where they run a six-week training course for blind people," he said. "They learn how to get around with a white stick, work at a telephone call center, and other useful activities."

According to his spiel, this place was only ten years old, but I could already see that Saray was in a state of disintegration. Peeling paint, cracked walkways, and broken windows caught my eye while I tried to keep my footing on rock-strewn paths.

On a hill between two of the buildings, several cement igloo-like structures stood empty. When I asked about them, he replied, "The original plan for the orphanage called for a children's petting zoo. *Insha'Allah* [God willing], this will happen one day."

We walked on, and he continued: "There are about 400 children and young people living at Saray. Nearly all of them have some sort of handicap. Some are mentally disabled, some physically. We also have two dormitories with normal children who go to school in the neighboring town. Saray is the largest facility in the nation. Our former prime minister, Turgut Özal, had this built. He wanted our country to become modernized and to have modern social work."

He went on speeding through his infomercial. But I slowed down to take in what I had just heard. Never having had a formal education in social work, I was in no position to make any sort of judgment about Saray at this point. I just had to wonder about all the rubble we were walking through.

The director waited for me to catch up with him as we walked briskly across the campus and through the windowless double-entry doors of the largest building.

Even as I walked, my mind raced, not really paying attention to the director's words. I needed some time to adjust my expectations. In spite of all our charity committee visits, I had never before visited any institution in Turkey, let alone the USA or The Netherlands, where most of the residents were so disabled that they were dependent on others for survival.

I thought of how Ken's mom had been born with a hip malformation. This was before the days when pediatric specialists knew that the hip and pelvic bones could be "trained" to form into natural joints. Her caring parents had been forced to put her in a body cast for the first twenty months of her life. Even so, she suffered all her life from a pronounced limp and then later painful foot deformities. I couldn't say, however, that I had any real concept of what life was like for her on a day-to-day basis. She was an independent, creative, and cheerful woman who tended to her garden and second husband in the suburbs of Southern California.

Then I thought of Dr. Tom Brewster, a fantastic professor whom Ken had enjoyed during seminary. Dr. Brewster was a dedicated Christian and an inspiring educator and traveler despite his condition: quadriplegic paralysis due to a diving accident as a teenager. Taking an electric wheelchair and lots of spare batteries, he and his amazing linguist wife, Betty Sue, had traveled the world over. Their practical "how to learn languages" curriculum, and their theories on linguistic and cultural adaptation and bonding, had inspired us both. From them, we learned how to take the role of learner (as opposed to "student") when coming into a new culture and linguistic setting. We learned that to learn a new language, one has to learn more than new vocabulary, but more importantly, learn the deeper meanings within the culture of what those words and phrases signify. Drs. Tom and Betty Sue not only taught us, but also modeled this for us. "Can't do this" was not in their vocabularies. "When God directs, all things are possible," they said, reminding their students of the apostle Paul's injunction in the book of

Philippians: "I can do all things through Christ who strengthens me" (see Philippians 4:13).

From there, I considered how Ken had left his university job four years before and begun manufacturing affordable wheelchairs for people with lower incomes. This, looking back, was a natural move for him. He'd had a growing dissatisfaction in his heart regarding his work as a teacher of English as a second language. He wanted to come into contact with the poor and needy. His opportunity came after seeing horrible suffering up close.

In 1991, Saddam Hussein started bombing Iraqi Kurdish towns, using deadly chemicals. Fleeing from annihilation, hundreds of thousands of Kurds ran with literally nothing but the shirts on their backs into the wilderness mountains of eastern Turkey. There, they fought to stay alive, but hundreds of men, women, and children died from disease, malnutrition, and exposure.

Five years after our move to Turkey, during one spring break, Ken found himself on the border, interpreting for relief organizations from The Netherlands, USA, and France. He told me stories of standing on a hillside and looking out on thousands and thousands of plastic makeshift tents and hearing the mourning chorus of those who were burying their dead babies under the rocks at the foot of the hill.

He came home changed. Because of his time on the border, he decided to leave teaching for a spell and begin a business that had socially redemptive ends. A physical therapist friend from Istanbul suggested that he manufacture wheelchairs. Evidently a huge need existed, not only in Turkey but the world over (the World Health Organization had recently posted the numbers of those around the world who are in need of a wheelchair and who have no access to one). This friend put Ken in touch with some disabled engineers who had developed a wheelchair model that needed to be replicated. This model was incredibly sturdy, as well as a fairly low-priced chair. Ken set up shop to manufacture them the following year—and KIFAS Ortopedik was born in 1992.

Ken was serving the disabled community every day, but I'd personally had little contact and really had no clue about what disabled people experienced or thought. I hadn't been in such a place to begin "learning their languages." And there I was in the midst of Saray with the director talking a mile a minute about how good the residents had it there.

"Wow," I said to the director and then figured a question might transition into something worthwhile: "How can it be that there are so many disabled orphans here?"

"Oh no," he was quick to reply. "The majority of these children are not really orphaned. They've been abandoned or left by someone in the care of Social Services. You know, children left in the garden of the local mosque or police station. Then these kids are brought here. We have a big, difficult job here. Did you know that there is even a waiting list of three thousand? Families are waiting to send their children here."

I stored this strange bit of information away as we entered C Block. We walked down a cold, gray corridor—deserted—and then up a flight of stairs to large metal double doors. After the director knocked sharply, someone from inside unlocked the door and let us in. We entered a beautifully decorated and warm gym room, and I was struck by the furnishings: all types of therapy equipment in bright blues, greens, yellows, and reds. Everything looked new, shiny, and ready to serve hundreds of children.

The large room, though, was completely silent, with no children or therapists to be seen. We had walked in unannounced, so after a few moments, the staff—all dressed in standard white medical uniforms—rushed out of the offices. I took a peek into those rooms and noted cigarettes still smoldering, half-empty tea glasses, and a daily newspaper, probably the popular , spread out on one of those large director's desks. The therapists stood stone-faced and at attention in front of the director and myself.

"Where are the kids?' I asked politely.

No one answered immediately but looked at the director as if he should answer. I realized that I hadn't introduced myself and did so. Again, no one spoke. In another attempt to generate some sort of dialogue, I continued: "What a lovely place this is."

"Oh, it's lunch break," said the person I supposed to be the head therapist. "They'll be here after lunch."

I then let them show me to various side rooms that were full of all types of workout equipment: parallel bars, steps to build leg strength, a "ball pool" (a large rectangular plastic enclosure filled with plastic balls—not unlike those you find at an American fast-food restaurant), weights, and a swing in the middle of the gym—"for vestibular therapy," one young woman explained. One room was dedicated as a fitness area for the staff and was also full of workout equipment.

One of the therapists quickly removed her headscarf. This was a government building, and strict separation of mosque and state forbade wearing headscarves. I noticed she limped as she walked—reminding me of Ken's mom. With her was another therapist who looked like a model in her fashionable, figure hugging sports clothes and modern makeup.

When I asked them to tell me a little about their work, first one and then another said that they "see children for therapy." I asked them if they enjoyed their work. After darting looks at the director, they nodded their heads. As if on cue, he excused himself to go to the restroom. Then, one after the other, they began telling me their complaints about the administration, about the other personnel, about their salaries. By the time the director returned, I was hard put to understand why any of them were working there. Their lives were desperate, it seemed.

"Too many uneducated, superstitious gossips," one woman said, then sighed and proceeded to recite a list of offenses against someone named "Mr. Mehdi."

I felt bothered, though, that I saw no children around at 11:00 a.m. in the morning. *These people feel bored and guilty,* I decided within myself, but said instead, "I'm sorry to have interrupted your schedule with my unannounced visit. I am sure your work with the children must be amazing, and I certainly promise to come back when I can watch you at work."

After being escorted from that posh and colorful unit with its surprisingly gloomy atmosphere, we found our way down corridors, up staircases, and around corners. I immediately felt like we had gotten lost in a labyrinth. We walked past numerous closed double wooden doors—the entrance to various wards. When I ask about those places, Mr. Director informed me that they housed children and teenagers who had various mental and physical impairments.

As we walked on, I just couldn't get over the smell. Something reeked: foul, dead. I couldn't put my finger on it but could see why so many of the windows in the empty corridors remained open even though the air outside was icy cold.

Finally we arrived at our destination: the sky-blue double wooden doors that opened into a ward the director called the "Spastic Unit." Walking in, I saw a mass of young children huddled together on a couple of mattresses that were pushed up against the far wall. It was a large dayroom—unfurnished, cold, and drafty. Some of the windows opened out onto the barren, brown grounds while allowing frigid air to flow in; other windows were cracked and stayed closed.

When I approached the children, I could see why the windows had been opened: the smell of urine and body odor made me gag.

Most, if not all, of the children looked like concentration camp victims: with shaved heads, open sores, and clear signs of malnutrition. Several of the kids lifted their heads and started to cry out, "Mommy, Mommy, Mommy!" Three of them rose up from the huddled mass and ran to me, throwing their arms around me and pulling me to the ground. Stiff with shock, it took a few moments before I looked around in desperation for some rescue, but my host had slipped back out the front door. And I saw no caregivers anywhere.

With considerable effort, I pulled myself up and, since they would not let go, managed to drag us all over to where the other children remained huddled. Some of these kids were trying to talk to me. I could see that they were unable to walk but still able to make perfect sense in speaking. Others were lying down or had their heads bent low over their chests, not moving. All the while, the other little ones held on to me as if for dear life. My hands, chest, and arms grew wet from their urine-soaked thin cotton pajama bottoms they wore. Again my stomach lurched. "Suck it up, Norita. You can do this," I whispered to myself.

Out of nowhere, a little boy came charging at me and started to pinch me. I was trying to fend him off when a young man in a white coat emerged from another door. He ran over to rescue me.

Pulling the boy off me and holding him down, he said matter-of-factly, "We've got to be really careful with this one—he's small for sure but can draw blood in no time."

"What's the 'pincher's' name?" I asked the man after he took me out back to the corridor where the director was waiting.

"Uh … Uh … Let me see," the young man said, and then thought for a moment. "Yes, that's Jemal. I am called Mr. Hal and am a qualified social worker."

When I asked him how long he had been working in that ward, he replied, "Six months."

"What about the names of the kids who were hanging all over me?"

" Uh … ummm," Mr. Hal said. "I think they were Alice, Jared, and Ninety-Eight."

"Ninety-Eight?"

"Yes. Would you like to see their bedrooms? I can tell you some things they need."

Mr. Hal led us into his office, a small room around the corner, after he had made an order of tea from an "aide" wearing a T-shirt and jeans—a boy who was obviously one of the older children living there.

After ten minutes in his office sipping tea, Mr. Hal and the director took me on a tour of the other rooms attached to that unit. The cement floors were wet, and the smell of sewage overpowered every other odor. It was icy cold in those inner corridors too. When I asked Mr. Hal what we could buy for the children that would be helpful, he replied immediately, "Blankets." When I asked if any kids had wheelchairs, he shrugged and pointed to a small locked closet near his office, then said, "There are a couple of chairs in there but not enough for the whole group. So we don't use them. Plus, who's going to be able to take one child out for a walk or anything, when all the rest are there needing our attention? I only have a couple of day-care workers and two night-care workers. Paperwork keeps me busy hours on end, as well."

I tried to compile a list in my head to report back to the charity. My category for "Needy" no longer applied.

Back at the door of the director's office, two other administrators appeared. They were to relieve the director, who had to make some important phone calls to the main office located in downtown Ankara.

So these two administrators—Mr. Youssef and Mrs. Melissa—escorted me out of C Block to another large single-story structure, the D Block. On our way, we passed several lampposts set in odd configurations on a broad field. Looking more closely, I could just make out, between high-growing weeds and bushes, what looked like little rectangles built onto the field.

"Oh, that field was going to be a miniature golf course," said Mr. Youssef, answering my puzzled look as he shrugged his shoulders while wearing a little mocking smile.

Later on, I learned that Saray was actually supposed to house regular, non-disabled wards of the state. But, with a desperate need for housing disabled and abandoned children, it had been converted into a residential facility for only the handicapped.

Soon we entered D Block.

Again, the stench here seemed overpowering. But this time, the sound of loud cries and moans caused me to turn to my hosts in alarm.

"Yes," Mr. Youssef said, shaking his head sadly. "This is too bad, but we don't have enough caregivers to look after them. It's a good thing they are handicapped, because they don't feel anything anyway."

I stood there, speechless. This man had just told me he was a certified psychologist.

I entered a room filled with children lying in and bound to metal cribs, their hands tied so tightly with cotton tights or rags that their appendages ballooned out into purplish-gray masses. Many of the children had also been tied around their middles. I could see their little stomachs bloated above these rag "belts." Wearing thin grayish pajamas, they looked like inmates from a medieval torture house—and the cries and moans only made it worse.

What is wrong with them? I wondered and then realized with horror that these children had all just been bottle-fed while lying flat on their backs. No one had held them to feed them, let alone burp them. Two of them were lying there with a half-empty bottle next to their heads. As I went from crib to crib, I encountered the same thing: vomit-encrusted children keening or moaning. Some of the children appeared to be at least ten years old; some older, some younger.

"I'm sorry, but I have to go!" I said and then made some lame excuse to get out of there as fast as I could. "Thank the director for the tour, and I'll get back to you all on what we can do for this place."

And without another word, I escaped out the door—only to discover two women in blue cotton coats sitting in the corridor, smoking cigarettes. They had finished their allotted fifteen minutes of feeding the ward of thirty-five children, and were now waiting for their tea to brew. Later on, upon reflection, I compared them to the therapists sitting in the gym in C Block two hundred yards away. Much like those individuals, these two women jumped up when two assistant directors came out the door to follow me, put out their cigarettes, and also stood at respectful attention.

I started to shake. The only thing I could think of at that moment was getting out of there.

I ran out of D block, down the walkway, past the administration building, down the steps, past Mustafa Kemal Ataturk's bust, and out the front gate.

An hour and a half later, after what seemed like an interminable bus ride, I walked through the door of our apartment, threw down my backpack, and collapsed onto the floor.

"Oh God! How dare You show me this? Isn't my life here as a Christian and a foreigner difficult enough? What do You expect of me? That place is … is … hell. Oh God, oh God, oh God!"

I ranted on for several minutes. Then, as is my typical praying mode, I finally stopped and tried to quiet my soul, attempting to hear an answer.

But heaven was silent.

Needing to share my day's experience with someone, I phoned Harriet.

"Oh, I KNOW, Norita!" she cried. "Janice and I were out there last week. It's too horrible for words. We've begun praying for the situation in a small group. It is so strange that you went there today. What does that mean?"

Two Weeks Later: Personal Journal Entry

Maybe the cold winter visit to Saray, maybe the emotional upheaval of seeing and experiencing so much suffering brought it on. I cannot say. But last night, I came down with the flu. Feverish and aching, I took to bed, but sleep and comfort eluded me.

Our apartment is insufficiently heated. We are waiting for the building to be outfitted with a natural gas heating system, but until that happens, we live a bit like campers in the wild. Every evening, we heat up the living room with a kerosene heater. We literally live together in that room: watching TV, eating, and playing games. Katrina is now a teenager and going to an international school. She is the only one who prefers her privacy to her comfort and hangs out in her attic room bundled up before a little floor heater. Just before bed, we turn off the kerosene heater and rush out of that room to our bedrooms, where we try to get dressed for bed as quickly as possible and snuggle down in our feather comforters. Sometimes I put a hot-water bottle in the bed a few minutes before bedtime. Before too many minutes, we are warm, cozy, and drifting off.

About 3:00 a.m. tonight, I got out of bed, shuffled in my slippers and robe to the now ice-cold living room. Curled up in a quilt in my "prayer chair" (an arm chair that affords me a panoramic view of west Ankara,) I could feel every bone and joint. I just couldn't get comfortable.

All of a sudden, I was overcome with a feeling of abject loneliness and desolation. I began to sob. I hurt so much. More than the physical pain, though, was a sense of being enveloped in a black cloud. Then, out of the blue in my mind's eye, the children in the wards at Saray appeared; it was as if I were in some way experiencing what they felt, as if I had become one of them. I cried for several minutes.

But then I recognized the "Voice"—God was speaking to me: these sobbing cries, this weeping was His, all birthed out of His broken heart. The tears that were falling were not mine alone, but God's as well. God was giving me the answer to a prayer I had prayed over and over again in the past: "Lord, show me Your heart. I want to want what You want, to know Your desires, Your passions."

After several minutes of sobbing, the desolate sensation passed, and I was transported as it were. In my mind, I saw a large grassy area with trees and animals and smiling children in wheelchairs; there were adults there too. All were sitting together in little groups enjoying the sunshine and the fresh breeze.

"You are to do this, Norita."

As is often the case when I have previously experienced what I call "God speaking to me," I argued in protest: "I can't do this. It is too great a task, too impossible "

"Nothing is impossible. Just trust Me."

I immediately felt peace and a small flutter of excitement. My aching joints no longer hurt; instead I wanted to run and shake awake my sleeping husband to tell him what had just happened. After a few moments, reason returned. It was too late, and I was in no state to fully understand what had just happened. I returned to bed and fell asleep.

This morning, I wake up feeling fresh and energized. What happened last night plays over and again in my memory. It is so real and compelling that, unable to contain myself, I wake Ken up.

"God spoke to me last night. He told me that He wants me to help the children at Saray and maybe even families. I tell you, I saw it. He healed me too."

Still half asleep, he yawns, says "Oh, Norita, you and your visions," turns over, and is out again.

I have to laugh, knowing he is referring to my habit of coming up with all kinds of ideas for projects and activities—some of which come into being, while others are still pinned to the drawing board of my imagination.

I punch him in the arm. "Come on. No, it's real. Something amazing and scary happened last night. God really cares about what's going on out there. I know that now. He's going to use us." I jump out of bed. "This calls for a good cup of coffee, and then I'm getting on the phone and going to make some calls. Come on, sleepyhead, time to rise and shine. God is on the move and we're movin' with Him."

CHAPTER 2

A Planting of the Lord

"Is not this the kind of fasting I have chosen: To loose the chains of injustice and untie the cords of the yoke, to set the oppressed free and break every yoke? Is it not to share your food with the hungry and to provide the poor wanderer with shelter—when you see the naked, to clothe them, and not to turn away from your own flesh and blood?"
Isaiah 58:6-7

Ken's initial response to my enthusiastic early morning declaration made sense. So I had a vision ... then what? Fleshing it all out with action would be the real challenge, as well as the proof that it was actually a commission from God.

Ken and I chose to live a life of faith that responded to a directive from God. Choosing a life direction, living in Western Europe, and then moving to Turkey were all actions born out of a sense of call. More recently, I had opened The Book, a bookstore in an upscale mall in Ankara, as the fulfillment of a literal dream. In the dream, I had seen a café-bookstore opening up on a street near our home. Students were reading books and magazines and talking about philosophy, literature, and culture. Definitely influenced by the tiny, quaint café-bookstores tucked away on cobblestone side streets in the West, I put feet to the idea. I raised some start-up capital, and with the help of several Turkish friends, who decorated and set up the café, opened shop two years before. It was a place where sometimes intense, sometimes lighthearted conversations flowed with the tea served to customers.

But in spite of our enthusiasm, we struggled to remain solvent. While my coworkers were outgoing naturals when it came to forging relationships with clients, I had to deal with the financing and shortfall challenges. It looked more and more like the lifespan of the bookstore was nearly over.

This new vision, however, was entirely out of my area of expertise. All I knew to do at that point was talk to God about it. As I did, direction came. God made a way for His love to come to Saray.

Harriet had decided to go out to Saray every couple of weeks to volunteer. She was assigned to spend time with teenagers who were mildly mentally challenged. She said that a German friend of hers, Karin, was also interested in going out on a regular basis. There were others. I spoke to Rose, a nurse. Would she be interested in going in once a week? She immediately jumped at the chance to serve.

I was happy that expats wanted to be involved, but I felt that Turkish participation would be intrinsic to the vision. I knew that Jesus wanted His people, expat and national alike, to be His loving arms and voice. I sat in the living room; eyes closed, and quieted my soul to listen to the Holy Spirit. Aisha's face popped into my mind. I knew that she was working part-time as a care-provider for a friend whose young son had recently been diagnosed with Duchene muscular dystrophy.

Before picking up the phone to call her, I let my mind drift back to the first time we'd met …

/////

"Let's talk," I had said as I plunked myself down on a large overstuffed sofa. Across from me sat Aisha—the seventeen-year-old caregiver of my friend, Judy, an American who had multiple sclerosis.

Judy's husband worked for a government defense-related company. His expat salary meant that they could afford full-time daily help. After meeting other American women who were part of my Bible study, Judy asked if we couldn't have the weekly study and discussion group at her home. So, every Thursday morning, we sat around in her living room, and shared, prayed, and learned together.

One day, Judy took me aside and said that her caregiver, Aisha, wanted to say something to me. After the others had gone, we met. Aisha sat perched on the other end of the sofa; her hands never stopped moving, nervously brushing down the sides of a silk cushion or smoothing her faded jeans. Although Judy had said that her caregiver was seventeen years old, I thought she looked more like twenty-five.

"Everyone thinks I'm crazy, but what I know, I know," Aisha blurted out. Her wavy long dark brown hair was pulled into a ponytail, and her long, dark eyelashes and intense brown eyes struck me.

"Whoa there," I said. "Slow down. I have no idea what you're talking about." I instinctively put my hand out to cover her hand.

"Okay, okay." She took a deep breath before jumping up to grab a small red-covered paperback from Judy's bookshelf.

"You know this book?" she asked.

"Yes, of course. It's the *Injil*—the New Testament," I answered.

"Well, I know it too," she announced.

"What do you mean?" I said, not quite sure what she was getting at. Aisha was a Muslim, as far as I could tell, and while pious Muslims say they revere "The Book" (the Qur'anic reference to the Christian scriptures), rarely had I met any who had actually talked about it that way.

Then Aisha launched into her story.

"When I was one, my mother left me with my grandparents in a village in the far east, near the border with Azerbaijan. Mom, like lots of Turks from that region during those years, went off to work in Europe. My daddy didn't go but instead stayed in Ankara looking for day labor.

"My grandpa—peace be upon his soul—was so sweet and loving. Most of the time, he was gone, however, selling things in towns and villages kilometers away all around the province. Grandma was supposed to take care of my older brother and me. She was so mean, though, and mostly left us hungry and scrounging for food from neighbors. Sometimes we'd even steal bread or an egg from the local market.

"When I was four, they sent me back to Daddy. He was supposed to take care of me, but as things usually are here, he left me in the hands of my aunts who were our neighbors. We lived in the same neighborhood I live in now. My brother stayed in the village where he could be put to work in the fields.

"All I remember from those years was how sad I was. Everyone was cruel toward me. My aunts always saw me as a burden and used to yell at me, beat me, or leave me hungry. Dad was okay when he wasn't drunk, but when he was ..." Her voice grew quiet for a moment and she looked away.

She took a deep breath and went on. "Most evenings, I was alone in our one-room house. It's on the other side of Ankara from here, up in those hills." She pointed out of Judy's wide living room window to one of the hills on the distant horizon shrouded in the cloud of pollution we had in those days.

"I remember we would eat something like bread and cheese, then he'd tell me not to open the door for anyone before taking off. He gambled and drank a lot, my mother tells me."

I sat with my eyes glued to this teenager, trying to get my head around the thought of a four-year-old girl experiencing so much upheaval and pain.

"I used to get so scared," she said, paralleling my thoughts. "I'd crawl into a large wooden chest we had, pull the lid down, and curl up in there until I fell asleep or Daddy came back."

She sat still for a moment and smiled. "One thing about that chest: it was where Daddy kept the fruit he'd bought at the bazaar. I still remember crouching in there and finding oranges. Mmmmm, what a treat to peel and eat that lovely fruit." She laughed.

"One night, a storm broke. The sounds—rain and hail came down in buckets—were like horses and dogs running across our tile roof. The wind blew so hard, and the noise was so big and scary. I was all alone, and I swear I heard footsteps scraping and a knocking noise just outside the front door. Branches from the bare oak tree outside kept hitting and pushing against the 'window.'

"Actually we didn't have glass windows. Daddy had stretched cloudy-colored nylon sheeting over the wooden sills to keep out the rain and wind. When it snowed or was freezing, we would stoke the coal heater in the center of the room. That's where we slept and ate. I still have an outdoor toilet like we did in those days." Her voice lowered as though our hostess, who was in the kitchen, would hear her. "Judy's toilet is wonderful, and her wheelchair too. She would never make it if she lived with us." She smiled slightly

Until that time, Ken and I hadn't ever been in a bona fide "built in a night" house like the home Aisha was describing. Thousands of these little homes crowded the valleys and hills surrounding the city center. From Judy's upscale apartment, I could see the red-tiled roofs across town.

Beginning in the early sixties, millions of villagers began migrating to the large cities. They traveled to western provinces and cities of

Turkey to find factory or construction work. Ankara's city government promised property ownership to anyone who staked a "claim to homestead." All the "immigrants" had to do was build a room of simple brick and mortar, and set up house. In the beginning, money was so scarce, people made do with only the barest of necessities. Glass windows were a luxury then.

"Anyway ..."Aisha continued. Her high, intense voice brought me back to the story. "Anyway, I couldn't take it anymore. I was so terrified, I ran to the chest, managed to lift the wooden lid, crawl inside, and close the lid down over me. I began to wail.

"I cried and cried and cried. At the same time, I kept peeking out the large keyhole in the chest. I shook, and sobbed, and peeked. I was sure someone was coming to get me and kill me.

"Suddenly the room outside the chest filled with a bright light. I watched in sheer panic as the front door opened. As I looked through the keyhole, I saw what looked like a telephone pole with a Man hanging on it, arms stretched out. I couldn't look away, but the next moment, He was down in the room. I didn't see any blood, but there were shining places in His hands and feet."

Sitting there on the sofa with Aisha, it was all I could do NOT to interpret her experience back to her. I knew whom she'd seen, since I had listened to other Muslim Turkish people tell me their visions and dreams about the Man on the telephone pole. I'd also learned that everyone's experience had something in it that was unique only to that person, so I needed to respect her interpretation.

"He started walking toward the box where I was hiding. I shook even harder and curled up with my head down, but heard the lid opening and felt Him lift me out. 'Who are you? Are you going to kill me?' I stuttered, but was so stiff from fear.

"He held me close, sitting me on his lap, stroking my head gently.

"'I am the Messiah,' He said. 'Don't be afraid.' Gradually I stopped shaking. 'I suffered for you. You do not need to fear.' He pointed to the window. 'Look over there and see for yourself.'"

"As I focused on the nylon window-screen, it was like I was watching a movie. There, this person's life was played out before me. I saw this Man do miracles, talk to crowds of people, and then be nailed to that telephone pole. I was totally absorbed in it. My heartbeat gradually slowed down.

"'Do not be afraid,' He continued. 'Your father will be home soon. You will see your mother again soon too. When you are older, you will have a son, and when you are seventeen, I will come to you again.'

"The next thing I knew, I was lying on the sofa bed. Daddy was there. I sat up and was so excited, I immediately told him what'd happened.

"I think he might have been sober that time, because I remember him saying, 'Oh my little girl, God sent you angels because you were so afraid. Hush now and go back to sleep. Go tell the imam about your dream tomorrow.'

"The next day, I ran up the hill to the mosque in our neighborhood. We are a certain type of Shiite—very modern and open-minded—and the mosque was one that was government sponsored and not from our sect, but I didn't think about that when I knocked on the door of the imam's house. He listened to me seriously and told me that I must have seen Saint Jesus—Jesus the Messiah. 'He's one of the prophets of God,' he said.

"I had never heard of him before, but from then on whenever I heard the name of Jesus invoked in prayers where all the names of the prophets are mentioned, I feel warm inside.

"Over time, however, I forgot about that night and didn't think about my strange experience again. Until ..." She stopped to catch her breath.

"Last week, Judy asked me to get her a book from that shelf. I noticed this other book." She pointed to the red-covered paperback titled *Good News* in Turkish. "I was curious. Judy's books are in English, so why was this one in my language? But when I showed it to her, she got scared and ordered me to put it back.

"'It's illegal for you to read that,' Judy said to me.

"I put the book back immediately," Aisha continued, "but something in me kept drawing me back to the shelf, to that book. 'Open and read' something inside me was saying. 'Open and read.' Finally I kind of prayed to God. 'I know this is probably a very big sin; this book is forbidden by the government, off-limits to Muslims. Please forgive me,

I just want to read one page and then I'll put it away.'

"I quickly snatched it up and opened to the first page. I read the first sentence and for a second couldn't move.

"'This is the history of Jesus the Messiah' was all I read; suddenly as clear as could be, I was four years old again. The memory of that stormy night and the Man's words flooded in. I couldn't put the book down and read on until I came to the end of the stories about Jesus.

"I told Judy what I'd experienced, but her Turkish is not so strong and I only knew a couple of words in English, so she thought she'd misunderstood me. She called over a friend, Sasha, to try to figure out what I was saying. Sasha heard me tell again that I'd already seen all the things I'd just read about; that as a four-year-old, I'd seen Saint Jesus. I could see that she didn't believe me—and she probably told Judy that. But I swear it's true."

She looked at me with such a pleading intensity that I could only stare back for several seconds before responding.

"Sounds like the Messiah I know," I responded. "God loves you and wants to come live in your heart. He wants a relationship with you."

"This is very strange for me," she answered. "I've got to keep on reading and trying to understand more about this prophet."

"Aisha," I said gently. "According to the *Injil*, Jesus is more than a prophet."

"What?" She grew serious.

I continued: "All the prophets show us what God expects from us. But only Jesus suffered for us and paid the penalty for our failures at doing what God expects—by dying on a cross. And only Jesus rose from the dead. He said, 'If you've seen Me, you've seen the Father.' He's alive today. All the other prophets were sinners like you and me. That's why all of them eventually died and are buried in graves we can visit."

"No!" she said. "Prophets are very holy, just like saints are holy. You know we Muslims have saints like you Christians do. What are you talking about their sinning? I can't accept that."

Without thinking, I had spooked her (language is the first "minefield"). She, like most people in the world, was afraid that if we disrespected in any way the reputation of holy men and women, we would bring upon ourselves negative, unseen vibes and consequences. I continued to reason with her, however.

"Well, you've got to accept that the prophets are all dead," I said. "Only Jesus is alive."

"I don't know. I have to think some more about this." Uncertain, she lowered her eyes.

I had to get off of my apologetic high horse and find our common ground: "Let's talk to God and ask for understanding from Him. He's the Creator of everything and all of us, and can show us the truth. Would you like to ask Him to show you more?"

"Oh yes." She smiled again. "I want to know what God wants me to know. Let's pray. Uh … what are your prayers like?"

"Because God is everywhere, and right here, too, we can talk to Him like we are talking to each other. I usually close my eyes to help me concentrate, and try to sit quietly," I answered.

Together that afternoon, we prayed. I talked out loud to God and simply asked for Him to lead Aisha.

A few days later, Judy phoned and said that Aisha wanted to talk to me again, that she'd come to a spiritual crossroads. She wanted to make some kind of a heart commitment.

Through another dream, she'd become convinced that she was to walk the path of life with the Lord Jesus—and Him exclusively. She'd seen two roads, which separated, and understood that she had to make a choice. But the road she chose was the road enveloped in light; somehow she knew that this was the "Jesus" road.

She told me this as we drove together to my friend Deedee's house. There, the three of us declared prayers of commitment to Jesus the Messiah. Deedee and I put our hands on her head and prayed for her to receive the Holy Spirit. Her new life of living with Jesus had just begun.

The next morning, she phoned again. She wanted to share what had happened to her the night before.

"I read some more from the *Injil* last night and crawled into bed. After not too many minutes, I felt a warm hand on my head. I started to cry. I wept for bad, wrong things I'd done; there are so many. I cried for a long time, it felt like—then fell asleep. When I woke up this morning, it was as if a different person woke up. So light, so happy. Jesus did this to me. It's kind of scary and totally wonderful at the same time."

/////

Now, six years later, I had Aisha on the phone, and she sounded excited, to say the least: "Come out and work at Saray? Oh, Norita Abla (Turkish for "older sister"), I'd love to! Maybe I can come for a couple of days a week. For years and years, I've wanted to work with poor, hurting people. I love children. Even if I only get out there one day a week, I'm coming. Can we go in tomorrow? I want to see for myself what we need to do."

I smiled as we hung up. It was time to get ready for whatever adventure God had in store for us. He, after all, is the One who promises to bring "beauty instead of ashes."

CHAPTER 3

Boot Camp

Blessed be the Lord, my rock, who trains my hands for war,
and my fingers for battle.
Psalm 144:1 (ESV)

With Aisha's permission, this chapter is her "initiation" story
As written in her own words …

All these "little lambs," as we call young children in our country, in row after row of metal cribs, cages really—some lying still, some writhing and twisting in spastic jerks and hitting the hard bars, some with hands clutching at the rails and whimpering. Filthy and stinking, they lie there with flies feasting on the open sores that cover their bodies.

I run to the bathroom as fast as I can—and throw up. Splashing my face with the cool tap water, I struggle to stop shaking. Suddenly I am four years old again …

I am so sad. Where is Mommy? Where have you gone? Why do other kids get to go home to their mommies when they are hungry or when they fall down and their knee hurts? Oh, why does Daddy go out every night? I don't like what he smells like when he comes home late. I don't understand why he acts so different when he comes home so late in the dark.

Daddy says that Mommy is in a place far away—"JUR-money." He says that someday she'll come home. Someday when she's made lots of money. When Mommy comes home, she'll give me some money too, and then I can buy one of those HUGE pink-and-white lollipops Mr. Ahmet sells. Sometimes I dream about those lollipops. Not the bread Erman stole for us the other day. No, the sweet, sweet lollipops.

Oh no. I've got to hide. I hear Auntie Belgin. I hope she can't see me in here with the coal. She always hurts me. My head still hurts. I hate her comb. Why does she have to comb so hard? My head is always hurting and bleeding because she is so mean with that comb. "Lice!" she screamed. I must really be bad to have those things in my hair. She said so.

"You filthy thing. I should murder you. How could you walk in here with all those bugs? You are your mother's kid, your good-for-nothing father's daughter. May they rot in hell for leaving you here for these months."

Is my mommy not here because of these bugs? Where is hell?

They do itch a lot. And if I don't let her comb my head, then she won't let me have any of that bread she was baking. I wonder if I'll get to eat some of that bread. Oh, it smells delicious. My mouth is watering. But she is mad today, mad at Daddy and Mommy. She said Mommy was a "whore." What's a whore?

Oh, I am so hungry. I'll go look for Big Bro. Maybe he'll pinch me dinner …

My face comes back into focus as I stare into the cracked bathroom mirror. "These children are me," I whisper to myself, then sigh and take a deep breath. "Norita Abla is waiting for me in Continuous Care," I remind myself, and then back I go.

The stench hits me once again, but I move in closer to one of the metal cribs.

"Aisha, what do you think? What should we do first?" Norita has joined me to look into the bed.

"Well, this smell is soooo bad …"

After a minute, we walk to the darkest corner of the ward. The worst-off kids lie there, motionless.

Norita covers her face with her hands and is quiet. Then, "Here is where we begin."

The sight of these kids, the smells … It's overwhelming, but standing there staring at the children covered in crusted vomit, liquid baby food, and snot, I am moved, and a silent prayer forms within me: *I know what this is all about. It makes sense. I can do this. These children are mine to care for.*

I know what has to be done, and stopping up my nose with one hand, I reach for the little boy curled up in the bed farthest from the door.

Having lain in his excrement and vomit for so long, his skin is literally marinated. Supposedly they are bathed once a week, but that's a joke. It is bath day, and earlier I watched two staff ladies fill a bathtub with tepid water. One boy, about ten years old, is lifted out of the metal crib, laid on the floor. His T-shirt and dirty diaper are removed, then he is dunked in the bath, taken out, wiped dry with a cloth and dressed from a pile of faded, thin-worn pajamas that lay on the concrete corridor floor, just outside the tub room. Another child, a teenage girl this time, is "bathed" the same way, in the same water, dried with the same cloth, and clothed from the same pile. So it goes until the water is a brownish-gray. Later I discover caked excrement on the bodies of the children after they'd been "bathed." The once-a-week dunking had little effect on removing it or the acrid smell.

I am on a mission now. "What if I work with these children here?" I say, having gone to the supervisor of the ward, whose office is in the big administration building near the front of the campus. "I just need you to tell the other ward workers that I am going to spend time washing the kids. Maybe once a day, maybe twice a day. I don't know. But I want to do this. I'll start with the fifteen children on the far side of Ward 1."

I make sure each child has fresh bathwater, fresh towels, and a clean bottom before putting on clean diapers. This was not easy to do, because the supply of fresh clean laundry is pretty limited. I sift through the supply, looking for dry and truly clean sheets and towels. When I can't find enough clean things, I sneak things out and wash them at home.

Bathing the children properly turns out to be an all-day job. Sometimes I ask ward personnel to help. They aren't too excited about this, but, because the supervisor came in and ordered them to, they manage to move their bottoms off the chairs in the corridors and help sometimes. Often I lift and bathe these kids—they are anywhere between the ages of six to sixteen—all on my own.

I am physically quite strong. Norita Abla once commented on how impressed she was by that. Until we got indoor plumbing two years ago, I hauled water daily from a public faucet a quarter mile away from our house. I used to lift Judy (an American lady who has multiple sclerosis) too, and she was one BIG woman.

I discover festering sores oozing from some children's hands, which stay clamped shut. No one exercised these kids' hands, let alone the rest of their bodies. Flies had left their eggs; maggots crawled out of ears and wounds. I am staring at hands blistered and red from what I later learn are fungal infections.

/////

Here is beautiful little Eva, for example. After bathing her, I dry her and apply ointment to her many sores. Her face, palms, backside, and scalp are covered. I'm so glad that Norita Abla's foreign friends responded to her appeal for help. Now I've got a cupboard full of large tubes of antiseptic, antifungal cream. I rub baby oil into Eva's parchment-dry, cracked skin. She seems to purr like the stray cat we've adopted.

After a few weeks of bathing the children at the end of the ward, it strikes me that the major reason their skin is so dry is that they're thirsty. No one checks if the kids have had water throughout the day.

Why? I wonder. When I innocently ask why the kids don't get more daily drinks, the ward supervisor has an answer: "Diapers stay dryer longer—less hassle, less expense. We don't have the time to change them every couple of hours." She is actually annoyed that I am offering extra baby bottles of water.

Back to Eva. I carry her to a bench in the corridor and sit her in my lap. There I do "nothing" for a while. She is a ten-year-old girl who can't walk, talk, or take care of herself at all. I hold her close, look into her eyes, and tell her that I love her and that she is very special to my God. Later, while she waits on a towel on the floor in the corner, I change her sheets and put her into bed. I sing her a song I learned at a children's camp where I had helped out as cook last year:

"Do you know that you are very special?
Do you know that you are a pearl?
Do you know that you are really special?
And in the hands of the Lord,
And in the hands of the Lord.
Do you know that God Himself?
Did you know that He gave His Life?
Did you know that it was for you?
Do you know that you are really special?
And in the hands of the Lord,
And in the hands of the Lord."

One day, not too long after we had begun our work, I am sitting holding Eva and singing to her when her face lights up with an ear-to-ear grin. I burst out laughing and realize that I am happier than I have been in years. Now, every day, I can't wait to get to Saray. The weekends are such a drudge and seem to last way too long, if you ask me.

/////

Twice-daily baths for over four weeks finally achieve a victory over the horrible stink of Continuous Care Unit 1. Air fresheners help too. And now it's a whole lot easier to come into the room. Other volunteers, friends of Norita Abla, now can come into the ward and start "loving on the kids" as well. Even the staff has started to follow what I do.

I start out my day by asking my Father God to lead me and show me what to do for this day. I phone Norita and tell her when we get together to talk about what's happening. Sometimes she has some suggestions, but mostly she listens. I think she goes out to her friends and asks for help for us, because within a short time, she's returned to Saray with stuff we can use or news of someone who wants to help us do our work there.

One of the most shameful things about my life is that I have not finished junior high. I'm always so embarrassed that I don't have a high school diploma or that I've not gotten any certificate which I could hang on my wall. Oh, I can read and write and do arithmetic. I used to get A's, but when my mother married me off to Aaron (quite frankly, I was still playing with dolls when that happened), school was no longer an option. I was devastated then and still long to finish my high school education.

As I sit here in the ward, I'm aware of so many things I don't know, so many classes I haven't taken to prepare me for this job. The orphanage higher-ups have university educations, some in social work, some in psychology. They talk about themselves as "the experts." but book knowledge alone doesn't mean a hill of beans when it comes to caring for these poor children.

Child after child is left to die a slow death. They have stiff, deformed bodies. I have never seen such deformities in one place before. One boy's back is curved into an unbelievable position, with his spine forming a near backward circle. His head faces behind his body, like a gymnast doing back bends at the Olympics. Another girl's spine is curved so much that when you look at her back, there appears to be a large C-shaped structure just under her skin. One older boy's body is so mixed up; his long legs are splayed out in different awkward directions and frozen in that position. He lies on his back day and night in that position.

From what I hear from the staff, these children will not live long. Some die from suffocation: when the lungs or heart are cut off by bones pressing the wrong way, or if they get a chest cold or stomach flu and vomit, then there is no way their lungs can work correctly—no way for them to be able to cough out their congestion to breathe.

I think about the dream I had last night. In my dream, I was back in Continuous Care 1 at Eva's side. I was putting my hands on her back as she lay on her stomach. Someone reached out from behind me, putting his hands on mine. Soon I was pressing down with my thumbs, starting at the top of the spine, applying pressure just where the hands directed me to apply—in a circular motion all the way down the back while following the bones on either side. Next I went to the shoulders, the hips, and finally the legs and feet. I woke up this morning, tired—after all, I'd been working all night in my dream—but feeling great!

I rush into the ward and make a beeline for Eva. First, I bathe her in warm water, wrap her in warmed-up towels, and then kneel down with her onto a small carpet I have unrolled for the session. I talk to her and tell her what I am going to be doing, that I'm going to put some baby oil on her and work to relax her cramped and stiff muscles. She lets me turn her over, and I repeat what I'd done in my dream. Her eyes are open and head turned to one side. When I look over to make eye contact, she lifts her head and grins and giggles. I want to dance for the happiness I feel. As I work, I sing now, fulfilled beyond my greatest imagination. Who would have ever thought that I was to be tutored by the greatest massage master ever?

—Aisha: Saray, September 1998

CHAPTER 4

"Let My Heart Be Broken"

The Lord said, "I have indeed seen the misery of my people in Egypt. I have heard them crying out...."
Exodus 3:7

"Let my heart be broken with the things that break the heart of God."
Bob Pierce, Founder of World Vision and Samaritan's Purse

Notes to myself after meeting with Saray volunteers ...

December 14, 1998

The full extent of the horrors at Saray can never be understood by an occasional visit or a brief investigation. Every time I go there, I see or hear something that changes my viewpoint a bit more. While my first impressions after visiting are strong enough to cause my stomach to lurch and my heart to cramp in pain, new experiences bring me time and again to my knees.

Rose, from Germany—newly married to her Norwegian artist friend, Sven—wants to use some of her nursing skills. They are here with a mission organization and, like us, looking for ways to serve in practical ways. She has begun taking the bus out to Saray once a week. Today was her second afternoon of feeding children who have been tied to their beds; I have just found her crying in the corner of an abandoned office at the end of the corridor. She tells me that she's just witnessed a four-year-old mentally handicapped little girl being slapped repeatedly because she won't stop crying. The guy doing the slapping wears a light-blue janitor's uniform. He's the "staff," hired at minimum wage to feed these kids. Rose's brief conversation with him convinces her that his IQ is pretty low as well. Apparently he's just following instructions from a higher-up supervisor.

What to do? When Rose attempted to stop the abuse by saying something to the man, a white-coated woman who was in charge rebuked her sharply: "Oh, you volunteers! It's because you come and show that girl attention that she's crying. You are only making our jobs more difficult by your meddling. You get them used to love and attention, and then they crave more, and then cry and disturb the peace in the ward."

Rose and I sit for a long time before speaking again, tears streaming down both our faces now. We speak our hearts to God: "We can't do this without You making a way for us. You are the God of breakthroughs. How do we deal with these walls of inhumanity? Show us what to do, please, Lord. Soften hearts here, God."

We know that we have no power or authority in the system, and honestly as a "can-do" American and "excellence-oriented" German, we are ready to pull our hair out and start throwing things. But bowing to intimidation before the people in charge will only reinforce the craziness and help no one.

"Help!" we pray.

It's clear to me now what we must do. Pray every single time we are out here. Pray for the children as we touch them and give those hugs—even in the face of criticizing staff. Those of us who can speak another language than Turkish can pray out loud and no one will be able to complain about us doing some sort of proselytizing. We've got to pray for the criticizing staff; pray for the poor guys who probably were treated just like they are treating the younger ones.

/////

December 17, 1998

The other German volunteer, Karin—Harriet's friend—has begun visiting the C Block. Two days ago, she walked into the ward only to be confronted by a distressing sight. Jon-su and Juneyt, both small children with cerebral palsy, had just been hosed down with ice-cold water while they lay on the cement floor. Legs and arms cramped and stiff from the cold, they were being hastily dressed in damp, worn flannel shirts and pajama bottoms. The kids were crying out; limbs were flailing. Obviously spastic, with bodies out of control, they were being jerked and pulled and, at times, thrown down by angry women in a hurry to get this unforgiving job done. Karin scrambled to find dry towels—doing what she could to get the children really dry and warm again. The chaos in the corridor reigned for at least an hour and left her dazed and churned up inside. She decided that she needed to be with someone else when she worked in that ward and asked if our friend, Bur-joo, would join her when she worked there.

A college student and new member of the Turkish Christian Fellowship, lovely Bur-joo always brightened our day with her sweet energy and cheerfulness. She exhibited a strong desire to love these children and did not shy away from touching or hugging them.

Today, Karin joins me while I wait for the bus home, across the highway from Saray's front gate. Although she is bundled up in her wool winter coat, scarf, and snowcap, her blue eyes are visible behind her frosted eyeglasses. She is crying.

"Earlier this morning, while it was still snowing, Bur-joo and I walked into the Spastic Unit," Karin says. "We were wearing all our heavy clothes and boots, so we actually didn't realize how cold it was in there at first. I am so slow to register what's happening, but after a couple of minutes, even I could see that it was icy in the big Sitting Room. Then we also smelled the awful mildew or urine or something. I can't quite describe what it smelled like, but it was bad.

"I know you told me to expect some really hard things, Norita." She is trying to regain some composure. "But ... But I am finding it difficult to describe this. When we walked in this morning, some of the children were huddled up together in the corner on the old mattress. No staff was around, but I saw the chai glasses on a table, so they had to be nearby. A girl named Kader kept trying to scoot under another little boy. She wanted to use him like a quilt, to get warm. This ten-year-old, Umit, wasn't having it, though, and kept moving away.

"Even though there's always something blaring in the room, the radio or the TV, it's strange, but the children never say anything about the TV shows or sing along with the pop songs. I even wonder why they bother turning it on. But they always manage to have the sound turned up so loud and blaring. I got a headache from this, I think.

"Then I met a boy named Husain. He was skin and bones. He just stared and stared at me. He didn't say a thing. Finally he squeaked out that he wanted me to get him cigarettes. Can you imagine? This boy is lying on his back on the floor and wants cigarettes. Later I asked the cleaner about this, and she told me that another janitor often comes in, sticks a cigarette in Husain's mouth, lights it, and then walks out. The boy—oh, he must not be more than ten—manages to smoke three-quarters of it before spitting the butt out and not burning himself.

"Husain's angry with me for not bringing him cigarettes. The staff is used to this, I guess, and don't argue with him anymore. It's a case of less food, more nicotine for him.

"I think that the main way that he communicates is by grunting and staring. He can speak some Turkish, but the sounds came out garbled, kind of like the sound you get when you fast-forward cassette tapes. His legs and hands are so stiff, and today he was shaking from the cold too. When I asked him if he was hurting, he nodded. Still he was insisting that I go out and buy him a pack.

"After I left Husain, I went over to the kids hunched up on the mattress. They were all quiet. A couple of kids turned away and put their faces to the wall. Bur-joo was whispering to another little boy named Yunus. He was crying. He whispered something back to her, and then she started crying. They hugged each other and couldn't seem to say anything for a long time.

"They found Murad dead this morning, FROZEN, in his bed. He was a one Yunus's closest buddy. Now he's gone and Yunus is alone again. But he's also afraid that Murad's ghost is hanging around. He's terrified that he might be next to die.'"

Karin continues: "I am stunned. A child frozen in his bed … What is this? How can this happen? Dear little smiling, intelligent Murad … How I was looking forward to getting to know him a bit better … Oh God, oh God … It's a nightmare over there, Norita. The windows are broken; the furnace and radiators are broken; the washing machines, centrifuge, and dryers in the main laundry are broken. There are layers of 'washed' sheets spread out over the ice-cold radiators—still wet, still stinking. They brought back a pile of so-called washed sheets, and when they picked them apart to dry them, there were still little piles of filth stuck on some of them. It's gross beyond belief."

Without losing any time, Karin and I make our way back across the highway and into the admin building. We have to find out how it is that the giant laundry facility found under the industrial orphanage kitchen has been shut down. All the clothing for Saray is washed in a big building on the other side of the field about eighty yards from C Block. Laundry is coming back to the wards wet. Wet sheets, wet clothes, and sub-zero temperatures in drafty under-supervised units. The personnel in the ward have tried to rinse out some and lay them over the windowsills or radiators to dry. The radiators are cold too, shut down for some reason. Nothing is even remotely dry.

I think about something Harriet said the other day. She and her Christian colleagues at Kucak, the Turkish Christian children's publishing house, had met in the morning to pray together for the situation at Saray. She told the group what she'd seen there. Soner, the young student they'd hired to write, had seen something in his mind's eye while praying: out of a large, dirty, turbulent sea of water, children were raised up and taken into a cloud of light.

"Father, show us what to do about this," I pray quietly as I walk into the assistant director's office. Mr. Mustapha offers us some chai and then listens as Karin tells him what is taking place in the freezing wards a hundred yards from his comfortable and warm office—we notice he has an electric space heater going full blast next to his desk.

"Oh that's bad. No one has told me about this. Let me check." And he picks up the receiver to phone the orphanage technical director.

Mr. Mustapha tells us that the foreman has already put a request into the main office downtown that he has been waiting days for a reply. He needs funds to purchase a new dryer. As far as the heating problem goes, experts are required to come out and look before any decision will be made. It's already been three weeks since he put the request in, though. The officials downtown say they have no money left to spend, either, and they'd need to make a special requisition for heating repair funds, which could take some time—several months is what they said—to be reviewed, processed, and approved.

After putting down the receiver, he says, "Mrs. Norita, why don't you start a charity, a Turkish group just for your volunteer work here? You would be able to raise money from all your foreign friends and use it so much more easily if you had a legal organization. I know of other non-Turks who've done similar things. Why don't you do that? You're actually not supposed to get onto this campus without a signed protocol between a bona fide organization and the Office of Social Services. Really, if you and your friends want to keep coming out regularly, then you need to be official. Start your own nonprofit."

I can hardly get my thoughts around what he is saying. We're talking about an emergency situation just a few feet away, and he's telling me that without a legal cover, we won't be able to stay long and might be prevented from getting on the campus.

I reply as calmly as I can: "Okay, okay, I get that, Mr. Mustapha, but you guys have a much greater need here. I want to see what I can do to help you. I'm going to my volunteer charity group. We don't usually have that much money in the coffers, but you never know. Anything's possible with God."

"Yes, of course, God is great, but He doesn't usually mess around with the government, and the government doesn't mess with Him." His cynicism drips from every word.

Karin and I commiserate with him—stuffing whatever critiques we have—and then leave. I am going to a charities meeting in two days and need to let the chairman know about this urgent situation.

/////

December 19, 1998

We've just finished our meeting and I can't believe what's happened.

This morning, I received a phone call from the British Embassy. The wife of the ambassador, Janine, had heard about my report on the situation at Saray, and wanted to make a donation. Their driver picked me up, and she, her husband, and I drove out to the facility. They needed to see for themselves. Evidently the contrast between the modern physical therapy gym and the wards was enough of a shock for them that, this evening at the meeting, I learned that they've earmarked not only British Embassy donations but personal funds as well. I'm to get together with Mr. Mustapha to research and purchase industrial giant washing machines, fryers, and centrifuges.

Although I have no idea what they cost, I'm floored by the speed and thoroughness of this gesture. I wish I could see Mr. Mustapha's face when I tell him on the telephone. We'll go shopping tomorrow.

If this news wasn't heartening enough, I had another surprise. Jonathan, the young British committee member who serves as the bookkeeper of the group, turns out to be an engineer on government contract. He understands institutional furnaces and heating systems. He plans to come out tomorrow to take a look and make recommendations. If we need to, we are committed to getting the laundry service out there fixed and working again as soon as is physically possible.

"Father, You truly see and You hear and You answer," I whisper.

CRY OUT

CHAPTER 5

The Best Things in Life Are Free, but ...

Religion that is pure and undefiled before God, the Father, is this:
to visit orphans and widows in their affliction,
and to keep oneself unstained from the world.
James 1:27 (ESV)

My personal notes continued ...

January 7, 1999: D Block—Continuous Care 1 and 2 (CC 1 and 2)

Aisha pleads, "The children need good paper *bez* [Turkish for "diapers"]. Mrs. Melissa told us the other day that they order big boxes of them from the main warehouse downtown that are delivered once a month. But take a look at this." And she pulls a large adult-sized diaper from her tote bag. "These are so big, totally un-useable. The kids are so skinny that no matter how much time we spend trying to fit them, wrapping them around the little emaciated bodies, everything leaks out. We're busy changing sheets, and within half an hour, everything is dirty again. I tell Mrs. Melissa. She says she'll pass on the complaint but that all the diapers are purchased from private companies who win the bids. She says not to expect that there will be any action on this anytime soon."

"Socks, socks, warm tights," Guliya breaks in. "My kids need something warm on their feet. They are running around on cement floors in their bare feet. It's cold in there. I went looking for their shoes. But I couldn't find them. Mrs. Hande, the ward matron, finally brought me to a back room and a large locked closet. When she opened it, I couldn't believe what I saw.

"It was stocked full of shoes and sweaters—most still in their plastic wrapping! She told me not to tell anyone that she'd shown me the closet. Compassionate people and stores give these away for the children at Ramadan, but I never see the kids wearing them—just rags. Someone must decide to unwrap the packages and put them on the children. Plus I can't be sure, of course, since I didn't see it, but I also think that the janitors take from these closets and dress their own kids with the stuff. They get paid a minimum wage and live from hand to mouth too. No one checks what happens to the donated clothes or toys after they are signed into the supplies desk in the admin building."

Guliya is my friend from church. She's not quite forty, and has shoulder-length, straight, light-brown hair and hazel eyes. She is for all intents and purposes a "divorcée." Married off by her family in a religious ceremony, her husband legally married someone else. He travels between two households, visiting the wives and children in each. Despite his alcohol addiction and her sense of rejection with sharing a husband, her newfound faith in Jesus has helped her begin to gain a sense of value and dignity. Her three children now maturing into adults have also begun walking with Christ. They are turning out strong and motivated to make a place for themselves in the world and walk with God through their difficulties.

Her nineteen-year-old daughter, Laliye, told me all this one afternoon when the two of us met to discuss the possibility of mother and daughter coming out to join the team. Laliye's name had come to mind when I was asking the Lord who should join our team.

Guliya, as far as I know, has never spoken with a counselor or pastor about her marriage or the troubles she's seen. Maybe someday soon, we can spend time talking about "personal" things, but right now, she is ready to fight for the "special" children she's started to care for in the Continuous Care 3 Ward.

"The children in Continuous Care 3 are my little lambs now. I want to dress them in the new clothes from the closet and then take some of them outside. I'm not official enough, however, to make that decision. Mr. Hajji, our ward supervisor, is away from his office today and I can't get anyone else to okay this.

"Then, when I asked about socks for all the bare feet, I was told that there weren't any on hand, and anyway, that some of the children have the tendency to try to stick their hands down their throats and try to swallow their socks or tear them off as soon as they are put on, so the best solution was not to put any on."

Joining us in the Saray staff cafeteria where we occupy one of the tables in the corner, Laliye adds, "Most of these children are just plain bored. They need to *do*, something. Just putting on clothes or diapers isn't enough. Let's do some crafts with them. There are so many things we could do. Remember all the fun things we did at Sunday school and at camp?" she asks me.

When Laliye was a little girl, she started coming with Guliya to our little Sunday gathering. She told me that, before those gatherings, she never knew that kids could have fun and learn at the same time. So many of the things we did in those years were as basic as coloring in pictures or gluing matches together. She apparently loved the experience.

Laliye has never heard of special education. She just knows that it can't be right to leave anyone all day long in a bed or room without any stimulation just because that person has disabilities.

It is my turn to say what is bothering me: "These rooms are so chaotic, so noisy and smelly." My "vision button" is turned on. "What we could really use is our own space—an activity room of our own."

Laliye, her long-lashed eyes sparkling, adds her own dream: "Shelves. Posters will go there—carpets, too. Maybe we can even get someone to build us a little kitchen. We'll buy a clothes washer and use it for smaller laundry jobs. We'll get someone else to donate a computer maybe, to go along with books and toys."

Aisha, usually a fount of ideas, has been quiet as we brainstorm. Finally she cannot contain herself and breaks into the conversation again. This time, I realize, she is expressing what is really uppermost on all their minds.

"Dearest Abla," she says. "I love working with these children. I seriously haven't ever been so happy doing anything else. But my family can't survive without me going to some sort of paying job full-time. When I worked as a housecleaner, I found situations where I could take my babies with me and still bring home enough to put food on the table. You know my husband's problems. One day, he's fit for working; the next, he's gambled away what he made the night before." Her face screws up as she tries to keep herself from getting upset by the thought. "It's a good thing we have the two rooms we live in built onto his father's house or we'd be out on the street long before now, but I have got to make money. If you can't find something to pay me with, I'll have to leave this team and go back to housecleaning. I don't even have my high school diploma to fall back on for some other kind of job. This all makes me so upset." The tears fall freely now.

I have to face the bottom-line question again. Ever since the beginning of the work at the orphanage, it's been hovering in the background of my mind. Extra food, diapers, baby-friendly detergent, lotions, medicines, clothes, and shampoos are all necessities that should be supplied by the state but are not.

Wheelchairs and strollers could mean the difference between being tied down 24/7 to getting out of the beds, even possibly getting into the afternoon sun for a few minutes every day. Renovated bathrooms would mean children could be safer and the whole process of bathing less traumatic. This all takes money.

But the greatest gift we make to this place is ourselves.

Whereas Rose, Karin, and I receive regular income through donations from our network of church friends who believe in our work, my Turkish friends have no such circle of financial supporters. Aisha, Guliya, and Laliye have responded to a nudge from God. They want to serve, but they have no income. The government might hire them, but then they would not have the freedom to go from ward to ward doing whatever they see needs to be done. They would just become the lowest member of the blue-uniformed janitorial totem pole, forced to take orders from an unengaged foreman.

A Blue Coat, as we've come to call them, comes by at that moment to inform me that I have a phone call in the main office. It is Mr. Jonathan from the charities group: "The new laundry machines are up and running, Norita. Just thought you'd like to hear the good news. The ambassador made good on his promise, and I was appointed to oversee the installation and to check out whether they work or not.

"And some other interesting news ... When we said that we were going to come in to do a voluntary assessment on the boiler room and heating problem, some bigwig in the Ankara office immediately sent out a crew of their own; they are beginning the installation of a brand-new system as we speak."

I hang up, thrilled and a little awed at what had happened in such a relatively short time. Later, I sat down and wrote a letter to God:

> *Father, thank You again. You gave the ideas; You put the people together. Morale will be restored because of this, but we still need to make a lot of changes. Each ward needs its own smaller washing machines.*

Now what am I supposed to do? All those friends in California have been such great supports in getting us going. They really understand these kids, but we need money right now and all this is costing so much. It takes months to raise funds or buy stuff and mail it. The committee here is too small and not set up for this kind of ongoing work. Help!

/////

March 1, 1999

I'm still trying to get my head around the invitation I've had from out of the blue.

I received a long-distance phone call: "I understand you run an orphanage. My name is Reverend George and I'm from Arizona."

"Well, actually no." I hastened to explain: "No one is allowed to run an orphanage except the Office of Social Services, which is a governmental agency. All rest homes, halfway houses, and institutions like that are strictly controlled and structured. We just volunteer out at one. Actually it's technically not really an orphanage but more a residence for children with mental and physical disabilities. Four hundred of them."

"Well, I'm the pastor of Christ the King Presbyterian church in Tucson, Arizona. There's a couple who are in my congregation, and they've heard about your work from somebody who knows about you. This couple wants to visit. So we are planning on coming to Turkey next week for a look-see. Would you be able to arrange a visit?"

The following Monday morning, I find myself driving Ken's company van and taking the reverend, and Becky and Gary Parsons out to Saray, where after the customary courtesy visit to the director's office for tea, they walk up and down the long drafty corridors with me. They enter overcrowded chaotic wards and are accosted with the same desperate cries for "Mommy" that I had been that first visit.

With tears streaming down their faces, this insurance broker and his intelligent, faith-filled, and activist wife walk out the front door and climb back into the van. I have little doubt that they have come to a decision.

They talk about getting necessities like vitamins, creams, clothing, and food supplements, about buying simple puzzles and books for the children who could use them. From Saray, we drive to Ken's wheelchair workshop—KIFAS Ortopedik—where the three of them are introduced for the first time to chairs made with Third World users in mind: inexpensive, easily reparable, but eminently durable manual chairs.

While there, I tell them about attending a seminar in the States held by an organization called MOVE International. My good friend—and mentor on the whole area of special needs—Desley, had set up a meeting for me with the MOVE founder, Linda Bidabe. This special-education program gets special-needs children off the floor, out of beanbags, and up on their feet using some specially designed devices called Gait Trainers along with child-motivating curriculum. Desley and Linda had arranged for a number of these mobility aids to be donated. Becky Parsons immediately thinks of ways that she could help facilitate getting the things to Turkey.

But she doesn't just want to send things. She knows that what the children need more than anything else is loving touch. She wants to come as often as she can to personally care for and hug the kids. She wants to go visit churches to talk about this place and recruit people to come for short periods of time—groups she is calling "Hug Teams." Their only jobs would be to bathe and hug love-starved children.

"We have been convinced that we are to start a program here. We want you to run it, Norita. Hire more caregivers. Money is really no object, as far as we are concerned. When you need things like diapers or lotions or shampoos or whatever, just let us know and we'll either send you the stuff or raise the money for you to go out and buy it. We've been praying about doing something with our money that will help orphans. Several years ago, we adopted three children from Korea. They've all grown now and are doing well. I think they'd like to come to help out soon. Our one natural-born daughter, Amy, and her husband would just love to come too.

"What you've started by getting into the wards is remarkable. We want to back you in this, both with money as well as manpower."

As I write this, I am shaking my head. "My God shall surely supply all your needs," the apostle Paul wrote the Philippian gathering of Messiah-followers, "according to His riches in Christ Jesus."

CHAPTER 6

Man of Peace

"When you enter a house, first say 'Peace to this house.' If someone who promotes peace is there, your peace will rest on them."
Luke 10:5-6

My personal notes continued ...

June 1999

Mr. Mustapha is only too pleased by my new foreign connections, but he and Mr. Youssef, another assistant director, remind me that we need to be more official. He doesn't want to have to bar the door to us one day because we haven't complied with Turkish law. I know I have to get to work on this, but I need someone to help me navigate bureaucratic waters.

After church last Sunday, I mentioned this to Serap, a new Turkish believer in Christ who lives in my neighborhood. She told me about a friend of a friend who worked for the city government. He supposedly has had experience in setting up nonprofits, and specifically organizations that benefit people with disabilities. We made arrangements to go visit him in his office.

Now here it is two days later, and I'm supposed to be meeting her downtown in twenty minutes. I'm already late and not at all a happy camper. Earlier in the day, with minutes to spare, I rushed home from grocery shopping and attempted to pull together any papers or pertinent documents I could use to describe what we were doing and wanted to do out at Saray. Ken found me standing at my desk as I stood paralyzed before a mountain of unfiled papers and reports.

"What have you got prepared?" he innocently asked.

I answered as calmly as I could: "Umm, I don't know. I've got my preliminary proposal somewhere, some photographs. Stuff like that."

"That'll never work. You should have a folder all ready with points you can show him. His time is valuable. Don't go in without concrete material to show him."

Our desktop computer, though still a bit of a mystery to me, holds pages of things I've written. Switching it on, I started to look for any and all relevant files.

"Oh, these need to be cleaned up." I groaned. "What's the word for 'foundation' in Turkish? For 'long-term care'? AAARGHHH … I'm running so late and still need to catch the bus to make it downtown in time."

"Why do you do this? You can't expect to go to a legal professional in such a state of chaos. He won't respect you. First impressions are very important. Your paperwork … You aren't prepared."

Ken had switched into his teacher role. I sank into defensive child mode inside, but finally nodding in reluctant agreement, I grabbed the folders off my desk and ran out of the house, flagged down a taxi, and now am sitting in the backseat.

There, I start to take stock of what I am doing. Frankly I am embarrassed about the chaos. I know I need to present a reasonably cultured image. First impressions are important here. As has happened too many times before, lack of preparation has only increased my stress. How will I be able to convince a Turkish professional that our work is important when I don't give importance to the details that make communication important?

I meet up with Serap in front of the seven-story city hall building. Passing through the security check found in every shopping center as well as government building, we ask the clerk at the front desk how we can find Mr. Sharif, the lawyer. She directs us to the fifth floor.

The ubiquitous fluorescent lighting in the entrance halls casts a grayish pall upon everyone who is crowded into the narrow hall. I smell stale cigarette smoke and diesel exhaust fumes.

We wait in line. With a capacity to hold only four people, the elevator leaves a crowd of us trying to get to offices in the upper floors.

"Don't think about how unsafe this elevator is." I have begun whispering to myself, nervousness heightened by the pre-appointment chaos and anxiety. I actually am not excited about having to meet a stranger—one more government employee who lacks imagination—as well as being in that new, crowded place.

"Nothing bad will happen. Nothing bad will happen." I begin repeating the oft-used Turkish "positive" proclamation.

"Gee, I hope we won't get stuck and be late for our appointment," I blurt out. Everything feels sinister.

When our turn to enter finally comes, we squeeze in. Two gray-haired men in suits and ties push in before the elevator door closes. As we maneuver inside to face the door, sardines in a tin, I struggle to take deep breaths. Body odor is now filling the steel-and-aluminum cubicle.

Why do I do this to myself? Next time, the stairs.

Opening onto a floor filled with several desks and storage cabinets, the elevator ejects us and we stumble to find our bearings. No one is there, so we walk down the soot-laced, dingy corridor until we find someone to help. Finding ourselves in front of a closed office door with peeling white paint, we knock and enter.

The room is smallish—little bigger than two walk-in closets—and crowded with desks. At these desks, typing away at electric typewriters, are four smartly dressed women. Their hair, nails, and clothing bring some semblance of class to this room. Upon closer scrutiny of the little nameplates standing on their desk, I realize with a start that they are attorneys. What a contrast between their offices and those of the many administrators out at Saray.

We are directed next door and told to walk right in: "He's there if the door isn't locked."

We then walk into another closet-sized room filled with clouds of cigarette smoke, the sounds of an ancient printer—nestled under a desktop computer—slowly spewing out a document, and the clacking of an even more antique Olympic electric typewriter. A small, pudgy, slightly balding man is typing vigorously with his back turned to us. His light-blue short-sleeved polyester shirt shows sweat stains under his arms and on his back—reminders that it is a warm afternoon in Ankara, and that there is no air-conditioning in the office.

Piled high with folders, newspapers, and documents, his desk nearly fills the room. Two straight-backed chairs fill the remainder. To the right of his desk is a small bookcase, filled haphazardly with books and binders.

Standing abruptly, Mr. Sharif turns to us. "Welcome. Welcome. Come in. Who are you?"

Sticking out my hand, I introduce myself, stumbling along in Turkish: "This is Camilla's sister, Serap. Camilla phoned you, I think, to let you know we were coming. I'm Norita Erickson. We have an appointment to discuss forming a legal organization. We want to serve abandoned disabled children. Kids who are living in state institutions. Kids and young adults who have mental as well as physical disabilities. We've already been there several months but have to get legal permission now to come regularly." It feels as if someone has opened my talk-valve. I finally get a hold of myself and take a deep breath.

Though my hand is still extended, Mr. Sharif ignores my gesture. After standing at attention for what seems like a long time, he leans forward, nearly knocking over a half-full glass of tea that sits precariously near the edge of his desk. He fumbles in his shirt pocket for his packet of cigarettes. He shakes one out, lights it, twists his head to exhale, then stretches his hand out for the greeting shake. When hand and open gaze are directed slightly to the left of me, I realize with a jolt that Mr. Sharif is blind!

"Welcome, yes, I've been expecting you. Serap herself telephoned me. Are you here too, Serap? Good, good. How's your sister? Mrs. Norita, you say? So you speak Turkish? Well, I can speak some English." And in English, he says, "My name is Sharif. I am thirty-four years old. I have two children. My wife, her name is Zelly. So it's good? What can I do for you?"

I launch into another explanation of our work and what we want to do. Midway through the first five minutes, Mr. Sharif cuts in, "What you need to do is start a charitable foundation. I'm sure you can come up with about $60,000."

I pick up on a tone that always sets me on edge. He sounds just like someone I meet at the open-air market—a hawker who recognizes a well-heeled foreigner as easy prey.

"Well, I'm afraid I can't just find that kind of money. Even though I am an American." I bristle at the all too familiar stereotype I know that most people in the world believe. "I just don't have access to such a large amount of cash."

"Right. So you say, but surely you could get your foreign friends to donate that kind of money." He has entered full-street-vendor mode. And I am ready to react. The hawkers always make me uncomfortable—relentlessly drilling me with offers until I end up buying whatever, just to get them off my back. I am absolutely rubbish at bargaining unemotionally.

"Nope." I take a deep breath, trying to remain calm. This badgering because I am a foreigner who speaks the language is one of the annoying aspects of living in Turkey. Sometimes when I'm tired, I just pretend I can't understand the language. This seems to stop them for a moment, until they run and bring someone over to translate. There is no rest for the wicked, I guess.

I screw up my patience and explain. "Look, in the first place, most of my friends are Turkish. None of my friends in Ankara have that kind of money. We have to start simple."

"Well, if that's the case ..." His tone changes and another persona emerges. Quickly, confidently, jettisoning the smarminess he's just exhibited, he becomes proactive. Now he explains Turkish law regarding foreigners and nonprofits. He tells me what needs to be done, with whom and where. He shows signs of enthusiasm now. "Write a constitution and documents of intent. Find people who are willing to be founding members and sign their names to all those official papers."

When I ask how much money I will need, he raises his hand to say, "Wait a sec," and then sits down and punches a few numbers into his desk phone. "Three teas, Ajar, and quick." Turning his face back to me, he says, "Please forgive my rudeness." He has neglected the "chai ritual." Every and all business appointments are punctuated with the hot clear-brown liquid served in hourglass-shaped small glasses. Chai makes the world go round.

"Listen, Mrs. Norita. You as a foreigner have a desire to help poor, neglected, handicapped children, Turkish children. You could be doing this in your home country, but you are doing it here. I am truly touched by this.

"I want to help you, to volunteer my time and knowledge. You just be here and help get the papers where they need to go to. There is a lot of going back and forth from the security police station where all the files and permissions are given for association. You will need to be very patient, and you'll need to have Turkish friends to help you get going on this. They will need to come to a few meetings and maybe donate a minimum membership fee. You can't and shouldn't do it all on your own in the end."

I am running over in my mind's eye just who I'm going to need to ask to sign documents with me. I'll go to church on Sunday with the goal of recruiting as many "cofounders" as I can.

Mr. Sharif is not finished giving instructions: "Come in some afternoon next week. I'll get copies of the required forms and paperwork, and we'll get to work." He stands up abruptly, now that our business is complete, but at that moment, someone arrives with a tray of glasses full of tea.

Mr. Sharif sits down again.

I want to encourage him and express my appreciation: "Thank you for your incredible help. I'm sure you are one of the answers to the prayers I've been praying for the children. You are our person of peace."

Mr. Sharif is silent for a second then jumps up and says, "Do you believe in God?"

"Why, yes, of course. Would you think me really strange if I told you that it was God who has called me to start the work for those children at Saray? God is love and He loves them."

"Yes, yes," he interrupts. "Those kids are there to test our faith in Him. Will we care for them or ignore them? It is a great merit which will be applied to the balance of good and bad deeds we've done in this life. As a Muslim, I believe that this counts for good in God's eyes."

"It certainly is the kind of response God wants from us all," I answer, "and blessing is what He will give—absolutely."

Before remembering his disability, I stand and reach over his crowded desk to shake his hand again. He leans toward me on the desk, his facial expression taking on a new intensity. I wait—our faces literally a few inches apart. He has something more to say.

"It was my faith and hard work and the help of some friends which brought me to this point in my life," he continues. "I come from a poor family in a small town maybe seven hours drive west of here. I was not sight impaired the first few years of school, but a disease attacked my retina, and within four months, I lost all sight. I learned Braille; I had a tape recorder to tape classes and I went to law school.

"Blind folk, the lame, deaf people in this country get little help here from elected officials or government offices. But if someone doesn't help you, you know, offers you a hand along the way, it's really, really difficult to make it. Some friends would sit with me during class and take notes. We helped each other pass the exams, however. I have an incredible memory. God rewarded me with that."

He goes on to tell me that he and his wife were brought together in an arranged marriage: "She tells me that she limps, but I don't see it. We get along just fine," he is quick to add while fumbling in the pocket of his coat, which is draped across his office stool. He pulls out a billfold and a photo: his bride. "I work hard, maybe too hard. I have high blood pressure, and people keep telling me I'm headed for diabetes. That could be true, but I can't change—and this is what I love to do."

I sit down again since Mr. Sharif is not finished.

"Ha! I've been working for the municipality seven years. When the mayor got elected two years ago, I thought, 'That's it for this job, Sharif,' since typically everyone stays or goes on the basis of their being members of whatever party is in power. My political party is the opposition one.

"But I have to tell you. Now my blindness has become an advantage. They're not going to throw me out. It would look bad to fire a poor handicapped man. Politics ..." His laugh is bitter.

I have to ask him: "Will our working together, me being a foreigner and a Christian and all, cause you any problems? "

"No one tells me whom I can or cannot work with. I make those choices. Your religion and beliefs don't mean a hill of beans to me as long as you accept me and don't try to shove some propaganda down my throat. What matters is what you are doing, and you are clearly serving people who are not even your own family members. I am Muslim, but an open-minded one, I hope."

/////

Early this evening, Ken is shaking his head as I recount the day's adventure to him. "Well, I honestly was afraid that you'd come home in tears, with news that the attorney wouldn't give you the time of day. This Mr. Sharif sounds like an interesting guy. You've got a ton of work ahead of you, but it sounds like you've found the perfect partner in crime."

/////

Not too many weeks later, we were gathered in Mr. Sharif's office to finish writing the first draft of our foundation bylaws and petition for recognition.

"So have you come up with a name yet?" Mr. Sharif was poised to begin typing.

"Actually some friends and I from church were talking about this, and Ari suggested we use the name of a flower. He suggested we use the Kardelen as our symbol. I loved this and want to name our group the Kardelen Team."

"That's perfect," Sharif answered and began typing in the new name for our organization: The Kardelen (Snowdrop) Association for the Care and Protection of Abandoned Handicapped Children.

"From what I know about the snowdrop flower and what I remember from my seeing days," Mr. Sharif said, "they are bulb plants which dot the hills and plains of Anatolia in the spring with white petals. These are the flowers which pierce the snow—literally snow-piercers as their name means in Turkish."

"Yes!" I answered. "They are a symbol of hope and new life, of 'resurrection' if you will. Just think how those bulbs have been hidden away in the cold dark earth for months, then come popping out to say, 'Hey, we are here. There is life hidden away. We are beautiful.'"

"Yes, I like that. We are on our way, Norita." Sharif chuckled as he finished off the document to be sent to the security police officer in charge of vetting and allowing civil society organizations.

I couldn't help but lift up a prayer of thanksgiving within: *Father, I bless You for this man, "Mr. Snowdrop"—a survivor. He is our "man of peace" for this hour. May many come to know You, the Prince of Peace, through the Kardelen Team. In Jesus's name, amen.*

CHAPTER 7

"Why, You Little Blankety-blank-blank!"

… The wrath of man does not produce the righteousness of God.
James 1:20 (NKJV)

My personal notes continued …

September 1999

Maybe if I had more training in social work, I'd be better equipped to take on this battle of bringing rescue to the children at Saray. I have so much to learn still.

Although I will never say it out loud, I believe that, with good ole "Yankee" know-how and plenty of money, we will change Saray. My optimism is boundless.

But reality has begun to set in.

Three and a half weeks ago, I arrived at the D Block and was on my way to the unit we have come to call the "Joy Room." (One of Becky's ideas is to prophetically rename the rooms to reflect what changes we want to bring there). Halfway down the long cement-floored, bare-walled corridor, I saw three ward workers. They'd set up a table and chairs in the hallway for their tea-and-cigarette break.

But there, lying in the middle of the corridor on the bare floor, was nine-year-old Clara, the autistic head-banger and ear-gouger. I had heard about her only the day before …

/////

"Oh God, I can't believe it." Guliya covered her mouth with her hand and rushed through the ward where I was working on her way to the bathroom next to the bedrooms. When she emerged a few minutes later, she asked for a bottle of water and then told us what she'd just seen.

"There is a girl—Clara—tied up in her bed next door. She keeps poking her right ear with her finger. The personnel don't know what to do about this. They fitted her with a little helmet so that when she starts head banging against the wall, she won't hurt herself. But she keeps sticking her finger into the ear holes of the helmet. She won't stop.

"I wanted to help her. I thought that if I just hold her and let her follow me around, maybe she'll stop hurting herself. So I started to untie her. Then I noticed there was something white in her bloody ear. When I looked closer, the white started moving. Her ear is crawling with maggots!" And with that, she ran back into the bathroom.

Later she told me that she had tried to clean Clara's ear out as well as she could and then covered it with a bandage.

"Maybe that's why she repeatedly stuck her finger in her ear," Guliya said.

"No," Aisha spoke up. "The flies are attracted to the dried blood in her ear. Her ear-gouging behavior has been her condition for a long time, I gather. That's why they are used to tying her spread-eagled into the crib. She can't bang her head or gouge her ear when she's tied up."

"Well, whatever the reason she pokes her ear," Guliya said, her voice filled with conviction, "it's clean now. I asked the staff to make sure the bandage gets changed regularly and for them to take her out of her bed and pay attention to her. Starting next week, I'm going to come out every day during the week and she'll get lots of attention from me."

/////

And there I saw Clara—the very next day—lying on the floor, trying to get one finger into the helmet hole. Toilet paper had been stuffed into her ear and bits were poking out of the ear hole in the helmet.

Sitting on a low stool next to the table were three ward workers, including a female I recognized—Hatoon. Cigarette in one hand, Hatoon suddenly jerked on a rope with the other. Clara's head bounced up and then hit the floor again. Hatoon had a leash around Clara's neck!

Guliya had told me that, with support, Clara could walk. Here, she'd apparently been laid on the ground and told not to move.

"Aaaarrrrhhhh!" I heard Clara say, and then she lay still for another moment before turning her head back and forth repeatedly while arching her back.

"What in God's name are you doing?" I shouted, running up to the three ward workers and grabbing at the rope in Hatoon's hand.

Hatoon dropped her cigarette into the ashtray and bent as if to pick Clara up. Even though the stool was fairly low to the ground, Hatoon had to hop off it. She was extremely short—exhibiting an obvious growth-hormone deficiency.

She wouldn't look me in the face at first, but then turned with a smirk. "What do you mean? I'm having a cup of tea and a smoke." Her tone grew haughty: "I'm a state employee and I have the right to smoke whenever I want to."

No lowly janitor here.

"Take that rope off her neck immediately," I said, my fury still building. "You're unbelievable. That is no way to treat a child."

Hatoon twirled her end of the rope, and then glanced at the girl whose painfully skinny legs were spread-eagled on the floor. Hatoon sighed with clear annoyance, then said, "Okay, okay, keep your shirt on. I'll take care of her when I'm done." She picked up her tea glass, drained it, and then lit another cigarette defiantly. The two other people sitting there, a man and a woman, grinned at Hatoon before leaving "to get back to work."

Blood boiling now, I ran down to the unit supervisor's office at the end of the corridor. The door was locked. Frustrated, I knew I had to stick to protocol and see him before going any higher on the bureaucratic totem pole to complain. I asked a man washing down the hallway with a mop where Mr. Hajji was. He said that he thought his boss was on vacation.

/////

After not too many days at Saray, I have figured out one of the ways that people who have power here manage to keep on top of the multiple frustrations. On the day-to-day level, the people in charge are not the supervisors or administrators or professionals with college degrees in social work or child development. Those people are usually unavailable; the reasons for their absences all "good." Sick leave is the number one cause of administrator absence with "yearly leave" weighing in at a close second and "meetings at the headquarters" third. Finding out just who is in charge on any given day is a learned skill.

I needed to talk to Mr.Hajji, the ward supervisor, and no one else. He is the young man in his thirties who told me once that he is getting his master's degree in education for special needs children. Aisha and Laliye told me earlier that there was a rumor circulating about him: he planned to open his own school and take in private clients even though this was technically illegal while he remained an employee of the state. Wherever he was, he was not to be found on the big orphanage campus.

/////

I asked about him every day for two weeks, but he was still gone. Then yesterday Aisha phoned me to say that she'd seen him in the cafeteria during an afternoon tea break. I caught the bus and was walking into his office not two hours after hearing that he was back.

"Sit down, Mrs. Norita." His voice was cool. "How are you? Your family? Work?"

"Fine, fine. I'm here to complain about someone, though, Mr. Hajji." The picture of Clara's head banging back down onto the cement floor resurfaced, along with the anger. "I'm here to complain about Hatoon. She had a rope tied around Clara's neck and was jerking on it when I came into the corridor two weeks ago. I know I'm only a foreign volunteer and not an employee, so there might be something I don't know about how things are run here, but surely this kind of treatment is not acceptable practice!"

"Now, now, I'm sure there's some sort of misunderstanding." He half-smiled at me with a look that said, "You are annoyingly petulant, but I have to put up with you anyway."

I could feel the ire rising against him as well and found myself wanting to haul off and smack the guy in the face. He should have at least shown a semblance of indignation at the way one of "our children" had been treated. Government officials always referred to the kids in the institution as "Our children. Our national responsibility. Our 'Holy Charges.'" Instead I was the recipient of his attempt at patronizing placation.

"Listen, you do something about this or I'm going to complain to the head director," I threatened shrilly. I felt myself quickly losing control.

He went to the door and called down the hall for someone to tell Hatoon to come to his office. A moment later she burst in, her head barely above the doorknob, her face roughly equal to ours since we were sitting. He then told her I had leveled a complaint against her.

She took two steps toward me and shook her finger at me. "Why, you little blankety-blank-blank! You big liar! I did nothing of the sort. You can't prove anything. You can't do anything to me. You're ... you're ... scum." She looked like she was going to punch me, and unconsciously I leaned back as far as I could to keep my face out of her reach.

"Now, now, Hatoon." Mr. Hajji's voice was controlled as he tried to cajole and calm her. "Could it be that Mrs. Norita was maybe mistaken? Surely you didn't have a rope around a child's neck. That would be very bad indeed. You tell me what happened. Maybe she can't fully understand the situation? Sometimes foreigners get it wrong."

But Hatoon was not to be contained: "There's nothing you can do to me. I'm a government employee. I have my rights. I'll complain that you've been slandering me. What ARE you doing here anyway?"

"Hey now, that's not polite. You don't have to shout," he ordered her to no avail.

I sat stunned. It was dawning on me just what Saray was: a world where everyone survived either by intimidation or by sticking his head in the sand. I lowered my head and waited until, tired from her raging monologue, Hatoon literally sniffed with her nose in the air and marched out of the office, slamming the door as she left.

I left completely frustrated. Gradually, as the anger subsided, all I felt was hopelessness.

I shared that as we gathered as a group to pray about this. I related the experience, still baffled and wondering what to do. Then Guliye shared something.

"Sister Norita, this week I learned that Hatoon is a product of the orphanage system. She was abandoned when she was little because of her dwarfism. She grew up in this system. I think she was even matched up for marriage with another of the people who lived here. She has a child of her own, and often claims that her one reason for living is that little boy.

"I honestly think that nearly all the people we are having trouble with here, the ones changing the diapers or feeding the kids, are themselves Holy Charges."

As I listened, I felt more and more miserable. My reaction of righteous indignation, while justified on one level, hadn't helped little Clara, nor her caregiver for that day, tiny Hatoon. That woman, though a mother with her own child, had never been loved unconditionally. She had no clue.

I prayed for her and wondered what I ought to do. Hatoon needed to know that she is precious in the eyes of God, too.

I wish I could say that today I am more patient and don't fly off the handle when in the presence of such blatant cruelty. I still struggle with it and with Jesus's admonition to pray for evildoers. But I have been so impressed by my Turkish sisters who are showing me how to use our tongues to gently persuade childish caregivers to be kinder and gentler. I've been time and again amazed at hearing words of encouragement uttered to women and men who I felt ought to be horsewhipped. The results of gentle admonition are visible, though.

These workers, when treated with gentleness and respect, listen and begin treating the children differently.

I could finally pray for her: "Father of the fatherless, bless little Hatoon. You know her heart. You know her real need. She needs to know You personally. But, God, please move her to another unit where she won't do as much damage to the children as she does now."

/////

October 1999

Today, I ran into Hatoon as I came onto the Saray campus. She passed me in a rush while on her way to the main office. She held her head high while announcing loudly for all to hear, "See, they gave me a promotion." When I asked one of the day-care staff who was lounging in the doorway what Hatoon had meant, he told me that he'd heard that she was being transferred to Block A Unit 6, which housed children who had moderate disabilities.

I ran inside the building to call out to her as she slowly climbed the stairs to the second floor. "That's great," I said, smiling, and gave her a high-five. I meant it with my whole heart.

CHAPTER 8

The VIP Lounge

For the kingdom of God is not a matter of eating and drinking, but of righteousness, peace and joy in the Holy Spirit.
Romans 14:17

My personal notes continued ...

December 1999

At Saray, everything is concrete and gray plaster. The worst housing holds the neediest kids. D Block is a large cinder-block one-story building found in the middle of the vast orphanage grounds. There are four wards; each one opens onto one of two long parallel corridors. These are only accessible from one entrance that leads into and through the back of the bustling kitchen where all the food prep for the institution takes place.

Nearly all the windows are broken, and crooked wooden frames allow for draught and dust. Two of the wards are furnished with wall-to-wall metal cribs: Continuous Care 1 and 2.The children—some as young as ten months, others as old as twenty years—are confined to these beds twenty-four hours a day, seven days a weeks, fifty-two weeks of the year, year after year.

"Generally they are housed here until they die," Mr. Mustapha says in answer to my question about the future of these kids. "Unlike our normal orphanage children who are sent out into the world to make their way after reaching the age of nineteen, these people are now wards of the state until they die—even the ones who have no mental impairment.

"But then, why would the mentally fine people want to leave?" he asks rhetorically. "They have everything taken care of for them here. Out in the world, it's a different matter. They'd die out there on their own. Their families have abandoned them."

D Block wards were designed with one hole-in-the-ground toilet cubicle and a bathing room that opens into a large rectangular room. This serves as the dayroom for Continuous Care 3 and the Severely Mentally

Retarded Ward (SMW1)—the children in these wards can get around on their own; some can even walk, but all day long, they are left in a locked room.

When I come up to that room, I peer through a double-reinforced window into their dayroom. I can see the three long steps that follow the length of the large room. At the top of the steps, a veranda-like section is divided into four spaces by chest-high brick walls.

In the Continuous Care wards, these four sections are packed with metal cribs; in the Severely Mentally Retarded wards, they are empty except for a child or two who curls up into a corner. He might spend his time playing with his diaper or picking the linoleum off the floor and trying to eat it. Down the steps and lying or sitting on the floor next to the door are usually ten or twelve other children. A couple of active kids stand at the window pressing their noses against the safety-glass panes and pounding for someone to come and set them free—all day long, they stand and pound. I am told that these particular children are "hyperactive." If they weren't given drugs every day, they'd have to be tied to posts. As it is, from time to time, some of them are taken out and roped to beds in their community bedroom across the hall.

More than 250 children are housed in this building. Most are tied up; most have never known a loving caress or soothing hug. "Father, have mercy. Father, have mercy on us all," we have begun praying daily.

Guliya, enthusiastic about bringing in more help, introduced us to a friend of her son. Taciturn but determined to do a good job, Demi has come prepared to work as a Kardelen Team member in that difficult ward at the end of the hall. Tall, with long wavy black hair and almond-shaped brown-black eyes, this beauty is eager to please but has yet to understand the extent of the neediness around her. Actually we all are being challenged in the same way. Every new experience of abuse or ignorance comes as a shock.

Although silent in our meetings, where the rest of us talk freely about God and prayer, Demi is a respectful Muslim. "In my family, tolerance and open-minded discussion were valued by my father when he was alive. And my fiancé has told me a bit about Jesus. "

Those of us from church are quite used to stopping what we are doing, pulling off into a corner, and praying about anything or everything.

Demi holds back from all that but recently asked me if her younger sister, Sharifa, could come join us too. Since Becky and Gary have given me free reign to hire as many helpers as I can, I view these women as God-sent no matter what their religious affiliation.

The other day on her way down the corridor to CC2, Laliye noticed a locked door leading into what looked like a large storage room. When she asked a worker about it, she was told that it was actually an unused ward.

"Lord, give us this room to use," Karin, Laliye, Aisha, Guliya, and I stood in front of the locked door and prayed.

Together we walked over to the office of Mr. Jemal, the recently appointed head director, who greeted us warmly. "What can I do for you?" he asked while his secretary brought us cups of tea. More than once, we had commiserated together on the problem of insufficient staff and poorly prepared caregivers. He then said the powers above, the men and women who made the decisions, really didn't have Saray on their radar screens.

After taking my first sip of tea this day, I plunged right in: "We would like to have permission to renovate the vacant room next to CC2. I think I can find the money from some friends. We'll make it a community playroom. We'll use it for games and exercise and some extra caregiving for some of the kids there."

"What room is that?" His office was less than a hundred feet from the D Block, but it appeared that he knew little about the actual facility. He said he needed to consult with his assistant directors (any one of the hundred people who sat behind desks in his admin building, I surmised). One of them would know about the D Block. He'd get back to us in a couple of days.

Two days, later we got the okay: "Do what you want to the room. But show us your plans before starting," we were told and immediately called the USA to share the news.

The Parsons in Arizona donated funds. Mr. Mustapha connected us to a local chapter of the Rotary Club in Ankara who agreed to pay for another part of the renovation. The remainder of the construction costs of the "Hope Room" was covered by our newly formed sister charity in the USA: the Friends of Kardelen Foundation.

Desley's husband Don, an artist and photographer, had visited us from Southern California last summer. Ken and he, along with little Michael and Ufuk, the son of Ken's foreman, had taken off in our Hyundai van to deliver wheelchairs to children living in a couple of villages and cities in the Anatolian outback and Mediterranean Sea. Don's church had raised the money to buy the chairs. He was able to see for himself how kids and their families impacted by physical disabilities were living in Turkey.

Don and Desley's relationship to their daughter, Megan, was truly inspiring. Megan had suffered severe brain damage as a result of high fevers brought on at the time of her childhood immunizations while they were living in the Middle East and working for a private company. Love, commitment to excellence in care, a caring church community, and their own personal faith meant that Megan had been given the very best in care and training. She, in turn, was one of those children who made you feel loved and special just by sitting and spending time with her. She was nonverbal but communicated love more articulately than the grandest poet could.

What Don had seen on this trip, plus his visit to Saray, had convinced him that he and his wife could start a foundation in the USA to help bring us funds as well as administrative advice. The timing for all this was truly providential.

/////

Personal Journal Entry

Today, the 5th of March, 2000, we celebrated.

Washable hospital-blue linoleum covers the concrete. The cubicles have been transformed into colorful spaces where children can be brought. We are doing all we can to make one-on-one care happen. So now there are soft activity mats and floor rugs. Tables and chairs mean that children who are not severely mentally impaired but physically limited can play games or be tutored in reading or math.

While this room was being readied to serve the children, I got a phone call from Peter Rinehart. He and his wife live in Ankara with their three small children and are very involved with the embassy-affiliated German school.

"You know that I love kids and teaching," he said. "Would it be possible for me to join you once a week out at the orphanage?"

I was thrilled. So we now have a math tutor!

A donated computer, a washing machine, and a kitchenette are all features of our bright yellow Hope Activity Center.

We repaired the windows, put up floral-patterned curtains, and were able to get carpets for the veranda sections. A large carpet factory was situated just down the road about five hundred yards from Saray. Aisha and I made a visit to the manager, who gave us a decent price reduction. We immediately ordered ten smallish rectangular blue carpets that could be rolled up and moved throughout our room to wherever an activity was taking place. Becky as well as the Boardman's sent bags full of colorful hanging mobiles: birds, smiley faces, and sparkly shapes. We hung the first ones over the beds in the wards so that the kids lying there all day long would have something to look at other than the gray ceiling. Now mobiles adorn the cubicles of the Kardelen Room, too.

/////

From the moment the washing machine was installed, it has been in use. Appalled by the generally poor skin conditions of the children—fungal infections, calloused and cracked skin, and many open seeping wounds—we researched possible ways to change this situation.

The orphanage typically buys their laundry soap by the ton from a local soap-making factory. This detergent is the worst quality and, combined with the extremely metallic hard water of the region, is one of the culprits behind the skin conditions (along with poor nutrition and rampant bacterial or fungal infections). We have been told that Saray's budget will not allow for better quality soap (or shampoo or bathing soap or cleaning agents, for that matter).

This week, we began our campaign against skin diseases by supplying large bags of detergent along with laundry softener. Even though the sheets are still washed with the old detergent in the industrial laundry "cavern" and are still sometimes damp and never all that clean, "our" T-shirts and PJ bottoms come out soft and smelling like lavender.

Then we bought boxes of tubes of fungicide and antibacterial cream. This fight is on.

When we first began designing our room, Aisha, Laliye, and Guliya asked me about pictures I showed them of some activity mats I'd seen at a center in England on one of my research trips. We showed Ken's wheelchair workshop seamstress, Alise, those photos and she has made several for us.

Alise is a stunningly beautiful young woman. Childhood polio had left her limping and, incredibly, socially undesirable. One of the few who had decided not to give up, she'd gotten sewing training and used her creativity to produce quality products; her multicolored children's cushions cost a fraction of the price of the imported catalogued therapy items.

We got shot-in-the arm encouragement from Down Under too. Red-haired and wiry, Bob—a retired factory worker and disability engineer from Australia—along with his wife, Marion, heard about this work from another Aussie friend of ours. After writing to ask if they could come, they showed up this spring in Ankara with their sleeves rolled up and ready to work.

Marion is a retired nurse, and along with two new expat volunteers from the States, Darlene and Sandra, spends nearly all her time in CC1, lovingly bathing, changing, and feeding the completely dependent children: the ones who can't walk, talk, or feed themselves. These middle-aged women are tireless and resourceful. Even though they don't speak the language, they are ace at communicating with touch and tone of voice. All three are mothers with grown children and are good at common-sense caring. The Kardelen Team is learning from them just by watching them in action. Sometimes they find themselves watching the Turks to follow their lead.

Bob is funny and passionate. He loves to talk politics with Ken and spends part of his week at the KIFAS wheelchair shop and part of the week at Saray. He loves to tinker and invent. He rigged up a special bike for Juneyt, who has cerebral palsy and can't walk on his own. This little eight-year-old has been transformed. We have to look out when walking down the corridor or risk getting run over by our local grinning speed demon.

Turkey, Australia, and the USA are not the only countries where our team comes from. Two couples, recently retired, come from The Netherlands as well. Frits and Yikkie, along with Clement and Suzie, are all grandparents who have decided to take their pension time and pay and do something useful with it. Typical Dutch—intrepid travelers and entrepreneurs—this year, they have decided that their travels should include making use of their practical expertise. While the women spend time in the wards with the smallest children as well as helping Aisha and Laliye, the men have decided that the broken-down and unused playground equipment could be repaired and repainted. In their sixties, they are full of energy and passion for the children. I need to spend a lot of time, however, explaining or trying to explain some of the irrationality of the systems at the institution, at which all of us throw our hands up in the air, shake our heads, shrug, and then return to whatever work we're were doing before the conversations began.

/////

Becky's Hug Teams always make a big splash when they arrive. Typically a team of eight led by her flies into the small Ankara airport, stays in a clean, comfortable five-star hotel, and with a chauffeur-driven rented van, travels out to Saray to spend several hours.

They usually first come to the Hope Room. There, we who live in the country meet them. The visitors come laden with gifts of toiletries and cologne, or soaps and sponges. They bring food and nutritional supplement supplies we can distribute. We are thrilled with the large containers of children's vitamins, packets of single portion oatmeal, and peanut butter.

They like to "bless" not only the Kardelen Team members but also those janitors/caregivers in each ward they visit. No one refuses a gift, and soon the smiling staff permits these guests to take the children out of their beds and play. Before too long, the Hope Room is full of caregiving volunteers: some sitting on rocking chairs with tiny ones in their laps, others on the floor drying off children who have just had a long, delightful bath.

Youssef, the psychologist, has begun to visit the room too whenever a Hug Team arrives. I translate for him since he says that he must greet and thank the Americans who have traveled at great expense to volunteer their services. He asks that no photographs be taken in the wards. He stands by the door listening when the group forms a circle and someone prays out loud acknowledging God's presence in the day's activities.

The Hug Team members all dress in the easily recognizable colorful uniforms found in doctors' offices in the States. It is said that "the clothes make the (wo)man" and their daytime uniforms have raised the status of caregiving in the eyes of the local staff and volunteers. After the first Hug Team came and could get a firsthand look at the challenges of our small team, they sent a package. In it were brightly patterned uniforms like their own for our team to wear. Now the eyes of Aisha, Demi, Sharifa, Guliya, and Laliye sparkle brighter, and their heads are held higher, because they wear the uniform of a professional. They are truly dressing for success.

CHAPTER 9

VIP Power

But God chose what is foolish in the world to shame the wise; God chose what is weak in the world to shame the strong.
1 Corinthians 1:27 (ESV)

My personal notes continued …

June–August, 1999

Germany, The Netherlands, Australia, and the USA share their best people with us. The most amazing contribution, though, comes from another "country."

Young women from a ward called A Block 1 have started showing up at our door. A Block is a series of two-story "homes" situated behind the administration building. Each building houses about thirty teenagers. There is a dayroom, kitchen, bathing room, and toilet at the entry level and bedrooms on the second floor. There is no elevator.

These girls are in their late teens or early twenties, and I get the impression they are bored to tears. The other afternoon, I counted seven of them sitting in the shade in front of their building in barely functional oversized wheelchairs. Another five or so girls were there too, some sitting on plastic chairs, a couple sprawled on the weeds outside the front door.

A couple days later, five of them rolled up to the Kardelen Room door. Uncle Bob, as they now call him, decided he could fix a couple of the chairs but also determined that these girls were perfect clients for one of KIFAS' Whirlwind Models—chairs designed for rough use, which have actually been modified by Third World users. Friends of Kardelen raised the money. Three weeks after the girls were measured for custom fittings, their new "chariots" were delivered, among them a bright red one and a dazzling bright pink one.

Three of these women have grown up in the state institutions since being abandoned as babies. Others were abandoned by their families after some years in their homes. Two claimed to be taken in by Social Services after their parents died.

Two of them are brought to the Government School for the Orthopedically Handicapped for regular classes a couple days a week, but most of the residents in A Block 1 have no reprieve from a futile and boring life. All day long, they hang around their rooms, smoke cigarettes, maybe watch TV, and gossip or complain. I hear that there are a lot of suicide attempts, though I have not been around when these took place.

The TV in the dayroom of A Block 1 is always on, but if it is a rainless day, generally only Gul (age eighteen) watches from her prone position on the couch. Her body, deformed into the shape of a large "C," means she has not been placed in any sort of mobility device that could handle her deformity. Such deformities are common here where children have been left without the early intervention and exercise we take for granted in the West. So either by choice or the decision of the "House Mother," she is moved from bedroom, to toilet, to the day couch by one of the male caretakers. This happens when he is not busy with other chores. If she is lucky, after she wakes in the morning, she is brought down the stairs and dumped onto the couch facing the TV; there she lies all day until nighttime when the new shift brings her back to her room. Still, she is happy to be there; until a few months ago, she was tied up in a metal crib in CC2.

One day last month, Karin and I slipped into the Rehab Gym in C Block unannounced. We wanted to check out what was happening there and what children were being looked after. No White Coats in sight, the vast room was empty again except for one person—a woman, who looked to be in her thirties, pulling herself along the parallel bars. Painfully thin, her taut, jerky movements were slow and seemed tortuous. Sweat dripped from her chin.

"I'm Mediha," she drawled in answer to our questions. "Although I'm from A Block 1,I try to get here every day. There's nothing else for me back in my ward." When asked about the therapists on duty, she snorted a reply. "Ha! Not a single one of them is worth anything. They don't care about me. They just get paychecks and sit around and do nothing, or worse are fooling around with each other when I need help."

It took her several minutes to express this, but anger propelled her even though she fell short of breath more than once. Her legs jerked with spasms. I was afraid that our questions had brought on a fit, so I wanted to change the subject. She, on the other hand, clearly wanted to tell us about her life and feelings.

From her, we heard the accusation that Saray is no different than any other institution in Turkey: among the staff, illicit affairs abound; residents are considered chattel, or solely a means to a paycheck; and the "residents" who are able to speak have little recourse to voice their needs or complaints.

"I, unlike many of the children and teenagers here, can read and write. But that doesn't make any difference. On this vast campus, we are treated not with respect but as inmates, like those in a penitentiary. No one asks me what I'd like to do on any given day. Not a single person considers that I would like to wear something nice and new. I am a number in this concentration camp. I have no one to go to who will listen without shouting at me, or worse, totally ignoring me. Why do you think the morale is so bad in our A Block House? Since there is no one to listen there, instead we turn on each other there sometimes. It's horrible. "

At that moment, the smartly dressed female therapist whom I had met the first time I visited came running into the gym. Glaring at all three of us, she directed her ire at Karin and me: "Just what do you think you are doing here? Does the director know you are here without permission and bothering the patients?"

I slipped into my ever-useful "dumb foreigner" role.

"Oh, there you are. How nice to see you." I smiled, playing the role of cheerful innocent. "I thought I'd come by and drink a glass of chai with you and hear more about your work. Do you have a moment for that today?"

Mediha turned away to resume her parallel-bar work. Forced by convention to answer positively, the therapist stuttered an answer and led us out of the gym down to her office. After a few minutes of awkward conversation and two glasses of black tea, I, genuinely curious about her profession, again asked about Mediha's plan of exercise and about her cerebral palsy. The therapist impatiently replied, "Exercise and more exercise is what a CP patient needs, so that's what we do. Don't concern yourself with details; these are the provenance of us professionals."

I decided it was time to go. We took our leave after thanking her for spending so much of her valuable time with us laypeople. As she accompanied us to the front door, I abruptly turned back into the gym room, in effect, dragging her behind us.

"Mediha, you are an amazing woman," I called out. "Your courage and determination are so awe inspiring. I love what you are doing for yourself, and hope I can be as determined about life as you are. Don't forget to come by the Hope Room in D Block. It's a VIP room. We'd love to have you there."

At that moment, her intense physical concentration gave way to a jerky wave and wide grin, which grew even wider when she caught a glimpse of the White Coat standing there with an open mouth. I turned to the therapist and said with a broad smile, "Oh, and you, too. Please come and visit us there. The chai is always steeping."

/////

Nina is the natural leader of the A Block women. Twenty years old and a fighter from the beginning, she's been in government institutions for five years. The police first found her and her six-year-old sister on the front steps of the Ankara State Hospital. They had run away from the southeast of the country, more than seven hundred miles away. Having survived polio at the age of five, she then found herself permanently crippled due to the fatal car crash that took her mother. Nina is the oldest of seven children, at a young age forced to fend not only for herself but her brothers and sisters and a violent, unstable father.

At fourteen, she witnessed her small sister being kicked down the steep stairs outside their home. This, as well as other domestic violence and abuse, was becoming a daily occurrence. So Nina—not wanting her darling six-year-old sister Meryem, to suffer what she went through when her alcohol-dazed father abused her—convinced the little girl to run away with her. Penniless, they begged a cross-country bus driver to let them hitch a ride on his bus. He believed their story: that they were orphaned by separatist terrorists who had wiped out their village and the rest of their family.

Within six months of being brought to a regular state-run orphanage by the police, foster parents took Meryem to a city on the southern border, an eight-hour bus ride from her sister. Nina was brought to Saray, where she was forced to live separated from Meryem and the others, with her only contact with Meryem a sporadic phone call.

Nina, while not physically violent or abusive to others, is emotionally volatile. At least twice, she has sent the entire orphanage administration into a panic by threatening to throw herself out of the A Block third-floor window. Her wrists bear the scars of more attempts. She is a handful.

It is a cool but sunny spring day, and a gentle breeze blows over the large Anatolian Plateau. A patch of grass, the first sign of our newly planted garden, shows green in the twenty square yards of space between the our room and CC 1. The color and light bring cheer to our work group. Our team, working together with another Hug Team, this time from Louisiana, is busy preparing some gift packages for the workers in the regular wards.

Sporting a long ponytail, bright-green T-shirt, and jeans, Nina is at our door. With her, our gym-friend Mediha and their buddies—Kezzie, Elif, Behide, Fatosh, Shen-gul, Derya, and Dilek—have all positioned rickety hospital-style wheelchairs so as to block the entrance. They are clamoring for glasses of freshly brewed tea. Determined in spite of the difficulties in mobility, they manage to roll their chairs through the utility entrance, down the corridor, through the CC1 Ward, and up to our front door.

Seeing them there, I feel frustration and anger rise up inside me. Not at them but instead at the system, one that does not prevent molestation and violence. When I visited them once, two of them pulled me aside and told me that sometimes they have to fend off not only unwanted attention from personnel but also the violent outbursts of emotionally and mentally ill roommates. Since the first day as a volunteer, I have heard too many stories of how stronger children have overpowered and abused other children, how at night some of the older ones go roaming unrestrained, how angry outbursts can turn murderous. I learn that many a child disappears: his or her body is found lifeless—cause of death undetermined. Scooped up and wrapped in a sheet, the corpse is buried in a field behind the orphanage without marker or memorial. Within a few days, someone else comes to take his or her anonymous place in the ward.

It is sickening to realize that disabled people are the most likely victims of abuse. Those who have experienced this treatment, sometimes go on to be perpetrators. If you are a physically disabled resident in a state-run home here, then you are a ward for life. Most victims of abuse in institutions feel deeply hopeless and helpless; they believe that they are solely dependent on hoped-for kindness and protection from their ward supervisors or administrators. Apparently no one uses legal means to try to stop abuse. When I asked Mr. Sharif about this, he concurred that he could find no precedent of a resident opening any case against a state employee or the ministry responsible for institutions. Mentally or physically disabled residents, even if they are over the age of twenty-one, would not be tried, nor the staff in charge of them.

Today, mentally bringing myself back from these dark thoughts, I smile and ask how they are doing, but Nina blurts out a command: "Let us in your room. We're bored out here. It's nice in there. We want to meet the foreigners." The other girls with Nina look at me shyly, hoping against hope that I will grant them favor. I am almost overwhelmed by the hunger in their faces—hunger for recognition, for connection.

"Of course," I say and have to move aside quickly or risk getting run over. In they rush—six girls in wheelchairs, three of whom need to be pushed by their roomies: girls who are obviously slightly mentally challenged but over-the-top ecstatic at their good fortune to be a part of this group.

I call out to my team in the local tongue: "Hey, everybody, come and meet the ladies from the A House. Aisha, Laliye, Guliya, take them around. I'll get them chai." In English now: "You ladies from the Deep South, meet the girls from the neighborhood."

The Hug Team ladies are from Louisiana. Molly is an occupational therapist who shows them photos of her own children and some of the children from her practice in Rustem. Judy has brought her daughter Sarah along to visit. They immediately seem to bond with Nina even though none of them speaks the other's language. Hugs and warm smiles create a wonderful atmosphere of acceptance and trust. The A Block girls accompany the Louisiana ladies into CC2 and watch as the Hug Team go right to work untying children, lifting them up, hugging them, and then giving them warm baths and dressing them in clean clothes, all the while putting sweet-smelling lotion on the children and singing songs to them in English. The rest of the day, the noise of laughter and chatter floats out of the windows and onto the weed-ridden and abandoned miniature golf course next to D Block.

/////

Karin, our German colleague, chooses to spend the majority of her time visiting in the C Block Spastic Ward. She gives regular updates on how the kids there are faring, with special prayer requests.

"Let's really pray for Jem," she says one day. "He is so hyperactive and dangerous."

I remember Jem's pinching attack the first time I visited the orphanage. Though little, he sure could draw blood.

We sit together as a team and pray for Jem, asking the Father to comfort and calm his little heart, to change him. Karin and Rose go back to the ward and, laying their hands on Jem, briefly pray in German that whatever is causing him to act so violently would be dealt with, in the name of Jesus.

A couple of weeks later, the ward supervisor runs into me in the orphanage cafeteria.

"How is little Jem?" I ask.

"Glad you asked," he replies. "It's remarkable. It's like he's gone through some kind of transformation. He doesn't attack with scratching or pinching anymore. He's become more polite. You almost wouldn't recognize that he's the same person."

"Halil Hodja, our group has specifically been praying for him."

"Prayer?" This secular Turk registers surprise. "Well, whatever you are doing, keep it up. It's working." He rushes off, a little spooked by this unconventional strategy but certainly glad for the results.

/////

Karin's work in the Spastic Unit also meant that three boys—Yunus, Juneyt, and Umit—were fitted for new wheelchairs. Their lives changed.

In their "made for rough terrain" chairs, they escaped from their ward and made their way over to the Hope Room. Every morning, there they were at the door of the room, staying until we close the doors at 4:30 in the afternoon. Laliye has begun teaching Yunus to read. Umit and Juneyt prefer playing games on the computer and just hanging out. They never seem to tire of just watching the ongoing show.

Earlier that year, after I spoke in a small church in Los Angeles, California, three women came up to me and introduced themselves. Two of them had been working with special needs children for several years. They told me that they felt a tug by God to leave the States for a few weeks, come alongside us for a month to pray for us, as well as to give some seminars in the orphanage on how to really care for the children. When I returned, I was able to set up the training sessions. Administrators were going to participate in several seminars as well.

Her first day at Saray, Paula—the most experienced of the women from LA—noticed Derya. This twenty-year-old had big brown eyes and unwashed stringy lice-infested hair. Her movements were spastic, and it was obvious that no one had taught her to walk, wash, or feed herself. One of the more physically able girls fed Derya like a baby.

Paula and the Turkish girl from church who served as her translator, Hij-ran, took off after our group morning prayer together to go over to A House. No stranger to lice problems, Paula brought special shampoo and asked if she could wash Derya's hair.

"Hey, Hij-ran, who's the American?" Nina asked while outside, smoking her morning cigarettes.

Paula introduced herself, and at that moment when Derya was rolled outside, her whole body jerked and extended tautly, and she made howling noises. Nina translated: "Well, look at that, she's wanting to know if you've come to see her."

With a wide smile, Paula asked Derya questions. Hij-ran interpreted into Turkish, and Nina translated Derya's answers for Hij-ran to pass on to Paula.

"Are you able to feed yourself, Derya?" Paula asked. "Have you ever been able to eat on your own?"

Derya answered via Nina: "No, someone always feeds me. I don't remember ever feeding myself." Hij-ran translated that back to Paula who nodded, understanding.

Rustling around in her backpack, Paula pulled out a sealed plastic bag. Opening it, she produced a spoon with a bent handle. "I knew I was supposed to bring this with me. Derya, let me show you how to feed yourself."

With that, she strapped the spoon onto Derya's wrist. An hour later, Derya was eating out of a bowl on her own for the first time in her life. You would think that Derya had won the lottery. Her eyes shone with joyful tears, while her mouth, wreathed wide in a crooked smile, worked overtime as she tried to express in speech what the rest of her body language made plain. Later that afternoon, the rest of us walked over to A Block to witness the transformation. We started dancing. Everyone was laughing, clapping, and encouraging their sister to do this wondrous new thing—feed herself.

My heart was so full at this moment that I could hardly contain the joy. "Thank You. Thank You," I whispered. "Thank You for bringing us here. Thank you for Paula, for Carol, for Doris. Thank You for Derya."

A week later, Paula stood in front of the gathered staff of administrators and caregivers to teach a seminar on nonverbal communication. She asked Derya to join her for this. In so doing, Paula honored Derya, who was able to show the gathered group that she understood what she was being asked and could give "intelligent" answers to questions Paula posed. Derya pointed to pictures that Paula had prepared using the Boardmaker nonverbal communication system. They were also able to show the staff the beauty of adapted utensils. Derya felt like the star that day.

What we got from this event, however, was not that Paula had brought Derya to a new level of personal freedom (which she had), but that Paula PAID ATTENTION to this girl who before this was just one of the 573 disabled wards of the Turkish state. She "saw" Derya, recognized her as the beautiful girl that she was, and reached out in love to serve her. Derya's joy erupted into a special powerful expression because someone loved HER.

I am reminded of the story where Jesus loves a blind man called Bartimaeus, who had been sitting for years begging on the side of the road. His healing began the moment Jesus RECOGNIZED him.

"Norita," Paula whispered, "we have to share with these girls about the Source of our love. We're leaving in a week. We've bonded with them, but they don't know about the ONE who will never leave them. We won't have finished our mission unless we can share Jesus with them. If we could go out and have a party or something …"

Sensing that this urgency she felt was from God, I talked to the others and we came up with a plan. My friends Cathryn and Andy Hoard lived in a penthouse apartment with a fabulous view of the city. They were away to the States for summer vacation. They graciously responded to my request to let us use their place for a luncheon, where we would take the opportunity to show the *JESUS* film, a movie depicting the life of Christ from the Gospel of Luke, to whomever was interested.

/////

August 12, 1999

I don't think any of us will ever forget today. We prayed and prayed that we'd get permission to take the women off the grounds and into town without chaperones. And for the first time ever, we got it!

This meant that we were able to bring eleven wheelchair-bound young women out of the compound. For some, this was the first time they'd ever left Saray except to be taken by ambulance to a hospital; for others, it was the first time in so many years. We even got permission to bundle Gul, the girl with the severely deformed back, onto the backseat of the van and then later sit her, however awkwardly, in a sturdy chair for the outing.

Karin and Rose, along with the van driver, helped get the girls into the van. Four of us met them on the busy, steep street outside the apartment building and managed to one by one lift them from the van into their waiting chair. Oh, what we would have given for a simple hydraulic lift! At times, it was harrowing. Keeping some of the girls from rolling down the hill was no small job when the brake feature on their hospital chairs turned out to be either broken or nonexistent. In a couple of cases, the wheelchairs simply responded to the law of gravity faster than we could apply the brakes. We laughed away our anxiety and got on with it as best as we could. One by one, the girls were then rolled down a too-narrow driveway into the underground garage where there was an elevator just big enough to accommodate one chair.

Women from the Turkish church greeted each guest when they arrived at the top floor. These volunteers had prepared a feast and were prepared to serve.

Fresh-cut flowers in vases, silver, porcelain, and crystal adorned tables on the vast penthouse balcony. We enjoyed a magnificent view of this city—prosperous, modernizing, and official—the capital city of this land. It is a metaphor for the entire country, where in spite of all the building and bling, masses of people lie hidden away and off the radar charts for the only reason that they are disabled and poor.

Ken and his foreman, Hasan, showed up to collect three of the wheelchairs that were in bad need of repair. They, with no time to spare, took them to his workshop, hoping to get them back before the women need to get back on the van for the return trip to Saray.

After lunch, all but two decided to join us in the Hoards' TV room.

"Ladies," Paula began. "We have been so honored to have gotten to know you all these past few weeks. You have become friends, and we will miss you a lot after we've gone. But we cannot be happy until we tell you why we are happy to be here and to know you.

"For years, I was desperately unhappy and without a reason to live, but I was changed by coming into a relationship with the living God. Life is so full of turmoil and pain, but only Jesus can change your inside, your heart, and give you joy that last and lasts."

Aisha then spoke a bit about her own childhood years, mentioning being abandoned for a time by her mother. Shen-gul, normally the quiet, thoughtful one of the group broke in: "Oh, I can hardly bear thinking about what has happened to me. How could my own father and brothers just drop me off at the orphanage?" And with that, she began to cry.

Next to her, Fatosh nodded, then she, too, began to cry. The amount of inner turmoil, rejection, and loneliness being expressed was almost more than any of us could bear. As grief surfaced, we struggled to honor the need to express this long-withheld pain while still offering them something good to take home.

Nina, as usual, took the lead. She was talkative and aggressive, keeping up a running dialogue with whomever she was sharing her story. She, however, divulged nothing of her own experience. Instead she made comments about religion and things she'd heard from others about Christianity. "I'm interested and know all about it," she boasted. "Turn off the lights and let's watch this movie."

From the first few scenes, Nina continued commenting. After watching the visitation by Gabriel to the Virgin Mary and the birth of Jesus, she shouted out over the music, "Stop the film."

We paused it.

"Are you telling me that a girl who was a virgin became pregnant and her Son, the Prophet Jesus, was born?"

After we nodded, she retorted with a flip of her long, black hair. "Why, that's absurd. Everyone knows that that's impossible. Mary was a virgin? Ha! That's crazy."

I thought to myself, *what a perceptive girl. And how unusual.* Devout Muslims would never question the Virgin Birth—there are verses in the Qur'an alluding to Jesus's birth to the Virgin Mary.

"Nina," I answered. "Your question is a good one, and you've reacted to one of the deepest mysteries that define our belief in who Jesus is and what He did for us. We should talk more about this later. There's lots to say; maybe we'll have time for that later."

"Humph," she sniffed. "We might be stuck in a state orphanage, but that doesn't mean we can be fed religion without us asking questions. We still are free to think. "

"Oh, I certainly hope so," Paula answered. "Let's keep on watching and see where this all leads."

Three minutes later, however: "Stop the film and come outside!" Hijran said as he burst into the room. "It's two minutes to the beginning of the solar eclipse."

News channels and newspapers have been broadcasting this special event. We were aware that this year, astronomers and enthusiasts had traveled from all over the world to the Anatolian Plateau where they had been promised a splendid clear viewing at 2:00 p.m.

We asked the women if they'd like to be wheeled outside again to the balcony to get a glimpse of the sky darkening and the sun disappearing for a few seconds. To our surprise, only two of them seemed interested. Some wanted to continue watching the film, but I was picking up a reluctant tension in the air.

"No, no, no! Not me," Nina stated.

"But why not? This is an historical occasion. It will be really interesting,"

"No!" she replied and looked away.

Shrugging my shoulders, I walked outside to join the others who had gathered for the celestial show. It was an awesome sight, to say the least—especially as we also had a unique vantage point and could look out over an entire city shrouded in a strange, dim light.

When we walked back in, I was again struck by the somber silence. All of a sudden, it dawned on me. They were actually terrified by the eclipse.

When I asked them if it felt kind of scary to them that the sun, moon, and earth had so come into alignment that the color of the sky had noticeably changed, Kezzie, the one with the turquoise-blue eyes and perfect features, blurted out, "This is a sign, they told me at Saray. I mean, one of the cleaners told me that the end of the world is near. The Judgment Day is coming. Of course I'm scared!"

Most Muslims, even nominal ones, have heard the Islamic teaching about the great and terrible day when the Prophet Jesus returns and everyone must stand trial for their good and bad deeds. Judgment Day and teaching about that future event was in everyone's mind.

Back out on the balcony, Laliye and Karin had gotten into a discussion about life and death and judgment with Hediye. She was one of the brighter ones.

Like Nina, Hediye was one of the physically disabled young women who had come fairly recently to the orphanage. A victim of a genetically transmitted disease, she'd had to leave nursing school two years earlier and was now confined to a wheelchair. With the progression of her condition, she had lost feeling in her legs, and was slowly going deaf and blind from tumors growing in her brain.

She was terribly depressed when I first saw her outside the D Block. A cigarette dangling from her lip, she scowled at us when we attempted to greet her. Thanks to Karin's insistent invitation, Hediye had made the enormous effort to get dressed and join us on this outing.

Here, the topic of conversation somehow turned to that ubiquitous Turkish pastime of fortune telling. Hediye revealed that her only joy came from reading her tarot cards every day. Fortune-telling—reading tea or coffee grounds—is an ever-present reality in Turkey, and while people laugh and say they don't really take much stock in this "pleasant pastime," there is a deep-seated faith in fate, fortune, and secret knowledge. Laliye told Hediye that the source of that divining power is not necessarily God, and that the Torah expressly forbids such activity. After thinking about this for a while, Hediye said that she didn't want to be involved in anything spiritually harmful. She decided to take out her tarot cards and burn them then and there. Surprised but ever-sensitive Laliye and Karin prayed a simple prayer of blessing over her too. She looked up at them. "I feel peace in me," she said.

Back in the entertainment room, everyone remained engrossed in the unfolding story of the *JESUS* film. Nina stopped making comments and was viewing intently. So when the doorbell rang and I informed the group that the van driver was calling us to bring the women down, a small rebellion ensued. At that point in the movie, Jesus had been tried and was carrying the cross. No way were they going to leave this film now.

"Go out and tell him to come back later," Nina ordered.

"Please?" the others pleaded.

Since all the wheelchairs had not yet returned from the repair shop, the driver had to wait.

Ken and Hasan arrived just as the story finished. Jesus, raised from the dead, talked with two men who didn't recognize Him, and He told them why the Messiah had to die. Absolute quiet reigned in the room until the closing credits.

The driver told us that he'd been getting calls from Saray asking him where the girls were, so we needed to bring our party to a hasty close. Paula and her sister, Carol, and their friend, Doris, took the final moments to hug each of the women and to promise to come back someday. Derya sobbed when she realized that Paula was leaving.

After that, it was a scramble and we got the women back to Saray just before sunset, leaving us all with lots to think about. That night, we said our good-byes to our California teachers.

Paula spoke: "You Kardelen women. You are awesome. I have watched you this past week. You are naturals, doing things with some of the most deformed and stiff children that I only learned about in graduate school. I so respect you all and want to see if I can't do something to help you get even better trained. You'll be hearing from me again. God bless you and we'll see you again."

/////

August 15, 1999

That night, those women in A Block were constantly on my heart. While standing at the sink in the kitchen at home, I suddenly could "see" them as members of our caregiving team. "They can serve in the wards where the smaller children are bed-bound." Excited, I didn't even realize

I had spoken out loud. "We could get them special uniforms or Kardelen T-shirts and maybe ask Becky if she'll raise some money for a small allowance for them."

Thinking I was talking to him, Ken looked up from his newspaper, raising his eyebrows in question.

"Oh nothing ..." I said. "Just more of this ministry puzzle is coming together." I grinned.

The next day, I planned to approach the girls in A Block House about this idea. But when walking through the front gate, Nina confronted me, rolling up to me before I could get too far onto the grounds. She'd been waiting behind the front gate.

"Sister Norita," she asked, skipping the traditional greeting. "Can I work for the Kardelen Team? I'll do anything. I can work in the kitchen. Whatever. Please. I want to work." Her big brown eyes pleaded.

"How would you like to be the leader of a team of women from A House?" I offered. "You would come over to the Kardelen Room at 2:00 p.m. every day during the week. Your job would be to run the kitchen. Make a batch of oatmeal and fruit and yogurt. Give each of the women their own bowl and small spoon and have them be responsible to feed children from CC1 next door. They can each choose a child, untie him or her or get one of the tiniest ones, bring them onto their laps and feed them carefully. We'll train you. Do you think you all would like to do this?"

She laughed. "Oh wow, would we ever!" And as she swiveled her chair around and prepared to speed off to her house to tell the other girls—there was no doubt in her mind that she would form a team even before the others have heard the plan—she promised something at the top of her lungs: "We are going to be the best team you've ever seen! You just wait and see."

/////

And they were amazing—the Kardelen Super Team. Every one of them contributed to serve the most desperate of the bedridden kids.

If Mediha's or Derya's movements were too jerky due to their palsy, then each would just hold "her" child on her lap while one of the other women who had no trouble with her own arms or hands did the feeding.

They treated each of the children in CC1 as if he or she was their own, such that they began visiting them and supervising their feedings on the weekend when we were not allowed on the campus.

Word got around that the A Block Kardelen girls were protecting the bed-bound kids. All of us were pretty sure that boys and girls had in the past been molested in their cribs. We had seen physical evidence as well as detected unusual frightened behavior when we began bathing them months before. Our complaints to the administrators resulted in some increased supervision during the week. Plus our presence seemed to discourage people breaking into the wards, but weekend guarding was lax with a greatly reduced staff presence. Now with the women becoming vigilant for their charges, incidents of sexual abuse in the CC1—at least over the weekends—had apparently stopped.

/////

The next day, not to be outdone by the ladies, speed-demon Juneyt blocked my entrance into the room. "I want to be a part of the team too," he drawled, head twitching this way and that but eyes never leaving my face. "I want to learn how to fix wheelchairs. I know that I can do it." At that moment, Karin, who'd taken a special interest in him, came up.

When I looked at her as if to say, "Can he do this?" she replied enthusiastically: "I think he can do it, or at least he should be given a try. Maybe Bob or Brother Ken can teach him some basics; we'll buy a set of tools, and maybe set up a repair corner in this room."

Two weeks later, they were in "business" trying to repair old wheelchairs retrieved from rarely used storage closets, as well as adjusting newly donated chairs.

/////

Although we are creating a space and program to be proud of, the orphanage administrators never officially recognize our "Hope Room" contribution. But it is still common for the director or sub-directors to bring visitors, politicians, or foreign dignitaries around to see the room and program. We are always introduced as volunteer "Mothers."

My personal friends, however, know and encourage us with kind words and donations. For example, the Dutch ambassador's wife, Elizabeth, visited one day with the team and participated in a birthday party there. Once, she brought along the wife of the Dutch minister. Over the course of the years, British, German, Japanese, and Swiss dignitaries, as well as American military, all passed through the gates of Saray on their way to volunteer in our special room. There, they were greeted by all the other VIPs who worked, played, and prayed there.

CRY OUT

CHAPTER 10

The End of the World

Therefore, since we are receiving a kingdom that cannot be shaken, let us be thankful, and so worship God acceptably with reverence and awe, for our "God is a consuming fire."

Hebrews 12:28-29

3:02 a.m., August 17, 1999

The ground heaved. Tectonic plates shifted. Western Turkey experienced the full effects of the shaking, and thousands upon thousands of people were buried alive when their apartment complexes or brick-and-mortar village dwellings collapsed.

With the death toll reaching past 15,000, and at least five major population centers affected, the Marmara Quake brought the nation to a standstill. Then, three months later, another powerful quake devastated more homes and businesses.

Turkey was suddenly on the world's radar. Foreign countries sent rescue crews and money. Relief agencies like Doctors without Borders and World Vision suddenly were at our doors, asking how they could help. Churches from Singapore to the USA sent groups who set up clinics, makeshift kitchens, tent cities, and container cities.

The day after the first quake, citizens and expats alike climbed into their cars and trucks, and made their way out to the closest affected areas to try to offer any kind of help they could. Our storefront church members became relief workers overnight and soon were partnering with folk from other countries.

Almost overnight, Saray jumped from a population of four hundred people to eight hundred. A rest home and another facility for mentally disabled adults were significantly damaged as a result of the quake, so all the residents were moved to Ankara. Someone hastily completed a two-story twenty-room building fifty yards down the hill from C Block. There, a small clinic was staffed by a team of four doctors and four nurses. The new residents—all adults—hung out while their files were updated and the administration decided just what to do with them. To begin with, there were fifty or so newcomers to the Saray population.

At the same time, Ken and I contacted two European Christian relief agencies with proposals for bringing relief supplies in the form of mattresses to people who had been severely injured due to the quakes. Within two months, Dutch Evangelical Agency for Relief donated a large cargo van. A Swedish society procured and shipped five hundred special light and bedsore-preventing mattresses for distribution in the affected region some four hundred miles from our home. This became the Kardelen Relief Project.

Aisha's younger sister, Stella, headed up the project. She was a smart, educated, and self-confident young woman who had a tremendous heart for poor people. She, like so many Turks after the earthquake, was clamoring for work and a way to help practically. Friends of Kardelen raised her support for five months, and off she went, accompanied by our van driver and brother from the church, Murad.

No easy task, this young team tirelessly traveled thousands of kilometers in all the affected provinces, networked with the necessary government agencies, identified who the really needy potential recipients were, and, finally, distributed the goods.

"Norita Abla, you have no idea what a mess it is out here," Stella told me from the field. "No idea. The guys 'in charge' are corrupt as corrupt can be, all wanting bribes in order to help me get information as to who is really needy. It's also a very good thing that Little Brother Murad is here with me because I am definitely NOT safe in the company of some of these officials. They can be really crude, and quite honestly, sometimes I just want to slap one or two of them in the face for the way they talk to me or look at me. It's disgusting."

When I apologized for sending her out into such an environment without enough prior knowledge of just how bad it could be, she answered, "Oh no, I'm not complaining. God is giving me the protection and the wisdom I need to do this job. When I need to, I'm fawning and obsequious; when I need to, I'm a lioness—just depends on the person facing me at the moment." She laughed. "In fact, this morning I was able to get into the military headquarters, which is the command center for the earthquake region. The army is in charge, actually. The commanding officer, Colonel Mehmet, listened to me explain my mission and then made me an 'offer.' He told us to leave all five hundred mattresses with them in the warehouse, and then when I had returned with the bona fide list of those who needed the beds, he would release them to us. This is going to take several days, but I think he's an honorable person."

"Wow," I reply. "Sounds like this is our 'man of peace' for this job."

She continued with a smile in her voice: "Just tell Murad, though, that he'd better slow down and stop driving like a maniac, or I'm going to find someone else to do the job. He doesn't take me seriously. And you're the boss!"

Murad got a talking to and promised to slow down and treat the van with more respect than he had been doing. "Sometimes there are no roads to speak of Sister Norita," he said in defense of his performance. "It's just pure mud and rocks. One good thing about that, though: I can't speed up there," he joked.

/////

May 2000

Stella phoned me at 8:00 p.m. "It's finished. And we're exhausted. We will be back in Ankara tomorrow evening. We've got photos and stories galore. We haven't killed each other or anyone else for that matter—though, believe me, there were plenty of times I wanted to do just that. I have seen some pretty terrible situations, Sister Norita. So much need and so few people who really care out there. Oh well, God knows. We prayed a lot, nearly every day, and Jesus helped us, I can testify to that. But it was hard."

"Really?" I said. "You were able to get all five hundred beds out to the ones who need them?"

"Well, technically. Actually the colonel changed the deal and said that we had to 'donate' 10 percent of the mattresses to the army. So, in actual fact, on our sixth and final trip to the command center, we ended up fifty short. I told him that I had fifty more people I'd promised a bed to, but he didn't respond to that. He just signed the release form for the remaining mats and said that I should be proud of the work I'd done. To tell you the truth, at that point, I was so tired, I was in no mood to get into a talk-fight with him. Everyone else tells me we came out ahead. After all, 'this is Turkey.'" Stella repeated the phrase we all used when faced with an absurdity here.

Turkey indeed. All I knew was that those Kardelen people were to be found all over this land and not just in institutions like Saray. God wanted to touch them one and all.

CHAPTER 11

Dr. Don Plays His Violin

Enter His gates with thanksgiving and his courts with praise; give thanks to him and praise his name. For the Lord is good and his love endures forever; his faithfulness continues through all generations.
Psalm 100:4-5

Personal Journal Entry: January 2000

A letter just arrived from Massachusetts. I can't imagine whom it's from but am pleasantly surprised when I look down to see that Dr. Elizabeth Hale, one of my all-time heroes, signed it. She's asking if we could host a group of volunteers from her church for a Hug Team type of service. Among her group will be nurses and a doctor. They want to know if they can prepare a training seminar on any medical subject that might be of interest to the clinic physicians.

Elizabeth and her husband, Tom, lived and worked for many years in a clinic in the outback of Nepal. Although she was a concert pianist and pediatrician and he a heart surgeon when in the US, they had followed God's clear call to be his serving witnesses in one of the poorest nations of the world. Tom's recently written memoirs, *Don't Let the Goats Eat the Loquat Tree,* stirred my heart, and meeting Elizabeth in person some years back in Amsterdam only confirmed my awe of these Jesus-followers. They successfully raised two talented sons who love Jesus too and are living abroad as well. Tom and Elizabeth returned to the US only to continue their lives of service by advocating for those potential medical missionaries who cannot get out to the world's neediest people because of the huge school debts they have incurred. This is a sad reality: school debts keeping qualified and committed people from leaving the country for long-term service. Short-term teams, however, are an option for service. The important factor here is to make sure that those on the field long-term are setting the pace and arranging the agenda so that actual help and service reaches those in the greatest need. Elizabeth knew this and wanted to send those who knew it too.

Any friends of theirs are definitely going to be friends of mine.

/////

Personal Journal Continued: March 2000

We have permission for the team of a doctor, nurses, and therapists to join us for four days. When they arrive, we go first to the clinic to meet Dr. Sinan, the person responsible for all medical interventions and care. He's a pleasant blond-haired, blue-eyed young man who has requested that Dr. Don, the physician in the group, give a teaching on a particularly common but often undiagnosed bacterial reason for stomach ulcers. Dr. Don has come prepared with a slideshow and handouts. One of the nurses, Lauren, has offered to give another seminar on the best way to recognize and care for pressure-sore wounds—the kinds of potentially lethal open skin wounds that develop on people who are paralyzed or immobile for long periods of time. She's also brought sample medications and bandages. We've decided to hold the seminars in the cafeteria and invite as many of the caregiving and administrative staff as we can, sure that this will be a great benefit to the entire institution.

Also in this group is lovely Ruth. In her early forties, short with a round face framed by short curly hair, she immediately smiles and makes eye contact with the women who come from A Block every day to feed the children. When she gets up to walk over and greet them, they are silenced by the fact that Ruth walks with a severe limp, throwing her left arm around to give her the balance she needs to stay upright as she moves. However, the women—as well as the person in charge of CC1: Nilgun Hanum—are forced to pay attention when we explain that Ruth is a qualified occupational therapist. Of course, we have to explain what that is, since there is no such equivalent yet for that career here. Physical therapists receive a few hours of training in topics relevant to OT, but are unaware of how vital a role OTs play in training and aiding those with any kind of disability to survive and in most cases to thrive. Paula's "feeding yourself" training for Derya would have occurred years before had occupational therapy been a normal part of the health and medical system here.

Ruth offers several good suggestions on better ways to feed the children. From time to time, she comes to me to ask if we need this or that supplementary machine or toy, with a promise to try to raise money in the States, buy the item, and mail it to us. She checks to see what children could benefit from a wheelchair and talks about helping the children to sit correctly. Seating and positioning is another of those very vital practical areas of expertise for most OTs.

More than the material or professional help she offers, however, Ruth is bursting with a story she wants to share and asks me if I would gather the girls together. She has a story she wants to tell them—her own.

Within a couple of minutes of listening to her, we are all blown away and in tears.

Born with obvious physical deformities in her arm, hand, and leg, Ruth was abandoned at three years old and left at an American state-run orphanage. Despite her shriveled left arm and leg, she managed to survive incredible rejection and the emotional torment of her childhood years in the orphanage.

A volunteer showed up from a local church and befriended her when she was twelve. This woman prayed with her and shared the love of Jesus with her. With tears in her eyes, Ruth looked around the group of girls who were listening intensely, then said, "You have to know that after I came to know Jesus personally, I knew deep inside that I was not alone anymore. My suicidal thoughts no longer took control. Gradually thoughts of self-hatred left too. When I left the state home, I was eighteen and ready to do something with my life, so I studied hard and went to school to train as an OT. There at university, in a group of students who met to pray and learn about their faith, I met an amazing man who fell in love with me and ..." She stopped talking for a moment to pull out a photograph of her family. "... We got married ten years ago. That's him and our three children."

The group is dumfounded. Nina finally expresses what is on everyone else's heart: "Wow."

Ruth finishes her story by saying that when she heard about Saray from a friend of hers, she knew that God was asking her to come—not primarily to give occupational therapy tips but to meet this group of women and give them the best news possible.

"God really does love you each individually. He's not far away. Just pray and give Him your heart. He'll do the rest."

Mediha's eyes have never left Ruth's face as I translate the best I can.

Little lights of hope flicker in the faces of every one of the seven women sitting in that circle.

"Jesus is ready to come live in your heart, in your life," Ruth says. "Trust Him. Ask Him to come. He's not outside the walls of this place. You do not have to live in loneliness and heartache forever."

/////

Dr. Don, an internal medicine specialist, was willing to do anything to help. Having worked for thirty years in a large public hospital in Boston, he is no stranger to the power plays and de-humanizing tendencies of large medical institutions. Now sixty-five years old, he's decided to spend as much of the rest of his life showing the love of Jesus in as many practical ways as he can and has volunteered at his church to chair their missions committee, besides being on various boards for nonprofit organizations. While his medical knowledge is surely prolific, he has so much more to offer. Dr. Don makes you smile.

Sporting a still full shock of white hair, and with twinkling blue eyes, he took out the violin he's played for more than forty years and begins playing a lively Mozart piece. He played wherever at Saray—in the cafeteria, in the halls, or in the wards. Staff, coworker, and children stopped what they were doing to listen to these wonderful, sometimes humorous tunes. Every now and then, Dr. Don played a familiar hymn, giving me the opportunity to worship there.

Dr. Sinan was enthralled and decided to bring his guitar to the campus. He entertained us with lively music as well—well-known Turkish folk songs. Dr. Don listened, and when he could, played along. Aisha and Laliye join their voices to the musicians, as did Nina and Mediha. What a joyful noise!

It was day four of the Massachusetts Hug Team Project, and we had invited all who could and wanted to come. Unbeknownst to us, the new director sent around a message that everyone except for one or two caregivers who must stay back to monitor the children was required to come to hear from the Americans. Unfortunately this meant that a number of cynical and frustrated attendees filled the rows in the seminar room.

After the slide show on bedsore treatment (picture after picture of gruesome infected wounds), the atmosphere in the room had begun to deteriorate. I started to hear snippets of Turkish snide comments—all directed at the Americans and the Turkish government.

Dr. Don, unaware of the atmosphere, was eager to talk and knew he only had a few minutes in which to share. About thirty of us were sitting in college classroom-type chairs in the large, drafty, dirty pink meeting room. He leaned over and whispered that he had changed his mind about giving the lecture, but that he'd leave the material with Dr. Sinan. Instead he wanted to try to encourage the staff by sharing a bit from his own personal experiences.

Instead of immediately launching into a speech, however, he picked up his violin and asked for requests. Gradually the group warmed up a bit. Some of the girls with developmental disabilities girls had joined us and were shouting out their requests for Turkish pop songs. He didn't know those, so they begin serenading us all. Dr. Don clapped for this impromptu chorus.

"I won't have enough time to give you the seminar I'd prepared in the States before coming, but I do have a few minutes and I want to tell you a little bit of my own story," he said. "Because I worked for years in a large hospital in Boston, I know how difficult a task you have before you to care for the hundreds of children, young adults, and now even aged people who live at this facility. I salute you for your dedication and hard work. Your task is not an easy one. Each one of you is a hero in my book.

"As a young college graduate with a degree in music, I was restless and unsure of what I should really do with the rest of my life. I had the great opportunity to travel some and offered to do a voluntary stint for a few months in Africa. I was recruited to help keep the books at a clinic in the remote countryside of Congo. Everything was strange and exciting. I still didn't really know what to do with my life. One weekend, I had the great privilege to visit another clinic some several hundred miles away. It was the home and workplace of an aged Swiss doctor by the name of Albert Schweitzer. He was eighty years old then; I was in my early twenties. He loved to walk every evening after dinner and invited me to join him one evening. Although he didn't speak much, I felt that I was in the presence of greatness and will never forget the joy I felt when he, upon learning that I played the violin, asked me to accompany him while he played the organ.

That is one duet that stands out clearly from all the other performances I've ever given.

"Being with Dr. Schweitzer reminded me of the One who cared for the physical needs as well as spiritual needs of poor men, women, and children. I realized that because Jesus Christ had shown me how to live, I was to follow His example and also dedicate my life to caring for the sick. Those weeks in Africa redirected the course of my life, and although it is not an easy road to follow, I am convinced that it was as a result of a high calling that I went into medicine.

"Because we haven't had much time today, I shan't speak longer but would be happy to answer any questions you might have." He finished, then waited for any responses from the audience.

Dr. Sinan asked about the medical topic Don had originally prepared to speak on. Don answered him with as technical an answer the moment permitted and then agreed to speak further privately when he handed over the slides.

"Just a minute," a young man in a white jacket spoke up. "Your talk was interesting, but I have something to say about it. While I can't say that my faith in Muhammad has brought me into this profession, perhaps if we lived in rich America, I'd be religious too."

Sarcasm and mockery suddenly reared their ugly heads. Those sitting with the man, a group of five or so white-coated health care personnel, began snickering.

Ken, who had taken off from his work to perform as this day's designated translator, found it difficult to tell the good doctor what this man had said. But by then, it was obvious from the behavior of that group that they were antagonistic, the atmosphere taut with contempt. I heard one of the other doctors whisper loud enough for his friends to hear: "Who needs you? We did not ask you to come and talk to us, as if you were some great savior from America."

Responding with great grace and patience, Dr. Don reiterated what he'd said at the beginning of his talk: "I can understand some of your frustrations. But I am impressed by your dedication under such difficult working conditions. I honestly don't know how well I'd respond if I were here in your shoes."

The white-coated man sniffed and sat back, satisfied that he'd made his point. I still felt embarrassed by his behavior and that of his "professional" friends. How is it that people who could be so hospitable could at the same time be so rude?

After thinking about this for a bit since the incident, I have come to some conclusions about one source of such bitterness: pervasive hopelessness—not only at the orphanage but also in the society at large. This lack of hope for the future is deep seated and lodged in the hearts of so many of the "nice" people. This state worker was, in other words, saying, "Nothing you could possibly say will in any way change our situation. I won't bother to care. I might as well mock your faith."

Time and again, I've had long conversations with Turkish friends who have careers in the service professions and who were extremely idealistic to begin with. Now they are disillusioned and cynical. Social workers, doctors, and physical therapists fresh out of university are ready to change their worlds and their country. Not long after working in an institution, these good, intelligent people seem to shed their ideals and altruism like ill-fitting coats. Now you become aware of some hard edges, cynicism, and weariness of soul. The "Well, at least I am a professional" superior sort of attitude emerges along with a materialistic priority about work. Unselfish caring and a passion for improvement are ideas that they assent to in speeches and conversation, but in actual fact, those virtues inevitably take a backseat to self-preservation.

The humanistic motivation to serve and help the desperately poor and needy, while praiseworthy, does not survive on its own. Soon the fears of being replaced at work by another professional or of being passed over for a promotion or of being transferred to some outback station controls all other impulses. Once clear, hope-filled enthusiastic eyes now turn dark, suspicious, and "blind."

We entered Saray thinking that perhaps we could offer help and some motivation to the staff there by presenting in-service seminars as well as help in caregiving. Nearly every seminar experiences those first years and our day-to-day observations showed something different. We observed and listened closely to what they had each been saying.

If they are trained doctors or psychologists, social workers, or therapists, they begin their careers working with commitment and creativity, but before too many days on the job, their goals change, get squelched, or are overrun by the tyranny of the urgent, and their coping mechanisms kick in: a) be present on the wards as little as possible; b) never touch a child if possible; c) try to get an office job in a building as far away from the children's wards as possible; d) never step out on a professional limb to improve the living conditions of those who are wards of the state—because if you rock the boat, you might lose status.

The week after Dr. Don and that team left, Dr. Sinan stopped me on the stairwell. "What is it about you, Norita? You're always smiling and encouraging and trying to help these children, but can't you see that this is a hopeless situation?"

"Sinan," I answered, "this is only hopeless if you don't have a relationship with the One who created the universe. A relationship with Him makes all the difference."

"Oh, I am an atheist. How could I have faith in a god who causes so much suffering? You know how these children are sick and dying. You saw how stupid those medics were at the seminar. Embarrassing to say the least."

"Ah, but the very fact that you recognize suffering or injustice as something essentially wrong, and something to be alleviated, tells me that you are closer to God than you think, for that is exactly what He thinks. God does not remain passive. He does not 'will' it. He is brokenhearted about it."

"How do you know what He thinks?"

"Well, I hear Him. He speaks to me—through the words in the Bible and in my heart."

At this, Sinan laughs. "No, don't tell me that God speaks to you?"

"Yes, and I know that He loves you and wants to speak to you, too."

"No, no, no." Sinan laughed again. "That's too much, but if He does speak to you, will you ask Him to bless me?"

"Of course, but I'm also going to ask Him to 'bother' you—so look out." I grinned and shook his hand before rushing off to catch the service bus.

He stood there shaking his head as if to say, "Their leader is crazier than all the other 'Kardelen Kooks' combined."

CHAPTER 12

The Eyes Have It

"The eye is the lamp of the body. So, if your eye is healthy, your whole body will be full of light."
Matthew 6:22 (ESV)

From my personal notes ...

June 2000

Communicating means everything. Learning to listen, learning to respond, and learning to express needs are the first necessary building blocks of nurture and life. As a mother, I found it a real challenge to be able to interpret just what my babies were wanting and needing; their cries for attention were loud and insistent. I had to figure out if the diaper needed changing or if one or the other of them was hungry or not feeling well. I had to pay attention. At times, every theory I had as to what was going on tried my powers of logic, intuition, and sanity. But eventually I could interpret the type of cry, the issue at hand, and supply a solution.

An attentive and caring mother will try everything in her power to find out the reason for the tears and bring comfort. A successful communication bridge gets crossed when a diaper is changed or the breast is given. Within literally seconds, child and mother create a space of understanding that stimulates and further encourages even more complicated communication as the brain of the child develops.

Developmental neurologists and scientists building on the research done on attachment theory tell us that even the high-pitched loving chatter and "baby talk" of mother or caregiver, the warmth of a snuggled hug, the response to hunger cries stimulate the brains of newborns and infants in such ways that their nervous systems and emotional health are positively affected. Research shows, for example, that mothers in literally every different environment, culture, and tribe speak to their tiny children in "mommy tones." Their voice range goes up, and all sorts of "nonsense sounds" are uttered—to the absolute delight of their babies. Electromagnetic patches attached to babies in laboratories register immediate heightened brain activity when Mommy starts to look baby in the eyes and coos. One study points to the fact that mothers who are sedated or depressed do not speak in higher tones to their children. Brain wave activity in these children is significantly less. Less positive stimulation from Mom means Johnny might not get what he needs in his formative months.

My first day at Saray, I was, first of all, overwhelmed by the realization that so many children were moaning or whimpering, and no one was responding to their cries.

The kids in the Continuous Care wards moan when they hurt or are hungry. We mothers are realizing that in those rooms, the children do not cry like normal children would when feeling these negative things. Many of these Saray children have learned that no one will come when they cry, and so one by one, they have begun to shut off to the outer world. Or if they learn that lusty, healthy crying results in a slap in the face, they might whimper quietly.

Some of the children have learned compulsive self-destructive behaviors: head-banging, playing with their filthy diapers, and eating what they play with, or shoving their fists as far down their throats as they can until they throw up whatever they've eaten at lunch. They make no eye contact, and register no emotion. If no one is going to pay attention to them, then they'll survive, if barely, in the little bubble of "self"—doing what in some strange way gives them pleasure, like islands in the sea of misery that seethes around their individual metal cribs.

Rather than change the care program to increase the ratio of caregiver to child, and provide comfort and stimulation, the Saray solution is to tie the children's hands with rags to the bars of their metal cribs. Now they cannot stick their hands anywhere. More than once, I find myself entertaining the thought, *How much easier if these precious ones had been in comas—or dead.*

I cry out to God for understanding. "What's going on here? How can You justify this, Father?"

So here's my homegrown theology. Surely there will be those who disagree with me, but I cannot "fit" the relationship I have with an incredibly loving Father, Son, and Holy Ghost together either with an Eastern religious thought that says, "All reality is suffering, and release from this is some form of peaceful coma," or with an emotionless deterministic view of God's will.

I have come to live with the understanding that makes the best "sense," both to my heart as well as my logical mind. Foundational to the theology of Jesus is that human suffering resulting from human choice and neglect is not God's will. Nor is it the result of personal karma. These children are not the reincarnations of other sentient beings. They are truly innocent, but mentally competent bad people have made choices that result in the suffering of the innocent, both before they were born and after. God's will being played out in time and for eternity is essentially about relationship: the "I-Thou" relationship. God's perfect will is that we carry these suffering people in our hearts and minds, just as He carries us in His heart and mind. His perfect will is that we develop relationships with them. This side of heaven, we are responsible corporately to love and actively care for those who cannot care for themselves. Not to do so is to be separated from God's perfect will.

In the course of making relationships, we are compelled to look for ways to communicate and assuage wounds. God's will is that we partner with Him to discover solutions to seemingly hopeless scenarios. In a way, we have to "blind" ourselves to the whole horrible picture. Only God is capable of taking in all the terrible things and situations of humankind. *What burdens He must bear,* I often think. *What tears You must cry.* I find myself praying about this. Deep inside me, I have this unshakeable conviction that God weeps, not only for the condition of His creation, but for the condition of those who call themselves followers of Jesus but aren't actually doing any "following." A significant number of so-called Christians have turned a deaf ear to His cry and call to seek first His will and justice. In this twenty-first century, we need to read the story of the Good Samaritan in the Gospels in such a way that we understand Jesus is talking about lifestyle change, about relationship building, and not just an occasional foray into once-in-a-while-feel-good-about-yourself charitable acts.

God is both team player and coach. He is looking for a team who will be willing to step onto what looks like and sometimes feels like mined playing fields, with the aim of carrying the balls to goals that stand shrouded in heavy fog. Only the One who sees in the dark can guide us across.

We have begun to ask for the grace to "see" only what the Father is giving us day-to-day instructions to do. I remember that in the Gospels, Jesus goes to some towns where He heals everyone who comes to Him; in other places, compassion focuses His attention. He doesn't heal every sick person in Palestine, but He does do what He sees the Father doing. He is responsive to suffering that "crosses His path" as it were: the blind beggar on the side of the road, the father whose son is an epileptic as well as demonized, the dead only son of the widow from Nain. He heals those who break His heart.

/////

Among the thirty-six cribs, Aisha finds six-year-old Gursel tied up with hands blue from lack of circulation. She looks into his eyes. One eye is half closed and glazed over. She smiles, and then, reading his name from the paper pasted above his bed, she addresses him. He blinks and turns his head to focus with his other eye. His skin is bluish and body little more than a skeleton.

"Lord," she prays. "I want to help this boy. Show me what to do."

When she unties him, he immediately puts his right fist down his throat. She picks him up and begins to coo to him. "Well, little man. What do you think you are doing with that fist? Open up and show me what you are holding so tightly."

She tries to open his little hands (which are the size of a two-year-old's), only to recognize that his hands are red and chafed. Later she carries him down the road to the clinic where she asks Dr. Sinan that could be. He says, "He's got some fungus problem. Who knows how long it's been since he's had a proper cleaning? No one puts the medicine on those hands to heal him. You must not worry about that, because if you do start to work with him, chances are you'll be infected too."

Ignoring the doctor's instructions, she begins to spend more and more time each day holding Gursel, applying ointment onto his affected areas and feeding him with bottled formula. Within minutes, he responds to her voice, turning his head and grunting. Now he knows when she is near and allows her to pick him up and cuddle him.

It is days now, and he is not responding by gaining any weight, which worries Aisha. Instead he is getting weaker and weaker. He continues to auto-regurgitate. Aisha finds him one morning listless and gray. A doctor walks over to the ward from the clinic and immediately pronounces, "He's going to die soon. We better get him off the campus grounds and to a hospital in town"—further implementing the unwritten policy to send children into town to die if there is enough notice rather than have their deaths show up in the yearly report statistics.

"I'll take him," Aisha volunteers. She gets her coat on, and riding in the orphanage ambulance, she holds little Gursel wrapped up in a blanket. They drive into the city center to the well-known hospital that is the designated medical facility for state wards.

Holding him in her arms, she rushes as fast as she can to the pediatric ward, where she is told to take a number to wait to be seen by a doctor on call. She waits and waits and waits, looking up with anticipation every time someone with a stethoscope comes out of one of the myriad checkup rooms, only to be disappointed by a "No, not yet."

The ambulance driver from the orphanage comes into the waiting room at lunch to say that he is hungry, asking her if she'd buy him a sandwich. He was hoping to get back to the Saray cafeteria, where state-sponsored hot meals are served to the staff, but he has been delayed by her insistence on staying with the child. He is annoyed.

Finally, in the early afternoon, Aisha and Gursel are ushered into a room to meet with one of the specialists. The doctor takes one look at Gursel and flies into a rage: "WHAT IS THE MATTER WITH YOU PEOPLE AT THE ORPHANAGE? G–d d–––t! You wait until there's no more hope and then send your doomed children here to die on us. I refuse to have anything to do with him. Take him back immediately. We have too much work here already! He should die on your watch, not mine!"

Shocked, Aisha clutches Gursel to her chest, starting to retreat out the door. After two steps, she turns around, walks back to the large desk, plants her feet firmly, and forces the doctor to look up.

"I don't work for the government. I'm a volunteer. This little boy, Gursel, needs help and he needs it NOW. I'm not leaving this hospital until you admit him and do what needs to be done to save him! If I have to sleep here in the corridor with him, well then, I'll do that," she snorts, fire blazing in her eyes.

The doctor takes off his stethoscope, lays it on his desk, and stretches his hands out in front of him, not saying anything for several seconds. Finally he says, "Look, I can't save this child. He's going to die. He's already in a severe state of dehydration." He reaches out to pinch the skin on Gursel's hand. It stays pinched up in a single wrinkle. "See?" he asks, and this time, his voice is gentle.

"I know that he's in bad shape, but isn't there anything you doctors can do?" Her voice breaks now.

The doctor looks long and hard at Gursel and then back at Aisha before answering. "There is one procedure we can try. It should have been done a month ago. We'll give it our best shot."

He has joined her team.

He snaps his fingers and picks up the phone. "I have a small boy here who needs to be fitted immediately with a stoma tube. I'll suit up and be in the operating room in ten minutes to do the procedure myself." He hangs up, and after looking into Aisha's shining, hopeful eyes, he shakes his head sadly. "Please don't expect miracles. He's in very critical condition and needs to be stomach fed and hydrated. I personally don't believe that he'll survive."

"You just do your stuff and I'll pray. God has a plan. I promise to look after him after you're done."

Aisha has a big smile on her face when she hands little bundled Gursel over to an attending nurse.

/////

Overjoyed when Gursel survives after a week in the hospital, Aisha is there to pick him up. Every day back at Saray, she walks over to the clinic on the campus to check his condition. The hospital doctor taught her how to monitor and set up his feeding machine. So now she makes sure it is always working properly. She tells me that more than once she has discovered that the night nurse on duty at the clinic didn't know how to set it up and would allow it to get clogged with curdled formula. She took it upon herself to teach the staff there how to properly clean and fill it.

Slowly little Gursel has pulled away from death's door, but something still bothers him. He is still so uncomfortable after feedings. One day, Aisha looks at the formula in the bottle she was giving him. "I wonder if he has an allergy to this." She brings that up with Dr. Serkin, who agrees that this could, in fact, be part of the boy's problem. When the formula is changed to reflect this theory, Gursel's response is so obviously different that one could only wonder about the years he'd suffered from gas and nausea but hadn't been able to tell anyone.

Today, as Aisha picks him up and bathes him before giving him his lunch, he turns his head to be able to look her in the face with his good eye—and he smiles.

"Oh, my darling boy!" she croons. "What a beautiful boy you are! Father, thank You for this little one who is special to You. Keep on giving him new strength and keep showing me what I need to do next."

/////

Tucked far away in the corner of that room crowded with metal cribs lies a boy who has obviously outgrown his bed. He is curled up in a fetal position; his only movements to try to stick his hand as far down his throat as he can. He was covered in dried crusts of vomit and stank to high heaven when Aisha first found him months before.

Typically the nurse on duty scurries to pass out various pills and medications to all the children tied to their beds in Continuous Care 1. She obviously has the hardest time with the boy in the corner. He looks scary with his eyes half-pasted shut and his hair all in a wad. She slows down when she gets to him, pinches her nose with her right hand, and screws up her face in repulsion. Tentatively she sticks out her hand with a little paper cup filled with some liquid: her job is to get him to swallow and then for her to get out of there.

He invariably turns away his face into the mattress, and she is forced to touch him, to try to coax him to open his mouth by pulling on his chin and getting him to lift his head a bit to swallow. Every day, the scenario is repeated. Nearly every day, she grows frustrated at him and yells. He turns his head into the mattress and winds himself into a ball.

The paper taped to the wall above his bed says that his name is Bahri and that he is about thirteen years old. Usually covered from head to toe in puke, he has learned what so many of these children learn: when nobody responds to your cries for help or hunger or pain, then you stop crying and go inward. All contact with the outside world will cease, and the only discernible behavior is repetitive and self-distracting, like head-banging or auto-regurgitation. For Bahri, the only contact he has with the world is his own hand shoved down his throat.

Somewhere deep down in her heart, Aisha hears, "Love this boy."

The first thing she does is spend extra time washing him. The face that emerges is unbelievably beautiful. He has fair skin, black hair, and the brightest blue eyes and longest black eyelashes she has ever seen.

With Bahri smelling and looking nice, even the reluctant nurses' attitudes start to change. This gangly teenager, although much taller than the other children in the ward, just fits onto Aisha's lap. They begin to give him his meds when he is securely curled up there.

Two weeks later, Aisha comes to me with tears in her eyes again; she has been hurt by insensitive comments made by state workers. Someone has started a rumor.

"They are saying that in actual fact Bahri is my real son and that I am posing as a volunteer to come in and take care of him because, of course, I would be too ashamed to have a handicapped son at home. They are saying that no one shows such love to any strange handicapped kid—that he's got to be mine."

We talk together as a team about hurtful comments and where they really come from. We hug her and talk her through the inner process of forgiveness against those who seem so callous regarding the boy.

She takes a deep breath and announces a new decision; interestingly enough, it has nothing to do with the staff but everything to do with her heart and Bahri: "I've made up my mind. No matter what, no matter how I feel every day—if there are huge problems at home, for example—I am not going to let that affect my attitudes when it comes to loving on the kids. At Saray, the children come first. No long, sad, or angry faces while here. They need our smiles and joy."

Aisha's heart, filled with hope, reaches out to this boy. She bathes him, dries him, hugs him, sings to him, feeds him, and changes him day in and day out. In spite of all her attentions, however, Bahri shows no relational response: no eye contact, no grunts or sounds to indicate he is experiencing anything (good or bad). Aisha does not give up easily, however.

Bahri's legs seem to have cramped up into a kind of permanent fetal position. When she picks him up, his body is rigid and only minimally relaxes in a warm tub full of water. He's been left in this bed for so long with no real physical activity that he is getting more and more deformed and stiff.

She tells me, "I feel so bad for him. What should I do? Every evening before leaving the ward, I come by his crib and stare at him, trying to make eye contact. I pray out loud, 'Lord, show me what to do for Bahri. Please send angels to care for him during the night.'

"Last night, I had a dream—a lot like the one I had about Eva almost two years ago. I am at Bahri's bedside and hear a voice say, 'Put your hands on his leg joints.' After I do that, I hear, 'Rub with your thumb gently, counterclockwise.' I do that, then hear, 'Good! Now do that on his back, his neck, and his arms.' I woke up this morning with hands and arms tired!

"I will start today doing what we did in the dream."

/////

Six Months Later

Aisha comes rushing into the Kardelen Room, her face beaming. "You know how I told you that Bahri's legs are now able to fully extend and he is not nearly as cramped as before?" We turn to hear her story. "You know how sad I've been, though, because he doesn't respond in any way to my loving on him, how determined I have been not to give up nor stop all the massaging and bathing and feeding?"

We nod.

"Well, yesterday I went home totally demoralized about him. No matter what I did, he was not reacting. He was like a living mannequin, and my heart was breaking. Last night, I told God how I felt: 'I can't go on loving him without any sign that he's receiving it. I'm all out of energy and it hurts too much to do this. Tomorrow, if he shows no response, I quit,' and I cried a lot.

"Well, this morning, as I walk down the long bleak corridor to Unit 1, one of the state workers comes out to greet me. 'Something's happened. You won't believe this, but that lump of clay that was Bahri has gotten up on his knees in bed and is making sounds! Come and see.'

"My heart starts racing. I walk into the large room from the far side opposite to where Bahri's bed is. I call out, 'Bahri, my dear one, my little boy?' I can't believe what I'm seeing. He turns his head in my direction, grabs the metal railings of the bed, and pulls himself up onto his knees. He's making new sounds. Something's changed. He even flips his head back, showing me something. I know what that means. He's saying, 'COME HERE.'

"Balling my eyes out, I run to his bed and scoop him up. 'Well done, my dear little boy, well done!' At that, he looks down, almost like a shy little kid, and his mouth turns up into a smile."

At that, all four of us sitting in the room begin crying. This is too wonderful for words.

CHAPTER 13

"I Love You, Murad"

Have this mind among yourselves which is yours in Christ Jesus, who, though he was in the form of God, did not count equality with God a thing to be grasped, but emptied himself, by taking the form of a servant, being born in the likeness of men. And being found in human form, he humbled himself by becoming obedient to the point of death, even death on a cross. Therefore God has highly exalted him and bestowed on him the name that is above every name, so that at the name of Jesus every knee shall bow, in heaven and on earth and under the earth and every tongue confess that Jesus Christ is Lord to the glory of God the Father.

Philippians 2: 5-11[1*] (ESV)

My personal notes continued ...

January 2000

I am a very unlikely manager for all that goes on at Saray. I love to be in the Hope Room and participate in all the activities, but somebody has to tell the story and share the work with the people who might care enough about these children to give. I get stuck with the job and sometimes get overwhelmed, quite frankly.

This new vision requires being good with reporting numbers and getting details right. I have to learn to write proposals. So I spend time crunching numbers. How much is spent on buying fruit to give children a better diet? How much on wheelchairs and play equipment, on diapers, on renovations, on insurance, on ..., on ..., on...? It is a long list.

More statistics and I am getting "seasick" and begin to slide into a state of fear, because the details seem to shout out another reality: we are nothing more than numbers.

"Lord, do we mean anything? Show me Your take on things."

---

1 *Probably the earliest extant hymn of the fledgling group of believers in Jesus Christ, here incorporated by Paul in his letter to the gathering of believers in the Thracian city of Philippi around 65AD.

/////

We have a Hug Team here from a church in Texas. It's always interesting when they can only be here for a few days and we hustle to try to get everyone involved doing something meaningful. It's particularly a challenge to find activities for men who are not used to bathing and diapering big kids. Often the men have it harder than the women volunteers if they have to do hands-on care.

But today, Brother Jake, a lanky, tall Texan in cowboy boots and a ten-gallon hat, asked if he could accompany me as we made the rounds of the beds in Continuous Care 1 and 2. He and I decide to just spend the day praying for the children in their beds. Jake, despite natural upbeat exuberance, is having a hard time with what he is seeing. Broken windows and chipped paint quickly lose their negative value in relation to row after row of teenage children lying in too-small metal cribs and staring at the ceiling or the mobiles we have tacked up.

"This is Murad," I translate into English out loud for Jake from the little sign above Murad's bed. "He was born in 1978 in Erzurum, over 1,000 miles away. It says here that he's been here since he was six years old. Now he's seventeen years old. They have labeled his problem as 'SPASTIK.'"

I look down into intense black-brown eyes.

"*Merhaba,* Murad, I'm sorry," I say. "That was rude of me to speak in English. My name's Norita and this is Brother Jake."

To my surprise, he answers in slurred but intelligible Turkish: "Yeahhhh. I understand. *Merhaba.*"

"Murad, how are you?" I start in with the polite Turkish greeting.

His large lean body jerks crazily in response to my touch on his shoulder. "Awww, not so good." I am afraid that he is going to seriously bruise himself on the metal sidebars of the bed. Both his legs jack-knife out, and one arm stiffly rises into the air.

"Murad, Jake and I want you to know that God loves you," I say.

"Nawww. He doesn't." Murad jerks his head away and faces the wall.

I think that maybe he hasn't understood, so I repeat myself. But with a violent shake of the head, he repeats, "Nawww. He doesn't."

"Why do you say that? " I naively ask. I still am so thick when it comes to relating to someone like Murad, who looks to most of the people here like he's mentally challenged but in reality isn't.

"I'm handicapped. God doesn't love the handicapped," he says and then turns his face to the wall.

"Oh, Murad, why do you think that? Who told you such a thing?"

"Everyone."

And my heart breaks again.

I begin to think about this boy's life—actually not all that unusual for a child with his type of disability in this country. Here is a perfectly good mind trapped in an uncontrollable body. But his body is not his greatest grief. What must it have been like for a six-year-old boy to be brought by his father hundreds of miles to be left in a large, friendless institution? He is a "prisoner" in a bed in a ward. Some of his so-called caregivers' act toward the children as if they are tending livestock. Some treat these wards of the state much worse, expressing the belief that their jobs are punishment from God and that Murad is one of the reasons for their "suffering." God definitely cursed him or he would not have been left to rot in a bed with no one to really talk to for twelve years, they rationalize.

WHAT COULD I POSSIBLY SAY TO MURAD?

I turn to Jake. "Please pray for him. He's pretty depressed, and I don't know how to comfort him." I close my eyes and fix my inner thoughts on God, pleading for words that will encourage the boy.

From somewhere within come these words: "Tell him that I became handicapped for him."

Oh, Lord, what does that mean? What will he understand?

"Just tell him."

I open my eyes and look down into Murad's face. "Murad, God wants you to know that He loves you so much that He became handicapped for you."

Surprised and not a little skeptical, he shakes his head and his eyes bore into mine. "Naw. Naw. I don' unnerstand."

I draw a breath and, confident God is with me on this, just begin speaking.

"Well, Murad. What's a handicap? "

He shrugs and looks at me as if to say, "What a stupid question!"

"Isn't it when you're supposed to be able to do something and you can't? When something that is normal for people gets lost somehow. It's a limitation. Like if I'm supposed to be able to see, but because of some limitation, I become blind. For us, disability in one way or another is a limitation of what is considered our normal human abilities. We become impaired, disabled.

"But think about God for a second. He's the Creator of the entire universe. He's the most powerful, intelligent person of all. 'Normal' for God is to be able to be everywhere all the time. 'Normal' for God is to be able to do anything He decides to do. When it comes to God, you could say that He's the healthiest, most able being there is.

"But God chose to become handicapped. He chose to set aside all His normal God-power, His God-knowledge, His mysterious God-is-everywhere-at-once ability. He gave all that away when He chose to be born as a little baby. His human name is Jesus, and being human was His handicap."

Mural's eyes never leave mine as he listens quietly, his body still for a moment.

"But God's love for you and me is so deep that He wasn't only willing to become human, but also to suffer as a human. Jesus the Messiah grew up and was rejected. He wasn't treated fairly or kindly. He hadn't done a thing wrong, and still people captured Him like an animal, beat Him, laughed and mocked Him, and tied Him down to a cross where they pounded nails into His hands and feet. He died like that.

"But, Murad, God chose to do that, to hurt like that, to die like that so that He would destroy the vile hold on you and me that evil has. To show you just how much He really loves you and me, he chose to do that to make sure that we would be able to go to heaven and experience new bodies and joy at His banqueting table. One day, we'll get the chance to sing and dance with Jesus because He rose from the dead and made an open door to heaven."

I can feel my heart pounding with the revelation once again of this Good News. After a moment, I ask, "What do you think about that, Murad?"

Murad looks up from his pillow and mumbles, "Aww, ah don knowww."

Yes, I think. *What can he possibly understand of what I've just said? Like all the children here, the many of the staff here, he's never even heard Your name before, dear Jesus. How ironic. In the West, Your name is used commonly, often even as a swear word. Seminarians and theologians have argued for hours about this or that aspect of Your name. This boy has heard the Good News about you summarized in two minutes for the very first time. Of course he doesn't "know" for sure.*

I explain to Jake what I'd just told Murad.

"I have been praying this whole time," Jake says. "The Lord is here with us. I know it." He wipes his eyes, compassion for this lonely young man brimming over the surface of his heart.

I reach out and touch Murad on the shoulder. "Murad, would it be okay if we prayed for you?"

"Sure, go ahead."

"Lord Jesus," I pray in Turkish, "I don't know how You are going to do this. But will You please show Murad how much You love him? Will You come with Your love and peace and touch him?" I hesitate. We are in a tightly controlled state orphanage. Any kind of religious activity or prayer is forbidden in this ward. Finally I whisper, "In Jesus's name, amen."

The boy jerks and shouts out excitedly in response: "IN JESUS'S NAME!"

So much for keeping a low profile!

I have to chuckle. "Okay, dear Murad, I'm going to come back again. Right now, there are other kids here we want to pray for. See you later."

He waves us off with an arm jerking in a "good-bye."

/////

February 2000

The Texas team has gone, and things are back to a more or less regular schedule. I walk in the CC2 ward and head for Murad's metal crib.

"Hey, Murad. It's me Norita, your big sister. How ya doin'?" I've prepped myself to be upbeat and cheerful, remembering how depressed he was before.

"GREAT!" he shouts, his body jerking powerfully.

"You are?" My happy-face façade slips in surprise. Tentatively I say my line: "You know, Murad, God loves you."

"YES, I KNOW IT!" He grins widely. This time I am looking into shining eyes.

"You know it? " I repeat stupidly. I am examining his body looking for some change. Same cramped crib, same smelly clothes, same ward overcrowded with severely mentally disabled children. I focus again on his face. "How do you know it?"

"I know it." He jerks his shoulder to try to grab hold of my hand. "I know it because He came to me and told me."

Murad has seen Jesus, and I have just seen Him too in the face of that beautiful boy living in a metal bed. I have to reflect again, however, on the Bethlehem story: animals in a barn, a feeding trough, angels, shepherds, the mother, the father, this baby—"EXTRAORDINARY in our ordinary." And thinking about Murad changes me. The worry crease between my eyes gives way to worship.

CHAPTER 14

Gulistan, Our Little Rose Petal

"I am a rose of Sharon, a lily of the valleys."
Song of Solomon 2:1

My personal notes continued ...

March 1998

Making the rounds in Continuous Care 1 is always such a challenge. We are just beginning to figure out a care program for these bed-bound children and still do not have a clear idea of what we are actually going to do. There is so much need and so few of us. Beyond that, we are amateurs with nothing more than a desire to change the situation for good.

I come up to a crib where a tiny girl is sitting cross-legged on her sheets and blanket. Next to her are a flower-designed pink plastic teacup, saucer, and plastic teapot. With wispy light-brown hair framing a thin heart-shaped face, her large brown eyes seem to dominate her whole appearance. They are, at this moment, unblinking and glaring, her lips set in a straight line.

When I greet her and tell her my name, she sniffs her obvious disdain. She is not interested in whatever I am selling today. I move on down the row.

Later on, I learn that little Gul—short for Gulistan ("Rose")—is nine. She has been in Saray for at least six years. No one wants to touch her or take her out of her bed because she has brittle bone disease, a genetic deformity in which the bones never gain their strength and healthy constituency. Everyone is afraid of being the one responsible for a bone breaking on her watch. She's sitting cross-legged because her bones and muscles have stiffened into that position. She, unlike the children in the cribs next to her, is not mentally impaired and can communicate when she wants to.

"Oh, you watch out," one of the day-care workers whispers to me. "That one has a mouth on her. She knows how to curse you up one side and down the other."

"Well, who does she talk to all day long?"

"Only anyone who comes in to give her food. She can eat with a spoon and fork, so she sits in her bed to eat. We change her diapers, though." The woman is getting defensive. She's not really proud of the scene, either.

Drawn to the little lost girl in the corner, Laliye soon proposes that we buy Gul a wheelchair. "I'll be responsible for getting her out of the crib and into a chair," she pleads with the ward director.

"Oh, alright, but if anything happens to her, it's on your head. Don't forget that."

The very fact that Laliye has taken an interest in her, and brought in a chair specially designed for her, starts to change Gul. The first crack in her armor leads to transformation.

Some months later, I'm surprised to find out that Gul has expressed a desire to learn how to read. Zeynep, another young woman from the church, joins our team, and she and Laliye have fallen in love with Gul, their new little sister. They are trying all kinds of strategies to help Gul take advantage of their times together.

"Norita." Laliye pulls me aside one morning in the late spring. "Gul prayed out loud with me yesterday. She says that she and Jesus are now friends, good friends."

/////

A Few Weeks Later

I feel tears threaten again as I relate this. That girl has changed. Whereas we have to be so careful that we don't do something that will appear to be religious propagandizing and threaten the government employees, she couldn't care less what they say or do to her. She's already experienced the worst. Today I heard her chugging down the long D Block corridor in her new wheelchair singing at the top of her lungs:

"I know that I'm of worth.
I know that I'm a pearl
I know that God loved me so much
I know that He died for me.
Yes, I'm a pearl in His Hands,
I'm a pearl in His Hands."

/////

Gul is an inveterate "Bossy Boots." When the boys roll over from C Block, she greets them as they enter the Hope Room and tells them what she wants to see done that day. "This is the VIP Room, boys. No messing around or funny business."

They look at each other, grin, and move around her on the way to the old desktop computer on the learning table we've set up. "Sure, sure, little sister," Jonah says. "We'll help with the feeding or whatever you want us to do. Just later."

She shakes her finger at them and says things like, "Well, just this time. But I know you guys. You'll do anything to get out of helping around here." Then she'll turn around in her chair and go to the little kitchen where Nina is preparing the afternoon snack to check the progress of the food preparation.

Gone is the angry, lonely orphan, and in her place has emerged a motivated, caring young person. Laliye and Gul's relationship has deepened into one of sharing about their deepest fears and hopes. It is quite obvious that the Spirit of God is here. The all-consuming need to think about self and suffered injustices has now been replaced by a desire to care for others and the revelation that she has been called to that.

Gul has taken a special interest in one of the newest residents, Bahar. This little one, a survivor from the earthquake, has just been transferred to Saray after being found under the rubble of a collapsed building that killed her grandparents. Her father is in prison for murdering her mother. Her only surviving relative, an uncle, brought her to the police station and said, "Take her. I can't be looking after a handicapped girl at this point."

Bahar cannot speak or walk and looks to be about four years old. Gul has adopted her. So when Guliya and Songul (our newest team member) bring Bahar into the VIP Room, Gul makes a beeline for her, greeting her and hugging her from her chair. Once her food is ready, Gul is right there, feeding her "little sister."

Nearly every week, our Kardelen Team gathers everyone together to talk about his or her life and to make plans for the days ahead. Gul rolls in from her ward and joins us. She prays along when we bow our heads in silence.

This day, we've had some news that has caused us all to sit up and begin to pray more earnestly. "Some of the expected funding for this project is being cut," I inform the team after receiving an email from a major donor. "Unless we find someone else who'll support our work, we will be forced to shut Kardelen down."

Zeynep bursts into tears. "But I barely started working here. I love this work, and yet I need the income to help support my mother and two younger sisters. You all know that our dad left us to fend for ourselves after my mother made the decision to follow Christ. Oh, what are we going to do? None of us here are rich enough to have savings. You know that, Sister Norita," she cries, wringing her hands in panic.

"Zeynep!" Gul has rolled up right next to her to fix her sternest look on her friend. After applying the hand brake to her chair, she folds her arms across her chest. "Zeynep!" she repeats. "Look at me." Zeynep looks up at the tiny eleven-year-old girl whose disability has kept her from growing. "Why are you crying? Don't you know that your heavenly Father knows exactly what you need? He'll take good care of you. Stop crying right now!"

Every person in that room at that moment is struck silent. God has clearly spoken to us.

Yes, I know that I'm valuable
Yes I know that I'm a pearl
Yes, I know that I'm valuable
And in the hands of the Lord,
And in the hands of the Lord.

/////

February 2002

It is an icy day as Siberian winds blow over the Anatolian Plateau. Gray clouds threaten snow. A line of four vehicles stands parked beside a barren hillside. Heads bowed, seven of us are standing holding hands at the tiny gravesite. Recently dug and prepared, it was purchased today. This is the first time I have been in the vast Muslim cemetery on the northern border of Ankara. Had we not followed the hearse dressed in green-and-gold cloth, we would never have found the spot. Here, among literally thousands of concrete blocks and headstones, we lay the body of our precious Gul, and my mind can only retrace the events that led to this day …

/////

This morning as I walked into our room, Zeynep comes rushing up to me in tears. "Norita Abla, Gul is dead!" She finds it difficult to continue but struggles on: "Today was her birthday. We were going to celebrate it specially. I've brought the little beaded bracelets she loved. But she's gone."

Laliye walks in then, crying as well. "I've just talked to Mrs. Melissa. She said that Gul was taken to the hospital over the weekend with some sort of bad cold. They found her dead in the morning—suffocated because her scoliosis was so bad and she couldn't cough."

By this time, word has gotten around some of the wards that darling Gul has passed away. Yunus, Juneyt, and Umit are at the door then.

We sit together holding hands and in shock. This is the death of one of our dearest children and it is so close to home. It hurts so.

Yunus speaks to us all at that point: "Look, you all, we shouldn't be so sad, because you know what?" He looked around at the Kardelen Team. "She's with Jesus now." He sighed. "She's free. Really free. Now she can walk, now she can dance, now she doesn't suffer any more pain—no more stretching exercises that don't really help that much here; no more fear of falling and breaking some bone. She's free." His eyes are lit with a fire that warms us all at the moment.

"Where will they bury her body?" I ask.

"I don't know," Zeynep answers. "I hear rumors that when a child dies here in the orphanage, if the family doesn't claim the body, then she is wrapped in a sheet and buried in a 'Pauper's Cemetery'—some field somewhere—nothing proper and no gravestone or anything to mark her passing."

"Maybe we can do something." I jump up and run across the orphanage grounds to see Mrs. Melissa.

"Well, this is highly unusual a request," she says after I ask if we could give Gul a proper funeral in a proper cemetery. "But since she was found as an infant on the doorstep of a police station, we have no next of kin registered. You have to agree to pay for the plot and gravestone, you know.

I'll approve this if you are willing."

We spend the rest of the day getting the paperwork signed, riding in an ambulance to pick up the body from the morgue, taking taxis to the city office in charge of burial sites, then traveling together to the vast cemetery on the north side of town.

Ankara has two cemeteries. One is a few acres large and surrounded by apartment buildings. The other—vast, many kilometers square—is situated on several hills. From a distance, anyone can see the rows and rows of white headstones. After following the hearse, we eventually find the Burial Ceremony Office near one of the many entrances. Burial workers lift the body out of the ambulance and onto a marble slab in a small sterile room. We are allowed to go in and observe as scarfed women in T-shirts and baggy trousers take off Gul's hospital gown and begin washing the body. Gul's broken and deformed body lies there, purple bruises glaring while the bright neon light magnifies the process.

After the washing ritual is complete, she is wrapped in a white body bag. Two workers come in and hoist the body into a plain pine coffin. They shift the coffin onto the back of a burial truck. We follow the truck as it winds through the many rows of graves to a recently dug gravesite.

Wrapped in her white grave sheet, her tiny body fits easily into the roughly poured container. Two workers fit the concrete slab over the top. The imam assigned to say the traditional send-off prayer stands at one end and repeats this litany at breakneck speed; everyone there says "Amin" and begins rushing to their cars or van to get out of the cold. We linger.

Now we are singing her favorite songs, her praise songs to Jesus. The mullah and orphanage personnel who have accompanied us stare. One of the staff who was in charge of Gul's ward, CC1, comes up to me when we, too, break up to get back to the waiting vehicles. "I have never ever seen an orphan be treated to such a send-off. That was amazing and beautiful. I have goose bumps and it's not from the cold."

"She was our darling, our coworker," I say. "We will miss her desperately. But she is in the hands of the Lord, dancing, singing, enjoying life as she has never enjoyed it before."

It is four in the afternoon, and already darkness is nearly here. As we make our way back to the city center where I'll be let off to catch a bus home, I am lost in thoughts about the day, about the year, about the work.

What a privilege to have known such a remarkable little girl.

CHAPTER 15

A Page from Hell's Diary

O Lord, all my longing is before you; my sighing is not hidden from you.
My heart throbs; my strength fails me, and the light of my eyes—
it also has gone from me.
Psalm 38:9-10

My personal notes continued …

September 2000

The phone rings. 11:00 p.m. Even though it's late, I answer since it's from Saray, but I'm not prepared for the news.

"Sister Norita!" Nina sounds frantic. "We've just heard from Hediye's mother."

Hediye's mother, Fatoshi, has taken her daughter back to Tunceli in the east of the country where she is also caring for another son. This young man apparently is also now blind and immobile due to the same disease that had left her daughter deaf and in a wheelchair. What a difficult situation. This widow believed that a place like the state-run orphanage and rehabilitation center would be able to take better care of her daughter than she can.

I remember Fatoshi. She came once to Ankara to care for her daughter. Besides Hediye's personal self-neglect, no health professional at this massive institution regularly checked for pressure-sore wounds on the bodies on the bedridden or wheelchair-bound children. The results are always emergency situations. These wounds become gaping, infected, and lead inevitably to death. Skin graft surgery is required as a short-term solution and can prolong life for years if the patient is careful.

At the hospital to pray for and encourage our young friend, Karin, Aisha and I managed to convince Fatoshi to take her daughter back home for the recovery period. We bought them bus tickets, and after three weeks in the hospital in Ankara and with the doctors' permission, they returned to home—fourteen hours away.

Now six months later, Fatoshi has phoned Hediye's girlfriends (the women in A Block).

According to Nina, Fatoshi says that the Saray administrators have ordered her to bring her daughter back to the orphanage to prepare for a transfer to another institution. When Fatoshi first brought her daughter to Saray, she relinquished all legal guardianship for her. Hediye, now a ward of the state, is scheduled along with all of the young people over the age of twenty-one to be transferred to another facility near the Carmel Sea within two days. It means that our Kardelen on-site team is scheduled for demolition—and none of us have heard anything about it.

My heart stops. "Noooo! This can't be true. There's got to be some mistake! Your work, our team, this will destroy you. No, there must be some misunderstanding." I think it must be a false rumor; Fatoshi often panicked about things. She must be mistaken.

"No, she sounded pretty certain." Nina has learned the details. Evidently a newly completed, fully equipped and staffed rehab center has just opened in another location—a six-hour drive to the northeast of Ankara. It was set up for adults, and now a group of fifteen young adults from Saray are being sent there—supposedly all of the wheelchair-bound over the age of twenty-one who live at Saray.

Nina's voice breaks; she is sobbing. "Oh please, Norita, we are desperate. We don't want to be sent away. This is going to kill us. We love the children. Shen-gul has thrown herself out of her chair and is crying on the floor. How can they separate her from her little Dilek? She's been like a mother to her. Mediha has locked herself into her room." Her crying grows louder. The phone goes dead.

I try reaching her by phoning the main operator at Saray, but no one picks up. Finally, fifteen minutes later, Nina phones again. Her phone needed to be recharged. "I can't stand this," she says. "I don't want to go. Can you help us?" she pleads. "We are demanding to see the deputy director. He's the one in charge. It's his doing. He has to give us an explanation of why we are being sent away the day after tomorrow."

I encourage the group to write a petition explaining all the positive things they are doing for Saray by working with the children in Continuous Care every afternoon. I am unaware of the small detail that, in spite of Nina's intelligence and oral communication skills, she suffers from a learning disability and has never let anyone know that she can't write. Her strength is her ability to talk about issues. She needs to talk to the people in charge.

I promise: "I don't at all understand what is happening, and it must be a mistake, but whatever is happening, I'll go down to see Mrs. Umra at the Department of Social Services tomorrow. Don't give up. We're not going to let you get taken away. You are part of our team."

Early the next morning, I find myself rushing up the stairs of the main office of the National Social Services and Child Protection Agency.

This is the fourth time I have spent any time with Mrs. Umra. Knowing the importance of cultivating a relationship with the people in charge, I'd gone to drink tea and discuss ways our group could be more effective in helping out. She apparently has the authority over all the facilities where people with mental and/or physical disabilities are housed throughout the country. At this time, I believe there are at least five such institutions. I know for certain that Saray is the largest.

She always seemed pleasant and eager to cooperate and collaborate, praising us for our commitment to the children. In her early fifties, she has spent the majority of her time working with her three assistants compiling facts about the institutions under her jurisdiction, as well as attending debriefing meetings with every new director of the national agency. (At this point, she is serving under the fourth person since her own appointment to this position.)

She had told us about her trip with a Turkish delegation to Germany to visit a home where people with developmental disabilities were housed. She also talked a lot about her daughter who was getting her master's degree in engineering and planning on working in the USA.

When I enter the room, she stands up from her desk; it looks like every square centimeter is stacked with files. I notice that she has not yet had her morning tea.

"Umra, please excuse my barging in like this. I know that you are very busy. But something bad has happened and I needed to talk with you." I am breathless, my heart pounding.

"No problem, Mrs. Norita." She has always spoken very softly with a slight tremor in her voice. "What can I do for you?"

"It's difficult. It's not about what you can do for me. It's about what's being done to the young people out at Saray. You remember I told you about starting to include some of the young physically impaired women from A Block in the Kardelen Project? As you know, they've been wonderful in caring for small bed-bound children. One of them makes a pudding in the afternoon and the rest—even the ones who are extremely spastic—go into the wards to feed their 'children.' I've arranged it so that we provide a little monthly allowance for them to spend on phone cards or snacks from the canteen. I've never seen people so joyful—or, for that matter, so good with the children—as these girls when they've got one of the babies or toddlers in their laps.

"Last night, in a total panic, one of the A Block girls told me incredible bad news: they are being sent away to the Carmel Sea to a new center. IN TWO DAYS! They were not consulted about this. They are adults and *not* mentally impaired, yet they are being treated as if they were."

"Uhhhmmm. I don't know what this is about," Mrs. Umra replies in her trembling voice. "I'll look into it for you. Please excuse me, I have a meeting upstairs."

"Yes, please help them. This isn't right." I feel that if I somehow keep talking, she will understand the urgency of it all. "They should at least have the opportunity to be spoken to with respect. They need to process this change by hearing about it and making some decisions about this on their own."

"Yes, yes, of course," she replies. "I'll phone Saray right away and delay this." She walks to the door, indicating that it's time for me to leave.

"Thank you. I'm sure the girls in A Block Unit who are being sent away would want to hear from you too. I'll let them know we were able to talk about this. They'll be so glad."

I walk out of the building onto the crowded boulevard feeling satisfied that at least something is going to be done to delay the transfer. I cannot imagine that my friend Mrs. Umra will let them down.

I phone Nina after returning home: "I've just spoken with Mrs. Umra, and she says she's going to do something about this. Please don't worry."

"Sister Norita, we still haven't heard back from Deputy Director Mr. Maurice. You need to know that when he's not acting as DD, he's the social worker who's in charge of our house. He knows us. We're leaving messages in his office and even on his cell phone. He's not answering. I know he's somewhere around here even though they tell us that he's left the campus.

We want to talk to him directly to hear if this is a rumor or not. We can't get up the forty stairs in the administration building to wait in his office or I'd do it now. But he knows that we need to talk to him. Can you come out here tomorrow and go in with us to talk to him? Maybe he'll respect you, and if you tell him about our work with the other children, he might listen."

I promise Nina that I'll come, and the next morning, around 10:00, I walk through the rusty, paint-chipped front gate. Parked in the middle of the lot and blocking the stairs to the entry is a large sky-blue school bus. Normally this old bus sits on a vacant lot behind the C Block.

Some of the boys, residents who typically hang out and beg for money or candy from visitors, come rushing up to me. Aras sticks his hand out. "Do you have any candy, Sister Norita? Have you seen John lately? He said he was coming by soon to play football with us. Where is he? Is he at home? Do you know his phone number? Tell him Aras wants him to come by." He is talking about one of the volunteers who comes out regularly to play football with some of the boys on the weekend. Today he has latched onto me as I make my way up the stairs and down the cement walkway toward the two-story building known as A Block.

Outside the two-storied pink stucco housing structure, Karin and Cheryl are talking to one of the other younger girls. Cheryl has been coming onto the campus for some months now with the express purpose of teaching and facilitating handicraft activities in A Block.

Cheryl cries out when she sees me. "Some staff person came into the girls' unit this morning and ordered them to put their belongings in a suitcase or cardboard box and prepare to leave for Hot Springs[2] by 10:30 a.m."

"No, this can't be!" I protest. "Don't they know that Mrs. Umra has ordered a delay?" My heart breaks, washing over me with the first wave of helplessness.

Screams pierce the morning calm. The windows of the girls' dorm are open and the crying can be heard all the way down the walkway to the front of the administration building. "Nooooo! Aahhhhhh!" someone moans. Out in front, either lying on the grass or slouching on the half-upright metal picnic table, other younger girls and some women in white coats are smoking or staring at us.

2 Hot Springs is not the actual name of the location.

One of them—energetic and off-key crooner Meral—jumps up and comes running to tell me the news. Her mental impairment always seemed greater because her face looked like she had been flattened from both sides, with eyes brought close and chin longer than normal. Today she has appointed herself to be the bearer of all tidings bad and good.

"All our friends, all the women and Murad and Ozgur too, all of 'em are going away today. They are going to a place by the sea. It's going to be very nice. Why can't I go? Do you think they will come back for a visit? They better. And they better bring a present. I was a good helper to them. Do you think I will have more allowance? I hope so. Shen-gul threw herself on the ground. Dilek is crying. They should just obey the directors." Meral chatters on, unaware of the extent of the tragedy taking place around her.

I turn and see Mr. Youssef, the main one who helped us in the first year of setting up the volunteer care program. He is rushing out of the administration on his way to the parking lot.

"Mr. Youssef! Mr. Youssef!" I am shouting.

He turns and waits for me to catch up with him.

"Ah, good morning, Norita Hanum. I'm sorry but I've got an appointment at the bank or I'd stay and talk." With that, he runs to his car and drives off with another colleague in tow.

I stand looking at his retreating back with my hand still slightly raised in greeting. Mr. Youssef is a member of the Turkish Association of Psychologists. Occasionally we would sit and talk about institutionalization and how things are done in America. I had only been able to tell him how friends had said that sixty years ago life for the disabled or the orphan wasn't all that much better in the USA.

He would show me articles he had read in English; he talked about change and wanting to have a better-run facility.

Now I am mumbling to myself: "He, more than most, will understand what it means to perfectly intelligent young adults to be treated as if they were mentally deficient and prison inmates. If only he would stay and we could figure this out together, we'd come up with a solution."

I turn back to see a rush of wheelchairs carrying their unwilling cargo out of the girls' dorm. The younger girls lumber along beside. From behind the administration building, some boys show up: Ozgur maneuvers his chair while balancing a small case on his lap; Murad, plastic shopping bag hanging from his chair, is being pushed by another much smaller boy, Koray. This chair was the one specially made by Ken to compensate for all the stiffened limbs and spinal deformity Murad had to live with.

I am reminded of one of our picnics in the small garden. Ozgur had made sure that everything was well watered and cared for. Murad was lying there in his new chair, grinning at everyone who happened by on their way to BR1. Murad's friend, German volunteer, was sitting next to him. Murad called Laliye over to tell her something.

"Sister Laliye, I can die now!" His announcement startled her.

"No, Murad. We don't want you to die. Why would you say that?"

"Waaaal," he drawled. "I have seen grass and flowers for the first time in my life. What more could I want? I could die, and die happy, right now."

Now Murad and Ozgur are being torn from their garden, their friends, and their new family.

Herding them all are two white-coated government workers. Several cardboard boxes and a couple of battered suitcases find their way to the minibus, and one by one, crying women and stone-faced young men are hoisted from their chairs and up into the waiting vehicle to be ignominiously thrown into seats. The indifference on the faces of the men who hoist the "goods" is hard to look at. But this is nothing in comparison to the angry look one of the White Coats, Hatijeh, wears as she shouts at Nina.

Nina has refused to get on the bus and keeps trying to throw herself out of her chair. "I'm not leaving. This is my home. These are my family. Where is Mr. Maurice? He's got to speak with us. We can't be sent away like animals."

"Get in the bus," Hatijeh orders. "Don't be such an actress! You're making us late. You are going to a nice place. You should be grateful. Get over it and stop making trouble."

It's all I can do to restrain myself from grabbing this woman's collar and throwing her to the ground. I do walk over and put my face up close to hers. "You have no idea what you are saying or what these girls are going through. Shame on you."

"Oh, and just who do you think you are to speak to me like that? I'm the person in charge here doing my job, and it's to get these people to Hot Springs. They are going to a newly built rehabilitation center—all new and modern just for them. Plus they will be near the sea. It will be like going to a hotel."

She turns around again and orders Nina to get on the bus. By this time, however, hysteria overtakes Nina. She's grabbing bunches of her long brown hair and trying to tear it out, her clenched hands stiff, all the while gasping for breath between cries and screams. Minutes later, one of the doctors shows up from the clinic with a hypodermic needle; two nurses hold her down while he injects her.

Then the now-unconscious twenty-three-year-old is hoisted like the rest into a bus seat, where her slumped body is shoved against sidewall and head propped against the window.

By this time, the parking lot has filled with spectators—staff workers and personnel, some normal school children sent to live in special dorms on the campus during the school year, the boys who had met me earlier, and some of the older girls. Many, including some of the state workers, are crying. Dilek, tears streaming down her face, stands mutely under the bus window. Above Dilek, her longtime surrogate mother, Shen-gul, cries inconsolably. Earlier she had broken our hearts when she'd asked with a wail, "But who will look after Dilek? Who will make sure that she doesn't eat too many sweets? She's diabetic. Who will make sure that she takes her insulin at the right time? Who will care for her like I do?"

While some children try to say good-bye to their older "sisters and brothers and friends," other blue-coated workers hover, under apparent orders to prevent any kind of fight or incident. Our volunteer team, Turks and foreigners, huddle, crying and praying for our friends who are being shipped to a place no one has ever heard about—a place as far away from us as the moon.

I am struck by another wave of desolation. Unbidden, a picture of people and children being forced against their wills to abandon their homes flashes into my mind. Was this not something like what had happened to the Jews when they were forced to leave their homes and family and travel to their deaths? Or any group, for that matter, who is forced into exile? My stomach clenches.

I walk off the orphanage grounds shaking, dazed.

All I can do is pray: "Lord Jesus, these are my sisters and brothers. You have brought us together. They are Your children. Nina, Medina, Shen-gul, Murad, and Ozgur—they know You. The others have sensed You. I will do whatever it takes to save them from this exile and imprisonment. Show me what to do. Because I am absolutely helpless and have no idea how any good can come from this horrible day."

By the time I get off the bus in the city center, I have made another resolution. I head for the office of our lawyer, Mr. Sharif.

CHAPTER 16

Hot Springs

Where shall I go from your Spirit? Or where shall I flee from your presence? If I ascend to heaven, you are there! If I make my bed in Sheol,[3*] *you are there!*

Psalm 139:7-8 (ESV)

My personal notes continued …

September 2000

Two nights after the group gets deported, I finally hear from Nina. She pours out her heartrending story to me over the phone:

"'We're almost there. Wake up. Come on, wake up!' Someone was shaking my shoulder," Nina says. "As I struggled to wake up, I could feel the soreness in my hip; that shot had left its mark and I was still so groggy after six hours on the road. My eyes hurt from the afternoon light. 'Please, pleeeeeaaase let this be just a bad dream,' I pleaded to God as my head knocked against the window. Outside, everything was brown and gray and there wasn't a building in sight. Norita, it's nothing but a garbage dump out here. We aren't anywhere near the seaside.

"The bus started bouncing and bumping as the driver took us up a narrow unpaved road. He didn't know where he was going and was struggling to bring the bus around the curves and bends of this mountain path. All of us had trouble keeping seated or protecting ourselves from falling on the floor. I mean, can you imagine spastic people like Murad or Derya? They were lying on their backs on each of the plastic-covered bus seats. Every jerk and sudden stop-and-go, every turn of the bus meant they were thrown onto the floor. One jerk of the front steering wheel and Murad's body slipped off the seat and onto the hard floor between the seats. Two minutes later, Derya fell between the seats too. I think she hurt her head when it scraped against her cardboard box. Then to make matters doubly worse, she got really carsick. Our 'minder' Hatijeh started off cleaning her

3 *Sheol: ancient Hebrew name for place of the dead.

up, but Derya threw up so many times that Hatijeh gave up and decided to wait until we got to Hot Springs before cleaning the poor girl."

I had been so angry with Hatijeh when they left Saray and the way she'd treated Nina there, that I was having a hard time imagining her show any compassion or mercy to Derya. Nina continues and paints a different picture of her: "You should have heard her, Norita. Hatijeh began swearing as our bus rumbled up the mountain. But when we arrived at the front door of the Hot Springs rest home, she lost it. As people came down the front steps in the dark, she started yelling at them about the lies and total incompetence of the government. 'Where's the sea? We were promised a nice place for these kids! What kind of a joke is this? It's not more than a prison out in the boondocks!'"

Hatijeh's outburst at Saray starts to make a bit more sense when I hear this. She had been told the bus would be taking these twenty-something's to a newly built rehabilitation facility situated on the Black Sea close to the city of The Hot Springs. She had been told that this new place would be fully equipped, modern, and have physical therapists, doctors, and program directors ready to give special attention to these, her charges with special needs: which was one reason she had no patience with Nina and the others when they'd put up such resistance to being sent away that morning. She was not happy that they had been forced to sedate both Nina and Shen-gul, but they had gone hysterical. She had hoped that once they arrive at their new home, they would be pleased with the holiday-home atmosphere they had been told to expect.

Nina continues telling her story: "When we heard her talking like this, all of us went silent. Derya began crying again. One of the guys from the home started in on Hatijeh , telling her to shut up and just let them get on with their jobs.

"One by one, wheelchairs were set up; one of the guys there carried us out one by one and plunked us into them. I was last out, and wow, did it hurt when my sore bottom hit that chair.

"But it was so strange when one of these people—I guess the director or someone in charge—looks at me and at his clipboard and says, 'So you are Nina,' and snickers! 'We know all about you,' he says. 'You can be sure that we won't tolerate any of your rebelliousness here.' I would have given him a piece of my mind, Norita, but believe me, my head and bottom hurt so much, I didn't really think about this until this morning."

/////

Two months later, Marion and our new long-term American volunteer, Cheri, were able to take a trip up to Hot Springs and had permission to bring some toiletries as well as bring the group outside into the garden area. This newly constructed institution had a sign out on the road leading up to the center, which read: "Hot Springs Rest Home and Rehabilitation Center."

Marion and Cheri described what they saw: "Anyone who visits will find a large three-story rectangular building in the style of most government institutions: the floors comprising rooms running along the four sides of the building and looking out over the large empty space in the middle. To enter the building, one must climb twenty stairs. To get from one floor to the next, a stairwell in the corner serves those who can walk. Still not completely dry, a steep 40-degree cement ramp rises along one wall, open to the floors below on one side. There are no elevators, no guardrails, nor are there handrails built on the corridor walls to help those who might have trouble walking. Every wall, door, or window is an institutional gray. There are no blinds on the windows, no handrails for the toilets, the majority of which are squatty potties [holes in the ground]. The Saray group, obviously younger than the eighty or so other residents, is housed on the third floor. The cafeteria is on the first. Two *alafranga* [modern] toilets are found on the second floor.

"Most of the residents are truly elderly. Some suffer from dementia. A handful of them have personal caregivers who had been hired by their families to look after their needs. The seniors shuffle along the corridors or are seated in the dayroom and accompanied to the toilet or bath or cafeteria. State-hired personnel look after the others. Besides the five women in their late twenties who arrived the previous month, this new group of young adults with special needs is added to the burden of the locally hired untrained care-providers. There are two 'caregivers' per floor—their jobs: to dress, bathe, and transport the patients to breakfast, lunch, and dinner in the large dining hall. In the evenings, a skeleton crew of four manages the center. They also have janitorial duties like changing bedclothes or washing the floors."

Even as I hear all of this, I remember Nina's description of their first night:

"As we were carried up the stairs and to our rooms, one by one someone begins to cry. Derya was the loudest, but Shen-gul and Mediha set up a wail too. 'Ninaaaaaaaa, what are we going to do?' All of us are angry. I mean, Mediha may suffer from cerebral palsy, which makes it sometime hard to understand her, but she is smart-as-a-tack intelligent and a fighter to boot. She pleaded with me: 'We've got to let Sister Norita know where they've brought us. This is a sham. Where is the seaside? Where is the therapy center? Don't we have any rights to where we're going to live? They must take us back to Saray immediately!' I promised I'd try to get in touch with you as soon as I could."

Thankfully Hatijeh had been allowing Nina to use her cell phone to call me.

"You have got to help us get out of here," Nina told me. "They lied about this place. There's nothing here. We're stuck out in the middle of nowhere—even far from the town of Hot Springs. There are no caregivers who know how to help us. All of us want to come back to our team there. We can't stand it. Help us! Help us. I don't know—"

And the call went dead. After repeated attempts to reestablish contact that night, I had given up and gone to bed.

When Nina phoned me again three nights later, after borrowing a janitor's mobile phone, I learned that Hatijeh's cell phone had died, and I heard more of the story of their ordeal:

"Of the whole group, Ozgur and Fatma were so doped up for the trip that they were barely conscious; they only began to understand what has happened to them the next morning when they woke up in strange beds. The small bedrooms barely have enough space for two single beds, so those who cannot crawl or walk are for all intents and purposes imprisoned—again."

/////

A Compilation of Nina's Stories to Me

At 8:00 a.m. one day, everyone is getting hungry. Nina and Shen-gul, who are able to dress themselves and take care of their personal needs, call out to their friends in the neighboring bedrooms. "Where are you guys? What's happening?"

Medina shouts from her room: "Here I am. Derya is missing. I need help to get dressed and get to the toilet. Where is everybody?"

Nina gets into Mediha's room and helps her get dressed before returning to their third-floor landing and shouting for someone to come help them. After several minutes, a man in a blue uniform appears.

"Stop shouting!" he orders. "We can't be everywhere at once. What's wrong?"

When Nina explains Mediha's situation, he sighs, goes into her room, picks her up out of her bed, puts her in her chair, and takes her to the toilet. In spite of the fact that he is a stranger who obviously is not happy about having to care for her, she submits to the ignominy of having her underpants stripped off, then being held over the toilet hole. But Mediha is lucky in that she can articulate her needs and thoughts.

Derya's level of disability means that she is less able verbally than Mediha or Nina. She cannot always completely understand what is happening to her. Often she finds herself in an untenable position like when she is taken to the toilet at night and left there. Two nights after the Saray group arrives at Hot Springs, someone takes Derya to the European toilet at the end of the second-floor hall, undresses her, and places her upright on the commode. Forgotten there all night, the poor girl is found shivering and whimpering the next morning by one of her friends who, also at great personal peril, has maneuvered the steep ramp to get to the more accessible toilet.

Members of the group more than once spend entire days in their beds; no one bothering to come and get them up, changed, or to the cafeteria. They stop drinking any kind of liquids after lunch, knowing that there is a good chance they will not get to the toilet in the evenings. If no one comes to dress them for breakfast before 7:00 a.m., then they get no breakfast. Toiletries, feminine hygiene supplies, and adult diapers are just a few of the basics they need, none of which are anywhere to be found in this facility in the forest.

One morning after a week of struggling, Nina gathers Mediha, Shengul, Ozgur, and Derya together. It is late morning, and they have just been dressed in day clothes. Hungry, thirsty, dirty, and angry, they descend to the director's office.

"We demand that you send us back to Saray," Nina begins.

Surprised, Mr. Bulent tries to get past the group, but they have blocked the entrance to his office.

"We can't get dressed in time to get to the cafeteria to eat. You close the doors and the food's gone after 7:30!" Nina shouts. "We are left on the commode all night. No one is helping us with baths or showers. We as women need special supplies. You don't help us get them. At least at Saray, we got feminine napkins. Here ... nothing. If you can't take care of us, send us back!"

"I'd heard you were a troublemaker," the director retorts. "There's nothing I can do. They sent you here from Ankara. The main office makes its decisions; we abide by them. They give us a budget to operate by; I hire so many people. These people are supposed to do their jobs. Just be patient. There is nothing else to say." He stands there, towering over Nina and Mediha with his arms folded.

"Look, Mr. Bulent, I don't know what you are talking about when it comes to me being a troublemaker. All I'm trying to do is get some help here. The night we got here, you weren't even here. We were so sad and sick and discouraged. I was devastated.

"You see, when we were at Saray, we were part of a group called Kardelen; they are our family. They gave us jobs. We looked after the kids in Continuous Care Unit 1 in D Block. I made the food for the afternoon snack. Derya here, in spite of her being spastic, worked together with another girl, Delik, and they cared for one of the babies in the cribs. Mediha, too. Murad had people visiting him from town. He got a special wheelchair from them. Ozgur had his own garden where he grew vegetables for our team, and he watered that garden every day. We had parties and fun. Now it's like we've been sent to prison and you and the others in charge are guards rather than helpers."

She tries to make eye contact with him when he scoots past her to get to the safety of his huge director's desk—that ubiquitous piece of furniture found in every government office; the throne for all the little kings of state. This in spite of the fact that the ever-present portrait of Mustafa Kemal Ataturk, founder of the Republic and father of all the Turks—including those who are state wards—hangs as a silent reminder that the government had accepted the responsibility to care for those who cannot care for themselves.

"I'm here this morning begging you to do something for us because I believe that God wants you to act," Nina says.

At this, he stops shuffling papers to look at her. She has rolled her chair up to his desk.

"Last night, I cried and cried, calling out to God for an answer to our misery," Nina says. "I told God that He'd abandoned us. I thought that He was only there in Saray; that our hearts could only be helped if we lived there—we'd been so happy there this past eight months. I fell asleep in my chair.

"The next thing I knew, I was sitting in the corridor. I heard His voice: 'Do you think that I am weak, my daughter Nina?' He said. 'I am not weak. I can do anything. Look at Derya,' He said. I looked up and Derya was sitting in her wheelchair, and all of a sudden, she got up, walked over to me, and started talking to me, clear as a bell. 'You see, Nina, if I want to, I can make Derya every whit as physically able as I choose. Do not despair. I am here and have not abandoned any of you. I am wiser than you all. Trust Me. Just be ready and don't give up.'

"It was so incredibly real, Mr. Bulent!" Nina flushes from the excitement of reliving the vision. "So you must be part of the plan. Maybe you're supposed to fight for us to send us back to Ankara. You're the man with authority. You're the boss here."

"I don't have that kind of power," the director counters. "The people in the capital are the ones with all the power. We just got assigned here. We are doing what we can." He looks down and stares at his desktop for a few more moments. "What about this 'Kardelen' group? Can't they help you? Ask them if they will hire a caregiver for your group. Every day, I get applications from the town. People need work. I think I could find someone who would be good for you all."

Even as he is speaking, Nina reaches over onto his desk and picks up the receiver of the desk phone.

When she hangs up, she turns to the rest of the group and says,

"We're not alone. Let's go and see if we can find something in the kitchen. I'm hungry."

The troop of displaced "Wheelchair Wonders" rolls down the hall to the cafeteria, ready to take on anyone who dares stop them from eating a good breakfast of bread, cheese, jam, and strong tea. Maybe this time they can even browbeat someone to fry them up some eggs.

CHAPTER 17

Courageous

For the Spirit God gave us does not make us timid,
but gives us power, love and self-discipline
2 Timothy 1:7

My personal notes continued ...

Nina has managed to get permission to phone from the secretary's office to tell me what is going on there. Sometimes the whole group crowds in around her to shout some greeting or more often plead for rescue. They are hungry for detailed reports of what is happening with us in Ankara, with the children, with progress on getting them released.

"Are you going to do something for us? We have to get out of here. How are the kids? How is Dilek?"

They hear about my attempts to get them returned: "The day you all were sent away, I went to see Mr. Sharif, barging into his office like a banshee. He tried to calm me down, but I was crying too hard. It took several minutes before I could tell him what had happened. He was so sad when he heard what I shared. I told him I wanted to register a formal complaint to someone in the government, so we immediately wrote up a report, notarized and all, and I took it in to the Social Services office the next day.

"Karin came with me when we dropped in on Mrs. Umra, who was civil to us. As upset as I was with her not doing what she'd promised, I had to keep my cool, because I had a proposal I thought she might agree to.

"First, we told her how sad we were that you all have been taken against your will to Hot Springs, and then we told her all about your amazing work in the BR1 and 2 at Saray. Now I have told her all this before, but she acted like she was hearing this for the first time, because she seemed surprised to hear that you had jobs and were so productive in caring in little ways for the bed-bound ones.

"Then I asked her to consider a new proposal—that if I could find the funding, would we be able to bring you back to Ankara to live in assisted living homes like they have in the States? And that this would be a project completely under the jurisdiction of the Social Services office, but that we would help with advice as well as funding the project."

I do not tell them how absolutely terrified I am by the challenge of finding the money, but I am also convinced something radical has to happen for these people. I can see in my mind's eye a fully accessible apartment that might even serve as a model for independent living—something not yet known in this country but wildly successful in many cities in the USA as well as Holland. I know as well where the vision comes from and sigh a silent prayer of thanksgiving as well as petition.

"She listened to us," I tell them, "and even asked her secretary to find out if there weren't government-owned apartments that could possibly be renovated for just such a purpose. She says that if we can find a place, she'll back us up.

"I'm talking to people in America about this. We have to find a place. We have to get you back here."

/////

December 2000

The "exiles" continue to try to make the best of their situation. We hire an on-site caregiver, Soraya. Every morning, she is to help them get dressed and out the door. She makes sure no one is left on the toilet. At least we can breathe a bit easier on that count.

Soraya tells us that the group is making new friends. She even makes it possible for Nina to regularly phone us.

One evening, Nina asks us to pray for Irem, a twenty-something who is paralyzed from her waist down and deeply depressed. This young mother of two small children hails from the central plateau city of Orrin, a ten-hour bus ride away. According to Irem, her husband in a drunken rage pushed her off their fifth-story balcony, leaving her permanently paralyzed. The greatest suffering for her, however, is that neither he, his extended family, nor her family, will shoulder any responsibility for her. They couldn't care less what happens to her anymore, claiming that her fall was actually a shameful suicide attempt, and they washed their hands of her by having her transferred to this facility. Once more, my heart breaks: another victim of satanic violence and rejection. State-run facilities are full of people with similar stories. Nina's love and friendship for her is so precious.

But Irem misses her children terribly and alternates from holding long crying jags at the dinner table to lying for hours in her bed with her face turned to the wall. Nina's compassionate heart can hardly bear this.

Beyond coming to terms with her new friend's situation, Nina has her own traumas from the past to process. Irem's sadness triggers her own, always just under the surface of her extroverted personality. She has had no contact with any of her other six siblings, and only every six months or so has she been able to speak with Meryem, the sister she'd run away with eight years before.

Recently, though, news from Meryem lightens Nina's heart. Now a teenager, Meryem has returned to the city of their birth to live with a compassionate and protective aunt. Her high-school teachers are taking her under their wing; they see that she is an intelligent and hardworking child, and are investing in her future by trying to prepare her for the rigorous and highly competitive university entrance examinations.

Irem and Nina begin spending more time together, sharing their heartaches and hopes. Little by little, Irem starts to change. She joins the group at mealtimes and makes it through the hour without crying. She listens to Nina's story of God coming into her situation at Saray. Three months after the "exiling from Saray," I start hearing good news whenever Nina phones.

It is these very reports that encourage me to keep praying for the group there and to continue lobbying on their behalf.

Some friends in the States who donate to the work at the orphanage are having difficulty understanding why I am so passionate about this group of women. Beneath their polite inquiries, I hear unspoken accusations that I am neglecting my duty to the children at Saray. I feel torn. How can I let the Hot Springs group down? I find it increasingly more difficult to communicate what we face from day to day. Sometimes even some of my expat or Turkish friends express skepticism about the problems and situations I share with them. None of them has ever had to deal with the incomprehensible decisions made by the administrators or with the underbelly of the Turkish social service system.

I struggle to communicate the realities of what we deal with, but I still feel that I fail miserably to adequately convey the enormity of this battle.

So I swing back and forth: believing in a great God who commissions and empowers, but also hearing "voices" of doubt and criticism and falling into discouragement. My times in prayer and reflection increase as I pour out these thoughts and frustrations to God. I pray continually for wisdom in not only dealing with the day-to-day Saray program but also now for the struggle at Hot Springs, and most of all for those who are sending support for the work.

Ken is a good sounding board and advisor: "Don't let the voices of criticism keep you from seeing what you must do, Norita. You are the one God spoke to; you are the one who needs to lead."

/////

February 2001

The phone rings at 7:00 a.m. "Norita Abla, are you there? Can you help? Oh God!" Nina is wailing into the receiver. It takes several seconds before she gains enough control to tell me what she is so upset about.

"Last night … Last night …" She is having trouble talking. "Last night I was in the hall when I heard Irem calling out for help. I rolled to her door, which was half open. When I opened it wider … When I opened it … When I … Oh, Norita, one of the men who works here crawled onto her in her bed and was hurting her … raping her." She is gasping for breath on the other end. "I screamed at him to stop, and he told me to shut up, that he was coming for me next. I kept on screaming until finally he got up. He zipped up his pants and came at me. But he just pushed me aside to get out of the door. He was drunk. It was horrible; I couldn't stop him. I was so helpless."

"Quiet now. Shhh ..." I try to calm her. "Lord Jesus, heavenly Father, please come to Irem and Nina now. Please wrap them up in Your loving arms. Holy Spirit of Jesus, we're asking You to put Your healing, loving hands on Irem and do something to help her right now. Stop the work of the enemy, oh God, please." Desperate, I pray out loud whatever comes into my mind.

After a moment of silence, Nina sniffs a muffled "Thank you." She says she will call back after she has had some time to sleep and talk to someone. I hang up the phone and cry out to the Lord my bitterness and hurt for these women. Even though I don't personally know Irem, I have come to respect and care for her through the eyes and hearts of her new friends. Another excruciating emotional explosion.

Two days later, I finally hear news. This time Nina phones me along with Mr. Metin, a social worker. She is not crying this time but shouting—angry and determined.

"The guy came for me last night, Norita Abla, but the Lord protected me, and he couldn't hurt me. I told Mr. Metin I was calling you today. He wanted to be here for this phone conversation."

"What? Wasn't your door locked?" I ask, feeling a wave of helplessness. Why couldn't I be there to stop this abuse?

She laughs scornfully. "Ha! That's the point. We are not allowed to lock our room doors. We don't have access to the keys. Only the people in the main office do. And those people are bad, bad, bad. " When I ask her to tell me what had happened, she continues: "This horrible man, Halil, the same one who hurt Irem, gets drunk and uses drugs with a couple of other workers, other hired help. These same people come from town to take care of us or the old people living on the first floor.

"There's this evil woman who's in charge of the place at night. She brings drugs, like cocaine, and alcohol, and gets high and parties with these guys. Then she lets them roam the floors. They have free reign to pick out bedridden or wheelchair-bound victims. Last night, he came with a gun and burst into my room. He was staggering and said he'd shoot me if I screamed or called out for help. I couldn't help it, Norita. I started shouting. It's a good thing I was sitting in my chair; at least I could move around, 'cause he pointed the gun at me from across where he was standing and fired.

"It was so close that I felt the bullet zing past my ear and heard it hit the wall. He shot again, but I'd gotten to the door and wheeled out to get free. I left him stumbling. Just in time, and luckily, Mr. Metin was in the building and came to see what the commotion was. He saved me. Halil ran outside and drove off in his car.

"He isn't the only one; there are at least two other workers here doing this. I learned today that this has been going on for months. Three of the residents heard the noise last night; today, one by one, they called me over to tell me their nightmare stories. This has been happening to them, too, at the hands of these horrible people."

She puts Mr. Metin on the line. "Mrs. Norita, you've got to help us," he says.

I ask him about what he knows about the situation, and when he confirms Nina's reports, I get angry. "If you knew about this horror, if you knew that these things were going on, how could you sleep at night? How could you let such things go on?"

He whispers into the phone, shame and self-justification vying for the upper hand. He explains his position. Originally from the capital city, he had been sent to the Hot Springs Rest Home as a staff social worker. While officially he has some authority as a government employee, in real actual fact he has little say in anything that goes on in the institution. Mr. Bulent, the director, is also from another city. They have no real power when it comes to confronting the locals who make up the majority of staff. This is a small self-protecting community. A gang of three men and one woman are getting high and/or drunk, and using their free access to the residents to do damage whenever they choose to. The director is too afraid of repercussions from the townsfolk, all relatives of these people, to make any kind of complaint. Their family honor supersedes any government employee's authority. Mr. Metin is willing to help Nina if she wants to do something. He explains that it would be dangerous for Nina should she call in the authorities from Ankara. He asks that I back her up somehow.

"You have to get her out of here somehow, Mrs. Norita. I fear for her life."

"I am going to blow the whistle," Nina says, as she has made up her mind despite the risk and her close call the previous evening. "They are terrorizing us, and it's got to stop. I'm not saying I'm not afraid. I am, but I can't get Irem's cry out of my mind, or what I saw that night."

That morning, I phone Sharif to ask what we should do. He suggests another lawyer, also sight-impaired, who would be perfect for this job. Mr. Heron agrees to take the case and within three days is on his way to Hot Springs to meet with Nina. Mr. Metin arranges for them to meet secretly, and he drives her into town to a pastry shop.

The next day, Nina lodges a formal complaint to the Department of Social Services. When the authorities in the capital read her charges, they immediately send two investigators to check out the allegations.

“Norita,” Nina says and then gives me a blow-by-blow description of the day’s proceedings. “One by one, the other women heard they needed to be ready to tell their stories. But they freak out at this! They are so afraid of reprisals and are refusing to say anything. Now I’m in a hard place. What should I do? We have to stop this horrible stuff, but I can’t force anyone to say anything here. It wouldn’t be right.”

After listening to and praying with her, I tell her not to worry about what the others will or will not do; she has called in the authorities on the basis of her own experience. That is enough. We pray together.

Later on, she phones to tell more: With renewed determination, she returns to the office to tell her story, what she witnessed, and why she thinks the others are afraid. Before she is finished talking to someone there, however, two of the women who had been abused are shown into the room. Begging that their names be withheld, they muster up enough courage to add more details as they relate their experiences.

That night, arrest warrants for four employees are issued. The news spreads quickly, and two of the accused skip town, including Halil. However, Halil is soon picked up by the police in a neighboring town. The woman, Edza, and another man, Jafer, are taken in for questioning. This means that they will spend some days in custody. The system here says that when you are under investigation, you are considered guilty until proven innocent. You might spend months, even years, in jail until your case even comes before the judge or there is an arraignment.

When news of the arrest warrants first hit the streets in the small town, a number of the townspeople who were related to the suspects react in anger. Their native sons have been accused. Shame comes upon them—all caused by “a disabled girl living up at the center.” Early the next morning, gunmen come to the home for Nina. Unable to break in through the front door, they manage to shoot off several rounds at the windows of her second-floor room before driving off, all the while honking their horns and leaving Nina and her friends terrified inside.

/////

March 2001

“Mrs. Norita.” This time, the voice on the other end belongs to Mr.

Bulent. "Nina's going to be sent to the rehab facility connected to National Hospital in Ankara next week. She's going to start physical therapy. This'll last for about six weeks. We hope you'll be able to help her."

No one ever comes out and directly says that they need to get Nina out of Hot Springs. I understand, however, that he is concerned for her, as well as for the center's other residents, as long as she is living there.

I promise to do what I can to arrange for her to have some visitors and a possible caregiver while she is in the hospital. After hanging up, I phone Elaina.

Elaina is one of the first people in Ankara to openly make a commitment of faith to Jesus in the 1980s. She and her teenage son and daughter and three tiny daughters are members of the small and fledgling church Ken and I joined when we first arrived in 1988. Although from ethnic Estonian background, Elaina unofficially married a Muslim Turk and had five children by him. When she insisted on going to church and taking her kids with her, he left her. Since they had never been legally married with state papers, it was no great difficulty for him to return to his other wife, also a Muslim Turk, with whom he then had three children in that family.

Until her life grew excruciatingly difficult, Elaina had not given much thought to what faith was all about. After seeing a newspaper ad for Bible study courses available by mail, she started reading the New Testament on her own. Believers in Christ visited her and helped nurture her commitment. Her husband could not stomach the fact that she had influenced her children to such an extent that they, too, converted, so he abandoned her. He threatened to disown his children should they choose to follow their mother. Although this meant incredible financial hardship, they lifted up their hearts to God and made the difficult decision to continue on the faith path their mother had chosen. Elaina's faith is strong; she knows the answered truth of the prayer "Give us this day our daily bread."

Now I hire her to locate a suitable apartment to rent and ask if she'd be willing to be Nina's practical nurse while she is in the hospital. Elaina is glad for the job and wants to help this girl she has only heard about.

"I have found a place, Norita Abla," Elaina says to me soon enough. "It's not too far from my home, so I could go there daily to look after the facilities and the women. The owner wants to rent to us and is ready to sign a contract today, if we're ready." When I ask about accessibility for wheelchairs and within the home, she answers: "There are six stairs from the front entrance to this first-floor flat, but they are wide and a ramp could easily built—and the owner is willing to do that for us. He is also willing for us to put some bars in the bathroom and make the toilet facilities accessible."

"Take it, Elaina. We'll get Ken and his foreman, Hassan, to do the work; by the time Nina is done with her treatment, we should be able to get her in. I'll ask Sharif about the details for the contract, since we should rent this in the name of our organization."

After I hang up, I breathe a prayer of thanksgiving, so grateful that we are going to be able to save at least Nina from the ongoing dangers of Hot Springs. She can get settled in and then prepare the place for the other women to join her.

Oh, the best laid plans of mice and men ... or who can fathom what the Lord has planned?

CHAPTER 18

Blocks

Lift up your heads, you gates … that the King of glory may come in.
Psalm 24:7

My personal notes continued …

March 2003

It has now been six years since I first stepped foot on the grounds of Saray. Various organizations have responded by raising needed funding, and at the moment, we have ten people coming in every day of the week. They have been given permission to hitch rides with the personnel buses, saving a tremendous expense for our little nonprofit.

We receive word that the Ankara Rotary Club has offered to completely renovate one of the wards in D Block. This is welcome news if it means warmer winters and cooler summers.

Mr. Shughar, the newest man to be called head director, decides to temporarily move all the children from all the wards in this building while the remodeling work proceeds. So, one sunny day in the spring of 2001, the Kardelen Team, working alongside the state personnel and hired janitorial workers, manages to move 138 kids, plus all the beds and stored supplies.

Along with the entire Turkish team, Karin goes with seventy-two of the children to E Block, situated on the northwest corner of the twenty-acre grounds. The maintenance office has sent a tractor and trailer that is being used to move the beds, although at one point, Guliya holds a little girl in her arms while sitting on a pile of mattresses.

With the exception of the administrators, all the able-bodied people in the vicinity file in and out of D Block, carrying dismantled beds, mattresses, and pillows. The children are carried from one ward to the next and laid on the floor until all the beds and rails have been reassembled on the second floor of E Block.

Karin drives the white Fiat van Kardelen has obtained for use for a relief project after the earthquake in 1999. Juneyt sits in the front seat with her while everyone carries things out from the old building and stacks them in the van. This day, our team provides invaluable help as an organizing and manpower force. We know that the chaos and discomfort will be difficult for the kids in particular, so we try as hard as we can to be cheerful and to refrain from complaining. As is generally the case when decisions are made about moving large numbers of children or furniture, the administrators in A Block somehow expect that the janitors/caregivers will organize themselves and finish the job. It seems as though no one has taken into consideration that the residents who are in the wards need to be moved, fed, diapered, fed again, and made ready for the evening and sleep. Supplying the missing link for care, most of our team stays on until the last child is safely in his or her new bed.

The downstairs rooms of E Block houses forty-nine men and women over the age of thirty who are mentally handicapped. Their previous rest home had been destroyed during the 1999 earthquake. Their presence adds a new element of danger.

Laliye says, "Sister Norita, we're scared. These men down here are really frightening us. They leer at us. They roam around without anybody supervising them. They don't know us and want to come upstairs to where we are working. I never see any qualified social worker or monitor around. I hate to say this, but they fit the profile of the guys who we suspect are wandering into unsupervised wards and abusing the children in their beds. Who will supervise them? Who will keep us safe?"

We make a group visit to the director of Saray. After sitting down in his office in A Block, we tell him of our fears and the need for people on duty to check up on the older residents.

"I've listened to your complaints," he responds. "First of all, Mr. Mustapha and Mrs. Melissa should have come to me if there was a problem. This is not your responsibility. You are just volunteer helpers. You have no authority in these matters." He looks down and picks up a pile of papers to sign. He is finished with the discussion.

We move on down the hall to Mr. Mustapha's and Mrs. Melissa's offices to tell them that all the personnel as well as volunteers in the second floor of E Block are frightened. They assure us then that no unauthorized people would be allowed to come upstairs. What can we do but take them at their word and relay the message to our colleagues? Their placations sound comforting at first, but before too long, we learn that, most nights, only one watchman is assigned to look after the entire building. Most of the time, he spends his time in the watchman's hut found at the side entrance of the grounds. We know that besides a rare visit from a doctor or nurse, no one else comes to check on things. We have no authority to change this situation, so instead we pray, "Heavenly Father, send your angels to watch over these vulnerable ones and protect them from 'the terror by night.'"

We have learned to pray these prayers of protection for the abandoned and vulnerable. We cannot be everywhere at once, nor do all the things necessary to keep evil from occurring, but God has given us an effective tool for change, the prayer of faith, and we must be vigilant to exercise this right to partner with God for good at every turn of the road we're traveling.

The upstairs floor includes one long corridor opening out onto a landing and the stairwell. On either side of the corridor are two-person bedrooms, into which six metal cribs can be crammed.

"Hey, Auntie Guliya, Sister Laliye." Jonah's high voice reaches up to our floor from the bottom of the stairwell.

Someone tells the women that boys from C Block are waiting in their wheelchairs at the foot of the stairs. After being carried one by one up the flight of twenty stairs, they announce, "We're here to work."

Juneyt's crooked grin is spread across most of his face. "Just because the Kardelen Room is closed, and we've been moved to other rooms, doesn't mean we can't get over here and help you all out."

C Block is only two hundred yards up a dirt path from our new housing unit. These guys plan to roll down to the kitchen entrance on the ground floor of E Block each day, roll to the foot of the stairs, and call out for someone to come and get them. They will spend their days in E Block, hanging around or actually helping with feeding those in the high chairs we've brought.

Not long after the children are moved to E Block, Steve Grant, sponsored by friends, arrives again from the States. Never one to sit around, Steve sets to work, and designs and builds a playroom space on the narrow landing. There, we put all our toys, books, paints, and coloring books, as well as our little music set. Within a matter of weeks, we are operating our supplemental special care program from out of that room. We do not know how long it will be before we move back to D Block, but as always, at Saray all must live from one day to the next while planning for every eventuality.

Everyone loves Steve. He is always cracking jokes. He's so playful with the children, respectful with the workers, and a firm leader with the construction crews. Fluent in Turkish from the ten-plus years he'd lived here in the past, he brings a stable presence for a few weeks.

Not surprising, the D Block remodeling project is delayed. We hear that new foundation posts need to be poured. This slows down the work, and no one has any idea when we can move back.

Lindsey Boardman, a recent Wheaton College grad, has come from California to volunteer for three months. After one day in the E Block rooms, she "adopts" Nagihan, a tall, fair-skinned, blue-eyed teenager with special needs—to play with her and care for her during the day. Nagi is nonverbal and non-ambulatory. After all, she has been left in her crib since being brought to Saray—so her lack of skills is not surprising. But Lindsey is patient and loving, and before too long, Nagihan comes out of her "isolation" to reveal a personality full of mischief and understanding. She still can't walk or talk, but she is there!

Having grown up with an older sister who lives with physical and intellectual disabilities, Lindsey has learned at home how to approach Nagihan and patiently elicit nonverbal communication. Her mother and father modeled the way to love, and she models it for us. In many ways, Lindsey introduces this VIP Nagi to all of us. She teaches us by example; giving us the opportunity to observe what good loving care looks like. Anyone who walks into their room cannot help but be touched by their relationship. The differences in their intellectual or physical capabilities are irrelevant.

As she gets ready to return to her home in the States, Lindsey asks me to read her journal. It changes me.

> *Earlier this year I was blessed with the amazing opportunity to spend three and a half months at Saray Orphanage working with the Kardelen Team. Although I had known about Kardelen's ministry for years, seen pictures of the children at Saray, and even met members of the team when they came to California last November, the experience surpassed my expectations in*

countless ways. It's hard to describe the impact that intense service-oriented work has when extended over a period of months. I was touched by the children at Saray, by the impressive number of Kardelen-hired workers and international volunteers who make the vision of Kardelen a reality, and by the work that God is doing in the lives of everyone involved. I have picked some portions of journal entries that give an idea of the daily routine. I chose passages that focus on the progression of my relationship with a 17-year-old girl named Nagihan. I cannot say enough about what a blessing it was to be able to be a part of this work.

Friday, Jan. 24: Week 1
Yesterday was my second day at Saray. In many ways it was a more positive experience than the day before, but in some ways it was much harder. Aisha gave Kristine (an Indonesian volunteer) and me instructions to bathe, massage, and change the clothes of the six children in the room next to her own. We set up in a small bathroom with an inflatable baby tub. We took turns using the bath with a child, and then dried them and changed them in the adjoining storage closet. We also changed their bedding. This was very good and satisfying work. The smell of the room improved dramatically as the children were brought back clean.

The difficulties, of course, were emotional. All but one of the kids were severely malnourished, and one of them is on the brink of starvation. His body is simply shrink-wrapped bones and tendons, his chest taut over his ribs, and his head out of proportion with his body. He is too weak to move more than his head. His name is Emin and he is 17 years old.

It was difficult not to weep while holding these frames, so fragile that it seemed as though any pressure would break them. The baths took almost until lunchtime. In the afternoon I returned to the room of clean children to supplement their diet with a small container of yogurt. It took as long for me to feed Emin as all the others together. I think that he is normally not given enough time to finish his bottles, or the liquid runs out all over his bed rather than into his mouth because nobody takes the time to feed him.

Saturday, Feb. 1: Week 2
Today I finally felt as though I made a little progress in the room where I've been working. For starters, Nagihan smiled at me this morning when I washed her face. Usually she is stoic, if not angry. Later in the day while I played with Ayşe on the floor mat, Nagihan watched us intently and smiled again. I was so happy that it brought tears to my eyes!

Thursday, Feb. 6: Week 3
The biggest surprise of the day came this afternoon when I was playing with Nagihan. She was leaning against me on the floor while I sang and shook a musical rattle when she decided to sit up unsupported, as straight as an arrow! She remained sitting for about 45 minutes without tiring. It was great to see her sitting up like a normal kid and focusing on our play.

Sunday, Feb. 16: Week 5
When I went to Saray this morning on 4 hours of sleep, I felt like I'd never make it through the day, but as it turned out, it was quite a good day, and included the surprise arrival of a Hug Team that I didn't expect until Monday. I spent the morning with the kids in the Sunflower Room (the name given to the room I work in, after brightly redecorating it). It was nice to have some actual playtime with Nagihan, Ayşe, and Serhat. I feel like I've become incorporated into the system now, as the Saray workers just drop off bottles and diapers in the room and expect that I'll feed and change the kids. This means I can do these things the way I would like them done, but it also means more time doing basic care and less time working on other things.

Serhat played happily with a hanging crib toy today that he hadn't shown any previous interest in. He enjoyed ringing the hanging bells. Nagihan showed some real interest in the mirror at one point, after having completely rejected it earlier. She's really funny about what she will and won't do—very strong-willed, which is great to see in these kids. One second she'll be smiling, and then all of a sudden her hand goes up, her face is frozen in a determined frown, and she wants nothing more to do with whatever is being offered to her. Her defenses are beginning to break down though. Every day she is more willing to interact.

Thursday, March 6: Week 7
It was another busy day in the Sunflower Room, actually a bit chaotic at times. Kristine and I were both there, so she brought Ayşe into the room, making seven kids to care for. Ayşe was just switched with a boy named Ali across the hall for some reason. Also Gul and Harry (from C Block) both visited the room because there was more going on there than anywhere else on the hall.

Highlights today: Nagihan leaned forward to be kissed on the forehead and also gave me a kiss on the cheek. She also had the experience of being able to choose what flavor of oatmeal she would like to eat. I made up two bowls, gave her a bite of each, and waited for her to indicate which she preferred. At first she was very confused and pushed both bowls away, but when she understood, she slapped her hand down in one of the bowls, so I fed her that one. When she realized what she'd done, she beamed through the entire meal. It was a great moment for both of us!

Serhat was in a happy mood today but Emin seemed a bit weary. He wailed quite a lot, and it's hard to know what he wants. I sat him up for a while in one of the big strollers and he really enjoyed that. I'm feeding him a lot of extra food but I can't tell that he's gaining any weight.

Friday, March 21: Week 9
Yesterday at Saray was highly emotional, beginning with a very hard encounter in the depot where the children are bathed. I went in to get a clean pair of pajamas for Emin and was horrified to witness the normal Saray bathing procedure. Lying on towels on the floor were a dozen children from a number of rooms, all thrown down haphazardly with limbs every which way. Two or three women were there. One had the job of stripping down a child from the floor and then another woman grabbed the child by one arm and one leg, like a goat, and carried him or her roughly into the bathroom. Thankfully I didn't see what went on in there. Not more than a minute later, the child was brought back out in the same fashion, and flung on the changing table, where the first worker, having already stripped another child, would now put a couple of diapers and clean clothes on the "clean" child. Of course there was no thought of trying to make the experience a

pleasant one for anybody—no warmth, no talking besides shouting among the workers, no lotion or powder. When the child was dressed, a mentally retarded adult who works in the hall took the kids back to their rooms in a broken stroller being held together with duct tape. I was horrified by the brutality, but could say nothing. Feeling completely helpless, I returned to the cheery Sunflower Room with tears in my eyes. When I think that these same children that I hold and sing to are handled in such a way when I'm not around ... well, it's too much to bear.

The rest of the morning, thankfully, was wonderful. Nagihan and I looked at some picture books and a puzzle, Arif got some exercise, Emin ate quite a bit of fruit and yogurt, and aside from a little tantrum from Serhat, everybody was happy. Even the tantrum is welcome because it shows that he is learning how to communicate and that someone is paying attention to him.

In the afternoon Penny, a physical therapist from Chicago, spent a few hours in the room, working with each child. Everyone was so interested in what Penny was doing that the tiny room was extremely crowded: Gene, Marian, Bob, Kristine, Marge, Margaret, Karen, Penny, myself, plus the six kids! I learned how to work on trunk support with Uzlem, neck strength with Emin, how to use the big therapy ball ... it was fascinating. The way Penny gained the trust, even of Nagihan, with her soft voice and her skilled hands was impressive. I am so excited about implementing these exercises in the next month!

Tuesday, April 15: Week 13
With the help of Jean, a recent arrival from Australia, we took a giant step toward independent feeding today in the Sunflower Room. We helped the kids hold their own spoons while we fed them their snack. Most of them aren't capable of doing this on their own, but Nagihan and Arif might learn with enough practice. I worked with Nagihan, who initially could find nothing better to do with a spoon than throw it violently across the room. Oatmeal was everywhere! After a good laugh we tried again, and once she realized that the only way she would eat was to get the spoon to her mouth, she complied beautifully! I can't wait to try it again tomorrow!

People like Lindsey encourage us to keep going and to keep looking for that key which will unlock these children from the inner prisons they have been condemned to. Like Lindsey does, her mom, Desley, Frits and Yikkie, Bob and Marion and Emily, as well as Sam, time and again motivate us to continue, to find the beauty "hidden in darkness" and to advocate with renewed vigor for these special ones.

Six months later, we move back to D block. The remodeled ward is newly painted, has new windows and window frames, and, best of all, boasts a combination AC/heating system. Funds from Belinda's group bring Sam back twice to oversee the complete renovation of the bath, shower, and toilet rooms in two of the other wards.

We have also been able to facilitate major projects by other local donors for washable, long-lasting flooring in the dayrooms and bedrooms of those units. My records over the two-year period of rebuilding show that at least $100,000 worth of materials and manpower went into our efforts to make Saray a better place.

We also have begun to invest in more local leadership. Stella was back from her successful earthquake project, and after directing KIFAS' program during the ten months we had gone on sabbatical in the USA, she was the right person to come on board and coordinate the Kardelen program, taking over from Annelies, the Dutch psychologist who had filled in for me when I was gone. Stella knew how to talk to officials as well as relate to the neediest of children and workers.

So imagine our shock when six months later, the new director, Mr. Murat, calls Stella in to inform her that that we have to leave our Hope Room. "As far as I'm concerned," he says, his tone cold and official. "You are here as volunteers. You have no status and should never have been allowed to have that room as your own."

Stella bites her tongue, wanting to give him a major comedown for his arrogance, but instead manages to gain enough self-control to plead for some little room where the team could hang their coats and meet. A week later, she gets the news that the team can use a large storage closet to hang coats and store supplies. No more Kardelen special room where we can go to hang out or where kids can come to play or talk.

We try to deal with the rejection, but are hurt by this new director's attitude. Other state workers just shrug their shoulders. Nylene, the supervisor for CC1, explains, "The people who are in charge of these places have NO idea what goes on from day to day. They don't know what you all do, because they read the reports of the ward supervisors who never mention your help but instead take all the credit for themselves."

Of course, Nylene does not realize that we know about her too. We have heard through the orphanage personnel grapevine that she, too, never passes on a good word about our Kardelen work, even though our team considerably lightens her workload and helps prevent serious incidents from damaging her reputation.

Once again, we try to encourage each other to continue on for the children's sake and not to think too much about what people in "high places" are saying or not saying about us. This is a humbling time—and a confusing time.

Short-term teams generally are real morale boosters. We can hardly wait for these teams to come. From them, the local team members learn that there is no barrier between classes or nationalities when it comes to serving these children with joy and creativity. In direct contrast, the administrators and people in authority never thank us, and some treat us with obvious contempt.

However, it isn't only us who never hear a "thank you." None of the paid direct-care staff does, either. We hear more than once the complaint: "Well, you know that I used to work in the office, but my punishment for insubordination was to be sent down to work in the wards. This work is definitely a demotion, actually a punishment."

Everyone is desperate to be recognized as a "good person who has done a job well," even the "lowly job of feeding and bathing disabled children." The gift of encouragement is sorely lacking. Instead the word of complaint and veiled accusation is the norm. We MUST overlook much incompetence and focus instead on finding something good among the people we are rubbing shoulders with every day. Not only will this mean that we can stay on the campus—even unofficially—but also that the atmosphere in our rooms will be affected. We must, however tempting it may be, particularly reject the role of gossips and "Negativity Networkers." We are going to be Pollyanna's no matter how bad the scene. Sometimes we succeed at this; other times, we forget to reign in the anger until after we get off the campus and out of earshot of the workers there.

But bad news continues to dog us. We next receive word that that the permissions being given from the main office of Social Services for short-term Hug Teams are now "under review." A new office has been set up in downtown Ankara where all petitions for visits to Saray are to be processed and approved under the name of the Office of Public Relations and European Union Contacts.

One by one, petitions made by short-term teams coming from outside the country are being refused. When Stella asks about this, she is basically told that all the new petitions have been improperly filed and need to be re-filed.

We communicate this to the people wanting to come, as we have groups scheduled to come from Korea, The Netherlands, and the USA.

One day, an American group from a church in Texas shows up at the gate assuming they can get onto the campus without any sort of long bureaucratic wait. They drive into the parking lot and manage to join us for a few hours before being escorted off by the guards who man the front gate.

I make an appointment to speak to the people in the downtown office. Two smartly dressed professional women lead me into their office. I tell them about our work and about all the benefits of the short-term Hug Teams. I speak to them about our association: The Kardelen Association for the Protection of Abandoned Children with Mental Disabilities. They are pleasant enough and listen respectfully. I am shown notebooks thick with petitions. The young woman who has introduced herself as a psychologist—attested to by the diplomas adorning the wall of her office—suddenly pierces me with a hard look and asks, "Why do these people want to come all the way here to spend time and money on these children? Don't they have orphanages or mental hospitals in their home countries where they can do good works? We don't need them here. Let's look at this petition. It says here that this man is a house contractor. What use do we have for house contractors in an institution like Saray? Or this one … a woman says that she is an artist. We have our own artists here who do projects in our hospitals or orphanages. "

So much for "Public Relations." Just what the words "European Union" mean in this context is beyond me.

Over the years, more than a few of the administrators at Saray have spoken just as critically of foreigners who have visited and wanted to do good. I heard this many times while sitting in one or another administrator's office in the A Block. The implication: there had to be an ulterior motive. No one spends vacation time and money to come halfway around the world to serve the "lowest and least attractive of children."

After a time, I start to get it about these people's attitudes: behind this type of questioning is a deeply held shame. These people are ashamed of the children, the smells, and the actual facility. Turkey is a magnificently beautiful country and the Ministry of Tourism wants the world to come to this land to enjoy the natural beauty, historic sites, and wonderful food, but no one wants anyone—foreigners especially—to see their "hidden" population.

I must force myself to gently answer that our only goal is to serve them and the children. We do not want to create administrative or logistical problems, but to help out in doing whatever is truly helpful. For many years, we worked very well with some of the administrators who saw time and again our goodwill. There were always naysayers who made it clear that we were not wanted at Saray. Shame caused them to state their opinions about us: "We don't need anybody's help. We have enough resources to take care of ourselves." Others were so frustrated by the fact that their petitions to the head office did not result in needed supplies that they, ashamed as they are about this, came "begging" to us.

I didn't understand why there is so much stonewalling of the foreign teams when the people at Saray who are in charge know what good had been brought there through the volunteers. Something just isn't right.

CHAPTER 19

Aisha and Ali Reza

Hear my prayer, Lord; let my cry for help come to you.
Do not hide your face from me when I am in distress.
Turn your ear to me; when I call, answer me quickly.
Psalm 102:1-2

My personal notes continued …

May 2004: A Story I Heard from Aisha

Twelve-year-old Ersen, Saray's version of the Artful Dodger, comes running into the clinic not long after Aisha arrives for work.

"Aishaaaaaa, Sister Aishaaaaa, come quick!" He is sobbing and panting, and then flops down on the carpet in her newly decorated playroom.

Some months before, Aisha had asked me if she could start working in the intake unit and clinic at Saray: "I've made my mark in the bedridden units; now Zeynep and the other Kardelen workers are doing a great job with the children. They are going in every day and helping out in such a way that the staff is learning how to treat the children better by watching them. I need to be in the place where I can make the biggest difference. Here in the clinic, I've discovered that many of the children who are on special machines are left unattended and their machines either turned off or clogged and not properly used. I'll make sure all the feeding machines are clean and running. But most importantly, I can be here when new children are sent here, or maybe meet with parents who are considering leaving their children here—to warn them before they do this.

"You know how traumatized they are—being left by their moms or stepdads or other people with no explanation or help in getting adjusted. Put like inmates into these bare rooms with barred, nailed-shut windows and no toys or people to talk to or be around. They are kept here for at least two weeks. Mrs. Nimet said this was the directive from the main office downtown—to 'get them used to Saray and to get them over the crying jags they inevitably have before being sent into the regular wards.'"

I bent my head and with her wept for every little Mary or Mehmet who had to experience so much rejection because of her or his disabilities.

"If I'm here when the kids get here, then I can force the staff to unlock the door to the 'intake chamber,' have them come into my playroom, and hug them and play with them to help them feel loved and cared for. I so want to do this. Please let me work there."

So thankful for such an amazing friend and dedicated nurse, I said, "Wonderful, Aisha. You will be brilliant at this."

Aisha had already presented herself to be used for this kingdom when she stepped through the gates of Saray for the first time. But now, young Ersen's broken cries almost do her in. Since the first year we set up the VIP Kardelen Room, Aisha has had a special place in her heart for impish but emotionally damaged Ersen, whom I like to call the Artful Dodger. From the first day, he loved to scoot in and out of the open doors of our room, carrying anything and everything he could stuff in a pocket or put under his T-shirt. We'd chase him down and get him to give the stuff back and chide him for his behavior. He'd grin and then walk cockily back down the corridor toward his A Block living quarters. Within a few hours, though, he was back, ready to do more mischief. We knew he was basically harmless, but we were always trying to run interference between him and the Hug Team members who unwittingly would leave wallets or stuff out to be stolen.

Now, some years after first coming on the campus, Aisha knows that Ersen's living situation is anything but friendly. She knows that he is so desperate for love and attention that he has now made it a personal goal to run away as often as he can, to be involved in petty thievery or vandalism, and inevitably to be beaten to within an inch of his life by the police or by one or the other staff after he gets brought back to Saray. He's famous for his bad behavior.

She has taken him on as a special love-project—giving him some attention and little jobs to do that bring some meaning to his incarceration there. She told me that she now so trusts him that she can leave her purse and wallet in his charge and he will guard them with his life, making sure that no one steals from her playroom or her belongings. He is truly happy when he is acting as her assistant doing odd little jobs for her.

Now, though, he is sobbing. She wonders what trouble he's gotten himself into.

"It's not me, Sister Aisha!" He gulps tearfully. "They've locked Ali Reza into the 'Pee Room' because he wet his bed last night. It's not fair. It's bad." Ersen buries his head in his arms.

"What's that? You mean little mute Reza who just got here a couple of weeks ago?" Aisha remembers the six-year-old little boy, clearly traumatized as a result of his recent abandonment to Saray. He had lived in the clinic for a few weeks, and she had tried to comfort the boy when he cried himself to sleep every afternoon after lunch.

"Uh-huh," Ersen says, looking up at her with eyes wide with confusion. "They put him in a room with Jemal—you know, that big fifteen-year-old. He's a blankety-blank. I hate him. And Jemal did … did … did … I mean … he hurt Reza." Ersen pointed to his buttocks, and then quickly looked down, cheeks flushed red.

Aisha put her pen down on her report notebook and told Ersen to stay put. "Don't come out and don't talk to anyone," she orders her "son." "Stay here and look at some of these books. I'll be back in a few minutes."

She runs down the stairs and the fifty yards to House A. There, one of the staff helpers sitting on a folding chair on the top step at the front door cannot keep her from running up the stairs to the one door in the entire building that is shut tight and locked.

"Mrs. Aisha, what are you doing here?" the man says, looking slightly uncomfortable.

The "House Father" is not around, and this underling doesn't know what to do with this woman who has blown in like a tornado.

"What's behind this door?" Aisha demands.

"Why, nothing. It's just a storage closet. Nothing's there."

"Then open it for me to see."

"No, I can't. I don't have permission. You don't have permission to be here anyway." His voice quivers.

"YOU OPEN THIS DOOR IMMEDIATELY OR I'M GOING TO CALL THE POLICE TO COME AND OPEN IT FOR ME!"

Jumping up, he produces a key and opens the blue-painted wooden door before running out of the room.

"I took two steps into this small room," Aisha tells me later, "and the acidic sting and stench of urine caused my throat to clench up and eyes to tear. Gagging, I made my way to the hunched-up, wheezing, and crying child lying on the lower bunk bed, and picked him up in my arms. As fast as we could, I got him out the door and to the bath. I bathed him and changed him, sitting him down on one of the other beds in the normal group bedroom. No one came to bother us this whole time.

"I went back into the so-called Pee Room to recheck that what I thought I'd seen and smelled was actually what I had experienced and wasn't just a nightmare. There were two sets of bunk beds and a small corridor carpet separating them in this closet. Every sheet, blanket, mattress, and inch of carpet was soaked and slick with urine. Piles of feces were sitting in the corners of the room as well. The Pee Room had been especially prepared as a punishment room by the older boys in the house at the order of the House Father.

"Can you imagine? Little defenseless Reza had been put into the clutches of an older sexually active boy at the order of this house director and then was being tortured with this filthy punishment. Why was he being punished? As far as I can make out, it's because he continues to cry and wet his bed. I went ballistic."

After bringing Reza back to the clinic, she rushes out of the building and down the concrete pathway to the main administration building, where she bursts into the director's finely decorated office.

"Mr. Murat, I am filing a complaint against the House Father for his horrendous treatment of little Reza." She can hardly speak she is so angry.

"Oh, please, calm yourself. You'll hurt yourself." Mr. Murat's voice is unctuous—he is a smooth politician now, as Saray currently houses 780 residents, and as the director, his first job is to keep some sort of peace. After he hears her complaint, he says, "Thank you for your sensitivity to this issue. We appreciate your coming to us to tell us what you've seen. But don't you worry your pretty little head. We'll deal with it. Good day." He nods to the door, in effect sending her away like a child.

As Aisha makes her way down the stairs and out the front door, her heart sinks. There facing her is the House Father, in a hurry to see the director. He glares at her but says nothing. This in itself doesn't bother her too much, but to her dismay, Ersen is standing there too. He has disobeyed her injunction to stay out of sight. Then, for all to hear, Ersen asks, "Did you tell Mr. Murat what happened?"

"Oh, why didn't you do what I told you to?" Aisha says to him after they are out of view and earshot. "Let me deal with this. Don't talk about this with anyone else. Now get back to your house and I'll see you tomorrow."

She returns to the clinic and busies herself with some of the nursing duties she's taken on while there until she can no longer ignore the uneasy feeling in her chest. Dropping the towels she had collected to fold, she runs back to House A again. This time, after she has run in through the front door and up another flight of stairs, she comes to a halt in front of an open door.

There is the House Father, wielding a long piece of 2x4 lumber and beating Ersen's hands and knees while shouting, "Why, you filthy little pig! How dare you go telling on us here? What happens in this house stays in this house! You deserve to die. You will learn your lesson never to snitch. You will suffer—"

At that moment, he turns to see Aisha staring at them. As quick as he can, he throws the 2x4 under a table that has been pushed against the wall.

"Listen, you poor excuse for a human being!" Aisha shouts. "I may not have the degrees you've got, I may not have the tenure, and I may be out of here tomorrow, but I am making dead sure that you are gone from this institution. Upon my life!" She looks at Ersen and says, "Ersen, come with me. We are going to see the house doctor."

With that, she turns and walks slowly down the stairs with the sobbing boy whose hands are swollen and whose knees barely hold him up. Her knees are shaking as well.

When Dr. Suleiman, one of the physicians on call in the clinic, takes one look at Ersen and hears the story, he explodes, "What are we going to do with such animals?" He echoes the sentiments of some of the state employees who have grown hopeless about inhumane practices becoming the norm here. They are upset but too fearful for their own jobs to carry on any campaign to see the ruthless ones ejected for good.

The next day, the kind doctor greets Aisha at the door: "Light to our eyes, Sister Aisha. The House Father has been transferred. Thanks to you, he's gone from here."

"I couldn't believe my ears," she later tells me. "No one who's been involved in such cruelty gets shipped so soon. But I guess they were afraid

I was going to go to the press, so they transferred him out.

"That afternoon, I walked into House A and directly to the Pee Room. The night before, someone had stripped it of all the beds and filthy bedclothes. The filth on the floor was gone. I could smell bleach mixed with the faint scent of cheap primer. That room was undergoing a lightning-fast overhaul. The next month when I checked again, it was fitted out with new wooden cupboards filled with the unopened packages of donated boys' dress shirts.

"Ersen has been told he must not come unattended to my room in the clinic, but we'll find a way to communicate. Ali Reza is the one I'm concerned for. He's still with the same boys. I don't know who is in charge now that the House Father has been transferred. I pray for someone good.

"As for the House Father—he has actually been PROMOTED to the main office. I don't care, just as long as he is far away from the children. And you know what? He was the one who never missed Friday prayers, who was always encouraging the kids to learn the prayers and to be a faithful believer in Allah. I hate hypocrisy. Religion is not supposed to be a cover-up thing. You can be sure that one day he will pay even worse for using God's name and doing Satan's work."

/////

A Few Weeks Later

Kimberly, an intrepid and determined pastor from the USA, snuck herself on campus at Saray by coming onto the premises with Aisha. They had met up at the statue of Ataturk in the city center and come together on the bus. No one questioned her at the front gate, and she just walked into the ward where Aisha was now working. She wanted to spend some time with Aisha and Laliye, who it turned out were about her same age. Kimberly loved to just hang out with them, and her presence and love for Turkey and Turks made them feel appreciated.

Kimberly was there when Aisha found about a new resident and called me: "Norita, please pray and tell me what to do," Aisha said over the phone, voice broken and pleading. "They've just brought in a teenage girl from off the streets and locked her into a room across the hall from my clinic playroom. She has been screaming all morning. After I went into the admin building to tell Mrs. Melissa, I was told to go back to the room and carry on with my normal program. This is what Mrs. Melissa said: 'She has to learn that she is here for good and not to be living like a wild person on the street. The only way we can deal with her and teach her the realities of this is to punish her for her crazy behavior. She is out of control, and the only way to stop this is to bind her and leave her somewhere where she won't hurt anyone.'

"When I told Mrs. Melissa that I had heard the orderlies beating the girl and screaming at her, she just shrugged and said, 'That is as it has to be. The girl won't learn any other way.'

"Oh, what can we do? I can hear her whimpering now. And a while ago, another orderly opened the door and threw a piece of bread into her as if she were a dog. There is nothing besides a mattress on the floor—nothing, nothing, nothing! Oh God!" And then she began sobbing. "They won't let me do anything. Not even clean her up or touch her. Please pray."

When she hung up, I got on my knees and cried out for mercy for this girl whose name I didn't know but who was terrified and being terrorized: "Give Aisha favor and make a way for her to serve this girl. Please, oh Man of Sorrows."

A few minutes later, after changing into her colorful scrubs (compliments of the American Hug Teamers), Aisha told Kimberly that she was going back to the director's office again with a proposal. A half an hour later, she returned, face set in a determined but triumphant expression.

"I told them in the office that I wanted to be responsible for this new girl—Noorgul—that I would sit with her and play with her and help her try to find comfort rather than fear, that I could achieve better results for her if they'd trust me to do the right thing with her. At first, they weren't going to let me do anything and said that they had more experience with this kind of unruly behavior and so on—the usual baloney—but then I told them that I could get someone to come and renovate the room, you know, paint it, put it new unbreakable windows and maybe soft padding on the walls for real out-of-control patients. In a way, I bribed them into letting me try something with the poor girl.

"They agreed. Now I better phone Norita Abla to see if she can find the donations to do this renovation, and then I'm going to get them to unlock that door and see what I need to do. "

She made her phone call, got me writing a proposal to the charities committee for some room renovation, and embarked on her mission of mercy.

"Give me the key, Ahmed," Aisha said after the orderly was summoned to her floor. She put the key in the keyhole all the while speaking clearly and in a pleasant manner: "Noorgul, my little Noorgul, your older sister, Aisha, is coming to rescue you, to help you. Don't be afraid. I will not hurt you. Don't be afraid."

When she opened the door, the scene that greeted her caused her to put her hand to her mouth to keep from screaming. The poor girl had hit her head against the window, shattering the glass and lacerating her head. She was covered in blood and lying there on the cold concrete floor. She had defecated during the night, and her hair and face were matted with this filth as well. She was curled up in the corner of the bare room, hands still bound by the ropes they'd used to subdue her the day before.

Aisha prepared a plastic tub of warm water with soap and washcloths to begin the cleanup process. As she knelt down beside her and unbound her hands, the girl lost any energy to resist and allowed the ministrations. Aisha began to sing:

"Do you know that you are so precious?
Do you know that you are a pearl in the hands of God?
Do you know that He gave himself for you?
You are a pearl in His hands, a pearl in His hands."

As she sang to Noorgul, the tension in the girl's body left; she allowed Aisha to wipe away some of the blood and feces. Gradually she was willing to be led to the shower room where Aisha washed and shampooed the teenager, all the while singing over her.

Noorgul, bandaged but calm, lay down clutching a toy bear on the floor mat Aisha had in her playroom. Aisha did not leave her the entire day, and then requested that she be given a hospital bed to stay in on the clinic floor until better plans could be made for her care in the future.

Mrs. Melissa stood at the door of the playroom. Shaking her head, she said quietly, "This is so good. We need ten of you, Aisha. If everyone could treat these people the way you do, we'd have no problems at all.

Keep it up, girl."

/////

"Invitation by the Man of Sorrows"

Pour it out
Drink offerings on the altar of love
Flowing down your cheeks, neck, and chest.
Pour it out
Slow in motion
Slow, still,
Softer sweeter
Sighs of deep
Calling to Deep
Signs of Deep
Calling to deep.
Notes in the treble clef
Reverb in the bass
You have traveled far to bring your heart-song to this temple
But not as far as I have.
Surprised to find Me in this pain-filled place?
Where else would I be, My Beloved?
Waiting as we compose
The Song of the Saints,
Lamentations
Complaints
Tears
Sobs
Silence
Until the Final trumpet Call
Until the Final DAY

CHAPTER 20

Everybody Dance Now

"Call me and I'll answer, be at your side in bad times;
I'll rescue you, then throw you a party."
—God, from Psalm 91:15 (The Message)

My personal notes continued ...

April 2001

As much as I am finding my emotional stride today, I struggle too. Aisha's questions never really disappear. Every time I come face-to-face with some sort of violence perpetrated against these children, I find myself emotionally wrenched for days. I image it's not too different from what happens when an honest cop has to deal with the aftermath of the senseless violence of gang warfare or the feelings that plague an aid worker who sees the result of horrendous wartime brutality.

I still do not forget seeing a little girl dragged across the floor from the leash around her neck, nor hearing stories of small ones being beaten because they cry, or kicked because they are on the ground and in the way. Sexual abuse, bullying, and tooth extractions or painful medical procedures without anesthetic are a common reality in the institution—as is slow starvation by throwing away food before a child could be fed.

Perhaps most heartbreaking is witnessing how residents, who have lived in this violent environment, have learned to perpetrate as well as perpetuate the cycle of inhumanity.

Word has filtered into each ward about us: we are here and will report whatever abuse we saw. Incidents have become fewer and fewer, which is truly heartening. We have lost any fear about speaking out against an abusive supervisor or state employee. After all, we are volunteers, and so not in danger of losing our jobs.

But speaking out against abuse only works for a short time: there is an outcry, the main office informed, a so-called investigation undertaken, and typically the incident will gradually be forgotten. Without severe punishment or serious retraining of the abusers, bad behavior resurfaces after so many months.

One day, Zeynep runs into the changing room with an announcement. "Norita, that prayer you've been praying for four years has been answered. The scuttlebutt around the campus is that over a hundred new caregivers are being hired. There should be enough hands to go around, at least to do the most important things. They are even giving them special training."

Two weeks later, a new host of blue-coated women and men walk into Continuous Care 1 and 2. Although technically janitorial staff under the direction of a middle manager for a cleaning company, they are to attend a two-week course on patient care.

Before too long, however, we see their excitement and hope turn sour: "This job is the lowest of the lowest job, and we get paid a pittance," Fatma says one day on a break. All the other women and men sitting there with her in their segregated corner of the cafeteria nod in unanimous agreement. "I just took the training so that I could get the job. I need work to put food on the table at home, and this was the only thing available. I only got hired because I know someone else who works here and she put in a good word for me."

I can see the telltale signs of fear, too, in their reactions to the children: "Perhaps the curse of disability will 'jump' on me, too, like the lice which we fight there." No training course here ever deals with the deep-seated beliefs they hold about the children or themselves.

We know that to make any long-term difference for the children, we have to reach these new recruits—but how?

/////

All of us in the team are inveterate party-ers. We never want to miss one—lots of music and dancing.

When it comes to Bible heroes, I feel the greatest affinity with King David, who danced "before the Lord with all his might." He knew how to party with God!

Often the picture I have before my eyes when praying "Thy Kingdom come; Thy will be done on earth as it is in heaven" is the picture Jesus gives of a wedding party. Let the revelry begin! We are loved beyond comprehension. We are loved no matter what color our skin is, what language we speak, what our gender is, and whether or not we fit to the genetic patterns of normalcy our cultures dictate. Sin and selfishness ushered in the long winter of suffering, but Jesus broke the hold the curse has on His creation. The Bridegroom paid an incredible price (in Middle Eastern terms—a Bride Price beyond compare) for His Bride and is preparing The Best Party Ever. All tears will be dried, all suffering glorified, all questions put to rest. By faith, we party today knowing that one day a celebration will take place for which we have no present words or imagination to describe.

So let's celebrate. Becky and Gary loved to do just that when she brought a Hug Team. She showed the Kardelen Team just how an extravagant and colorfully decorated cake would electrify the atmosphere in our Kardelen Room.

It turned out that Aisha was our party-planner-par-excellence.

"You know," Aisha says one day, "not a single one of these children ever had a birthday celebrated before. But with more than four hundred children here and the funds we raise, we couldn't possibly do individual parties. Not only that, you know I never had a birthday party until I was twenty years old and I had Christian friends. Nobody celebrated me until then. I will never ever forget that day. I would bet you that most of the Blue Coats aren't likely to have had birthday parties, either. Let's celebrate them too. We'll organize group birthday parties for each ward, even the ones we don't work in every day."

Soon Aisha returns after talking with Mrs. Melissa.

"I got us permission to start in whatever ward we want to. I just found out that Ali, one of the janitors, is a *saz* player [Middle Eastern stringed instrument that sounds a bit like a banjo] and has a complete electric speaker-and-microphone set. He's willing to play dance music."

The day comes. Ali sets up his speakers in Ward 7, filled with the happy chatter of twenty-five teenage girls who are curious about what is going to happen. Aisha arrives with bags of goodies, soft drinks, and something in a large rectangular box. We, with the enthusiastic "help" of some of the girls, decorate the room with streamers and balloons.

As soon as Ali begins playing a well-known Turkish pop tune, some of the kids start to sway and dance. Their caregivers sit in chairs against the wall, talking quietly among themselves, looking rather annoyed that their daily schedule has been disturbed.

Karin empties a plastic bag, revealing bottles of bright-red nail polish and yellow and green hair bands. Zeynep begins doing the nails of one of the girls. When the other girls see this, a near riot is narrowly averted.

"Me, too! Me, too!" the girls shout.

I do what I can to "organize" the waiting line. "Don't worry, girls. There's plenty enough to go around. We're having a party today and that means dressing up. We're doing it together."

Aisha runs up to Fatma, the caregiver holding up the wall with her frown. "Come on, Fatma, don't sit there like a stick in the mud. Let us do your nails too."

After a startled, shy mumbled response of "Yes," she becomes the next in the long line of red-nailed beauties. Then Aisha grabs Fatma's hand and pulls her into the dance line along with all the other girls. I can hardly believe my eyes. Fatma is smiling and showing us just how the dance is to be done. And within minutes, the wall-sitters are on the dance floor, holding hands with those they've been reluctant to touch before. Everyone is trying to keep the rhythm, and even though they really are not succeeding there, the laughter drowns out every cry of "ouch" from someone who's had her foot stepped on in the chaos.

Ali lets anyone come and take the mike and sing along with him. The ever-popular *Turkey's Got Talent!* show has nothing on what happens here in this place far from the public eye. Kids like Emma and Ebru sing with such abandon that they go hoarse.

Laughter, noise, and controlled chaos means everyone is letting off steam. Later we learn that violent outbursts and incidents between the residents drop in the wards where we hold parties.

The cake ceremony is ready to begin. An elaborately decorated cake is carried out by blue-coated Mehmet and Murad, and set on a table in the middle of the room. Everyone crowds around the pink-, red-, and white-creamed confection as Aisha lights the single candle placed in its middle. One by one, the girls are invited to come up and blow out the candle to the tune of "Happy Birthday"—who cares if we sing it thirty-three times?

It happens that Fatma also has a birthday this month. She is invited up and blows out the candle, then helps cut and serve the portions.

Written in big letters on the cake for all to see is the traditional Turkish blessing: "It is good that you were born!" The Kardelen Team then begins in unison our theme song for birthday parties: "Did you know that you are so valuable? Did you know that you are a pearl? Did you know that you are valuable and in the hands of the Lord?"

Everybody loves a party, and once news gets around that Kardelen is about parties, we are inundated with requests from every ward. We make it a priority now. May every child here, young or old, get to be celebrated; may every worker, whether high or low, know that she or he is beloved.

Soon it's the end of May and we are holding a party for Continuous Care 2.

On my way there, Laliye and Guliya catch up with me, each carrying bags of toys and wrapped packages for the staff workers. As we stand outside the building talking, the sun breaks through the clouds and we feel its warmth like a wool blanket.

We walk into the Kardelen Room to find that the rest of the team has prepared the garden between our room and Continuous Care 2 for the event. Bright throw pillows in yellows, reds, and blues have been placed on the ground, and the blue-coated women from the ward are bringing children out of their beds to be cradled in their laps while they sit on the pillows. Jonah and Juneyt have joined us and are sitting in their wheelchairs. Even the entertainer, Ali, has set up his equipment in the small space under the tree that grows in the center of this garden.

This day, all the children are out of their metal cribs, cleaned up, and seated in the laps of the caregivers, who sway with the music if they can't get up and dance with a child in their arms. The noise is happy noise, and nearly all the children as well as caregivers are laughing along. There are daisies growing along the wall, adding a glorious yellow to the greens, to go along with the browns of the earth and tree.

Suddenly I remember the vision I had back in 1997 and can only shake my head in awe. Here we are, young and old, disabled and able-bodied, all enjoying the warmth of the sun and peace. And we who have been called to announce the Good News are once again filled with wonder at the One who takes "the foolish things of the world to shame the wise"—the One who loves to throw a party for His kids.

CRY OUT

CHAPTER 21

Limbo Land

I trust in you; do not let me be put to shame, nor let my enemies triumph over me. No one who hopes in you will ever be put to shame, but shame will come on those who are treacherous without a cause.

Psalm 25:2-3

My personal notes continued …

Since 1988, our family has actively participated in the life of what is today called the Liberation Church of Ankara. This gathering of believers in Jesus Christ is primarily a congregation of Turks. Some of the members used to call themselves Muslim. Others, while having been born in ethnic Christian homes, now claim to have a personal relationship with Jesus. Some who are active participants have had little contact with anything religious before hearing and accepting the news that there is a God who loves and forgives and changes lives. They speak often of their lives having been changed by God.

All, including foreigners like us, have at some point in time recognized that God loves them individually and deeply, that He showed His love by entering into our time-space broken world as a human being. Jesus was born with the express purpose of living a life totally in tune with his heavenly Father, of teaching those with spiritual hunger what his Father really was like and that there is the possibility of knowing His love and guidance, and of dying a criminal's death as the sinless sacrifice for all the sins of everyone on the planet. We understand that the perfect, holy Creator sent His Son into the world to provide a way for imperfect, self-centered humans to be united with Him forever.

In his little gem of a book, *Life and Holiness*

> Sin is the refusal of spiritual life, the rejection of the inner order and peace that come from our union with the divine will. In a word, sin is the refusal of God's will and of his love. It is not only a refusal to "do"

> this or that thing willed by God, or a determination to do what he forbids. It is more radically a refusal to be what we are, a rejection of our mysterious, contingent, spiritual reality hidden in the very mystery of God. Sin is our refusal to be what we were created to be—sons of God, images of God. Ultimately sin, while seeming to be an assertion of freedom, is a flight from the freedom and the responsibility of divine sonship.

Jesus died in my place on a cross. Then, three days later, He rose from the dead, not only as a testimony to His divinity, His perfection, but also as a sign that the ultimate enemies of us all—death, sin, and unseen spiritual powers—have been conquered. Because Jesus is alive, we also "live"; His life is made visible in and through our lives when we choose to walk with Him. He gives us His Holy Spirit. This privilege of relationship with God has been "poured out," the Scripture says, on the whole world (see Acts 2:17). This means that this relationship is not bound by genetic, national, ethnic, linguistic, territorial, or temporal boundaries.

We come together to worship on Sundays because we are passionate about the message embodied in the crucifixion and resurrection of Jesus: that message of forgiveness and validation regardless of who you are or what you've done or has been done to you. Life found in present relationship with Jesus is the basis of deep hope. This is good news for everyone everywhere.

Still, unlike thousands upon thousands in sub-Saharan Africa or Latin America, there are only a handful of people and churches like us who openly meet for worship in Turkey. Fully 99 percent of the population claim to be Muslim, but in actual fact, only a very small percentage practice the religion and an even smaller percentage—less than 2 percent—call themselves Christians of any persuasion.

Our pastor, a Turk named John, and his wife Flora, lead the church. Now in his mid-forties, he is an intelligent, capable pastor whose preaching gifts are obvious as he opens his Bible each Sunday to teach and preach.

John came to know Jesus the Messiah after many years of searching for hope and reality. On his journey of faith, he traveled through periods of fervent Islamic practice, then about-faced to committed atheistic Communism. It was a totally unsought-for supernatural encounter that jump-started his search for God in earnest, though.

"I was on a crowded bus when, all of a sudden, I saw a pillar of bright light in the middle of the bus. No one else saw what I saw, but I heard a voice saying 'I exist. I am God.'"

Getting hold of a Bible, he began reading the New Testament. Then, one day while reading the book of Romans in chapter five, he read these words: "But God demonstrates His own love toward us, in that while we were yet sinners, Christ died for us" (Romans 5:8 NASB).

"The light went on. I knew that I could not, try as I might, live a righteous holy life that would please God. It was amazing to understand that God's love was so great that He Himself made the way for me to be embraced by it."

/////

Early 2002

William, a man who'd answered a missionary call on his life and moved with family from Korea, was active in talking about his faith. One Sunday, he brought his new friend, EP, to church. They sat in the back row and watched the service proceedings. EP also began visiting William's home for special conversations about faith. William characterized him as a "seeker."

EP came to our Sunday meetings over the course of several weeks. Then he disappeared from the scene. When asked about his friend, William replied that he couldn't contact him and had no idea where he was. He was sad and continued to pray for his safety and spiritual search.

A couple of months later, Ann, our lovely Turkish Kardelen volunteer who lived on the coast, tells me that she's just read in the newspaper about a book that supposedly is a daring exposé. The allegation in the book is that foreign missionaries are spies, agents of Western governments or the CIA who are trying to undermine the stability and sovereignty of the Turkish Republic.

"Norita, you, Ken, and Pastor John are accused of being undercover agents, seeking to destabilize the Turkish Republic," Ann tells me over the phone. "Even the Kardelen Association is named. My name is there as being a board member." She goes on to read from the article: "'EP's exposé, *In the Spider's Web—Six Months among the Missionaries* has reached the shelves of our bookstores today. In it, investigative journalist EP, who spent several months posing as an interested potential convert, shows how the foreign missionaries are setting up cells around the nation—there are thousands of cells according to EP.'

"Norita, this book is full of lies, but people in this country are so gullible they believe anything in print, and no one so far has been able to challenge this type of libel."

A few weeks later, while giving a series of lectures about God's love for Muslims to students at a Bible college in Scotland, I receive an urgent phone call from Ken.

"Pray, Norita. This evening, Pastor John, along with some other foreign and national Christian leaders, has been summoned to be on a televised talk show to answer charges that EP has made in his book."

That evening, Pastor John and two other church leaders faced the author. Also invited was ZB, often brought onto TV shows as an "expert" on religion. Next to him sat NS, a woman who was the titular head of a mysterious congregation called the Turkish Orthodox Church—a church set up by Mustafa Kemal Ataturk at the start of the republic. He wanted to provide an alternative for Turks who had converted to Eastern Christianity and who were being encouraged to move back to Turkey.

These three speakers were vehemently accusing missionaries and Turkish Protestants of anti-Turkishness. Fraught with tension and rancor, the TV program gave these people the opportunity to propagandize the nation in anti-Christian thought.

EP began by heatedly charging conspiracy and bribery: "I have here in my hand," he shouted, "absolute proof that John is the paid lackey of Norita Erickson."

He held up before the camera a copy of the receipt I had signed for Pastor John's donation to the Kardelen Association; a receipt required by the security police and the office monitoring nonprofit organizations. Pastor John looked dumbstruck. He had no immediate recollection of the receipt, although he assured the panelists that he had indeed donated to the Kardelen Association—not received a donation. Ignoring him, EP began shouting out that Pastor John was a heinous traitor to the republic and should be ashamed of himself.

I felt the first sinister fingers of fear when I watched the videotape of the program. What had at first been a suspicion now became sickeningly probable. Only I would know that this receipt was one of all the receipts we collected from members of our association and that we, per government regulation, turned them into the government office that monitors charities. Now I knew for certain that EP had had access to information he could only have gotten by going into our blue notebook at the police headquarters. His access to receipts was final proof of something I'd begun to suspect when he mentioned the names of the board members, using the initials and full names, which were only those to be found on our official required documents. He was not working alone. Someone in the security police was helping him.

/////

I often helped out our official board president, elderly and retired anesthesiologist Dr. Feriha Wegter, by doing the legwork, taking all the required paperwork documenting our decisions and finances down to the Office of Charitable Associations at the Turkish National Police Building. Our blue binder notebook was there among the hundreds of those belonging to other nonprofit societies who had to be legally registered.

This notebook held our official bylaws and project descriptions, as well as detailed information about each board member and dues-paying member. Ken and I were board members, and so was Ann, who traveled hundreds of miles from a sea town to attend the yearly meeting. Pastor John was a member; HB, another Turk, and his Jewish-American wife, Willa, were as well. Per government regulation, all the founding members of this association had been Turks. They all were members of the Liberation Church.

Turks are required to carry an identity card. On it is stated your city of birth, your parents' names, and your religion—that is, "Muslim" or "Non-Muslim." Many of our church friends had legally changed the "Religion" statement on their cards. For some, this had meant being subject to some ridicule by the Office of Identity clerks. For others, it had been a straightforward, simple process unmarred by negative comments from either disapproving family or officials. Some Turks approve the loosening of religious stereotypes and modernization of their country's laws, and call for a complete scrapping of the identity card or the religion line on the card. Others remain highly critical of other countrymen who choose to express publicly their religious opinions.

From the very beginning, Mr. Sharif, our lawyer, made extra sure that we complied in every way possible with the association laws. Many times, the police had cracked down on front organizations: "civil associations" that were involved in illegal activities; so we felt we needed to be as transparent as possible in order to preclude any official opposition.

Mr. Sharif prepared the papers and official announcements required by law, and I took the stuff down to the police headquarters. Reports and minutes of meetings were registered at the main office on the third floor of the seven-story building. Any procedural objections would come back to us a week or two later, but generally we'd had no problems.

So when, in 2002, we began to receive subpoenas to appear in court for one or another infraction of the regulations, Mr. Sharif was the first to say, "This makes no sense. According to the laws, we've done nothing wrong. Why are they taking us to court?" And he'd write out a petition and send me downtown again to present it to some person sitting behind one of the twenty desks crowding the room called "Association Monitoring."

I would be sent away with the words, " Okay, we'll look at this and get back to you in a few weeks." In the meantime, the court date would come up and we would have to petition for a postponement. This happened seven times.

"Norita, I don't know why we're getting the runaround," Sharif said, wiping his brow. His tiny office was filled with cigarette smoke, the heater on full blast. Ann had come to Ankara on the overnight bus, a thirteen-hour ordeal. I took her with me to talk to him about our legal difficulties.

"Every time we get called to court, and even if we win a case, we have to pay all these court costs," he continued. "It makes me sick that money you've raised for your charity is being spent on what I think is some sort of harassment case. Somehow I get the impression it has to do with you being a foreigner and that there are so many people on your membership list who are foreigners or else church members.

"Now, mind you, I have no proof, but at our last public association meeting, there were an inordinate number of police 'observers,' plus didn't you tell me that one of them was videoing the proceedings as well as taking footage of every person who attended?"

When I started to sputter in indignation at the lack of basic freedom of speech in this "democracy," he cut me off with a "You've been here for this many years and still don't get it? Do not expect open and honest dealings. This is Turkey. Nothing is easy as it seems from outward appearances."

Ann spoke up: "Maybe Norita is running into stone walls because she's a foreigner. I'll go down to the main office with her. I have a relative who works there who should be able to direct me to the person who can help us. I'm sure we can clear this up tomorrow."

The next day found us sitting chatting with the middle-aged policeman chief who, after giving us tea, sent us to speak to someone in an adjoining office.

We walked into an office with six desks arranged in a rectangle. Behind each desk was a young man wearing the regulation white shirt, black tie, and black trousers. Each guy appeared to be working away diligently amid stacks of notebooks and papers. After Ann introduced us and told them that we needed some direction regarding several legal issues, one of the men left for a few minutes before returning with our blue notebook stuffed with paperwork. He started to read it, then called over another colleague to show him some of the papers. They got up and left the room. Ten minutes later, they returned, faces grim.

Man One: "You are in big trouble. I don't see that there is any way you can get out of these problems except to shut down your organization. Otherwise, quite frankly, you'll be stuck in court for years."

Then he gave an unsatisfactory answer to my questions about specific infractions of the law: "This is a complicated legal issue which demands a judge's decision."

When I explained that our lawyer had filed objection after objection to their legal team's summons but that we'd not gotten anything in writing that helped us get to the bottom of the problem, he retorted, "You won't understand this and would be better off not trying to."

Not for the first time did I begin to think I'd been transported into a Kafka novel. I couldn't understand all the legalese, nor did anything make any sense to me. I could see that Turkish law was quite different from American law, and that I was in way over my head when it came to running a local organization. It was so confusing that even our lawyer wasn't going to be able to help us.

That afternoon, Ann and I returned to Sharif's office with the discouraging news. Sharif was quiet for a few minutes, then brightened up and said, "The law says that if you disband a charity organization like Kardelen, you may transfer all your assets to another like-minded organization."

Ann finished his thought by adding: "Why don't I start another group in my hometown? That way, our headquarters and board of directors will be local there. I know nearly everyone in our town; the mayor and police department people are friends with my husband. You can carry on your work here at Saray and Hot Springs. I'll just be the titular head and sign the official papers.

"This will help me build up our local outreach with families affected by disability. There is so much suffering that goes unheeded. People affected by Chernobyl contamination or struggling from the effects of close-family marriage. Our group will gain status. We already are known in a positive way for wheelchair donations and village visits. Thank you so much for sending that American physical therapist, Penny, and for Annelies, the Dutch psychologist. She phones me regularly and asks how we're doing. She definitely is an encourager. She plans to visit me soon too.

"I know!" she said, then snapped her fingers. "I'll just call the new association 'The KARDELEN BROTHERLY LOVE Association.'"

When I heard this, I felt a weight of unwanted responsibility begin to fall from my shoulders. "A great solution," I commented and Sharif agreed.

Without wasting one minute, we huddled together to write down the details in legal language with the goal of disbanding the Ankara-based organization and setting up the one that would be headquartered in Ann's town and chaired by her.

/////

This had all happened before the TV show with Pastor John. Still, we asked ourselves why they were singling us out. It made little sense. We were aware of opposition and knew that the unseen powers wanted to discourage and stop us.

Civil police agents began showing up at church and taking down people's names, then showed up at their homes during the week, making veiled threats about those who attended our church and what might happen to them.

After this, ZB and NS spent no little time speaking out against us both on university campuses as well as in military training sessions, claiming that foreign missionaries were as much a threat to Turkish national sovereignty as the Communist separatist militants who were wreaking havoc in the southeast regions of the country. They spoke at student gatherings organized at the largest universities in a land where young, gullible college students were told that the foreigners and Christians were teaching falsehood and that they were disseminating New Testaments in order to stir up division and ignorance in the land.

The invasion of Iraq was portrayed in books and television series primarily as an attempt by evangelicals to take over the entire region for devilish purposes. The propaganda portrayed Christians kidnapping children in order to harvest their organs for patients waiting in the USA. George W. Bush was vilified in several books as a mastermind evil leader, with us as his agents.

The TV series were one thing, but it began to get a little more uncomfortable when we learned that we and our friends were under surveillance.

One Sunday, Sami slipped into church, disheveled, unshaven, and shaking. After the service, he pulled me aside.

"Norita Abla, please, please, be careful. What are you doing? Do you know they know everything about you?" His voice was low and broken.

"What? What's happened to you? Are you okay?" I tried to calm him down.

Sami was a translator, researcher, and writer who had been coming on and off to the church for several months. Three months earlier, I'd approached him about giving our son Michael, now eleven, some private computer lessons. He came over every Saturday, spent an hour and a half teaching, and then left before it got dark to go back to his tiny office/apartment in the city center.

"Yesterday after leaving your house, I took the minibus home and was walking up the stairs to my flat when three men dressed in jeans and T-shirts jumped me, threw me into their car, and drove me outside the city limits."

"What?"

"The whole time, they were interrogating me about Ken and you. 'We know that you are visiting the Erickson family every Saturday and that you just came from their house. What are you doing with these Christian missionaries? What kind of a traitor are you?' They shouted at me, insulted me, and started hitting me too. I told them that I was a Christian too and had every right as a Turk to believe as I wanted to.

"But they wouldn't listen. 'You're scum and we'll make sure you don't hide behind this claim to civil rights.' They threatened me again and then said, 'You tell Norita Erickson that we know ALL about her and her spying for a neighboring country, and we will NEVER let her get away with it. She's bad, bad, bad.'"

I listened silently, shocked to hear they had labeled me as a spy. Though I had never been to Turkey's neighboring countries, I was ethnically related to a border nation the Turks consider their enemy. I mulled over the potential dangers to my children and husband, as well as the staff of Kardelen. I felt concern and sadness for Sami. He really looked and sounded bad.

I went to talk to Sharif. *Surely our lawyer can give me some direction.*

"Don't I know how ridiculous these charges are, Norita, but there's nothing I can do. You ought to open up a slander and libel case against EP. Since my name is mentioned, I'll be a plaintiff too. As far as your friend Sami goes, I have to say I have doubts. Who's to know whether he was really beaten up or if he's not working for the secret police and has been instructed to scare you? There's something you should know, however.

"I got a phone call yesterday from the administrative head of the city legal offices—I mean, from my immediate boss. He interrogated me about you and warned me not to have anything to do with you, that my involvement with you and Kardelen could cause me to lose my job.

"Now don't worry. I don't think they'll let me go, because they know I'd go to the press and say that they are depriving me of employment because I am blind. I mean, I can play that game too. In any case, you need to know there's stuff happening which is bizarre and mean, and I think that maybe you've not been wise, that you should have kept your church friends away from Kardelen."

Then Aisha found out why the team and I were experiencing so much opposition at Saray. The secretary to the director had told her that men from the security police headquarters had come out to Saray and, in so-called closed meetings, warned the administrators about me, saying that I was going to try to convert Turks, pay them lots of money, and get them to work against the Turkish Republic. She said that some of the people laughed when they heard the accusation, while others promised to do what they could to protect their wards.

"Imagine, Norita," Aisha said to me, "these agents are essentially claiming that Kardelen is seeking to convert children with extreme mental disabilities, most of whom can't even speak, to American Christianity: that somehow we're going to get paid per head for every name we offer as 'converts.' I think the people with the real handicaps are the officials. They truly need their heads examined."

We opened a joint civil and criminal lawsuit against EP for libel. Six months later, we learned that we had lost the case, that his accusations would be construed only as suggestions, as possibilities, rather than actual statement of truth. It was discouraging to say the least.

Now, as I reflect and write these thoughts, I wrestle with my own conflicting feelings. I am angry, and the anger is fueling poisonous thoughts against EP and against the bureaucrats. Even though I say that I believe that everyone is a sinner in need of the Savior, I am so easily slipping into the role of the Only Righteous One, ready to send down thunderous judgments. I must pray again and again, "Lord, have mercy on me, a sinner. Forgive us our sins as we forgive those who trespass against us."

Pastor John, after attending a Turkey Human Rights Watch meeting, tells us privately, "Everyone there is saying that we as Protestant Christians are losing the propaganda war and that public opinion is rapidly becoming more and more negative to foreigners and Christians."

One night, tense and fearful, I get my grandfather's autobiography down from the bookshelf. This little book time and again has encouraged me when things seem to be going so wrong.

Looking at his photograph inside the back cover, I am suddenly taken back to my living room on Chariton Avenue in west LA. The year was 1953...

/////

Los Angeles: 1953

"Come here, dear daughter," my father called out excitedly. "Look, this is your grandfather, the pastor. He's just come from a place very far away. From the Middle East. From where I grew up. I will show you on the map."

Not much older than a toddler, I found myself being scooped up by a white-haired man. My face rubbed against the itching wool, and I smelled the faint odor of mothballs. I heard the excitement in Daddy's voice as he communicated in the language he sometimes spoke with Mommy.

Only years later, after Grandpa had written his autobiography *I Shall Not Die*, did I understand the importance of this stoop-shouldered man. He, his wife, Nouritza, and my then infant dad had miraculously survived extermination in an ethnic-cleansing campaign in the latter years of the Ottoman Empire. In his memoirs, Grandpa wanted to honor the miracles and messages from God they'd received both during their flight from death as well as in the years that followed when he served as pastor to various refugee congregations.

That day, he held me tightly and began to weep. In halting whispers, his voice broke. For a long time, with eyes shut, he prayed out loud. Then he put his hand on my head. Finally, in a tongue I could understand, he said, "Good, good heavenly Father. Here is little Norita. Touch her. Speak to her. May she come to know You. May she be Your servant. Use her for Your kingdom's sake. In Jesus's wonderful name, I pray, amen."

I squirmed down and ran off to play.

Now, more than thirty years later, I am back in the country of my Grandpa's birth, serving the One who had called us both.

I also think about Grandma Armenouhi, my mother's mom. She, too, had survived that holocaust, but as an orphan. I used to love hanging out in her kitchen and watching her make the most amazing dishes. In her late sixties, she contracted Parkinson's but chose to live alone in her home with a variety of caregivers. She would lie in her bed, listening to Christian radio in her latter years ...

/////

Limbo Land

Los Angeles: 1973

"Norita, go look in top drawer of dresser. Checkbook is there. Bring here."

On spring break from university, I was visiting. Grandma, once so strong and active, was lying down to rest.

She whispered from her bed: "I got letter this week from Pastor Mordecai from Tehran. He say orphanage is almost finished. He need money to pay bills. Here ..." I took the letter from her outstretched hand. "Help me write check, then you go to mailbox and send it."

At seventy-two, she was weakening physically before my eyes, but her spirit was as strong as ever.

"I have dream last night," she began speaking after I'd returned. "Long time now, I not think about these things. In dream, I back in old home. I was young girl then. I was hungry. So hungry. In dream, I see brother, dear Harut. He was on ground pulling up grass and eating it." She stopped speaking and lay there staring into space for a while. "You know he and my father and mother died on the road to Dar-El-Zor."

I nodded, knowing the story of the deaths of my great grandparents along with hundreds of thousands of others in the wilderness of southeastern Turkey.

"No children should ever have to be hungry like that." She'd roused herself to speak in a stronger tone. "Whenever I hear about orphans, about hungry little ones, my heart breaks. I must give what I can. God, He tell me to help. I got money now; I can give."

Grandma and I used to spend lots of time together in her kitchen, where she'd "recruit" me to help her can peaches or make bread. While I never developed a great passion for cooking—how could I ever spend time away from a good book?—I did love to hear her stories, which she'd tell while kneading bread or sewing a dress. One question kept surfacing when I was a teenager, struggling to understand my faith in Christ and living in a competitive and individualistic world like America. The civil rights movement was changing the nation, and I was trying to understand the teachings of nonviolence and the struggle for equality.

"Grandma," I had asked her one day. She was up to her armpits in flour and having me chop onions for her specialty meat pie, *lah-majoon* "Grandma, you lost your whole family in the genocide. Well, except for your little sister who was married off to a Muslim and left there in the backwaters of Turkey. I know the stories of all that suffering. How can you live with all those memories and feelings? Aren't you angry?"

She kneaded the dough for a few seconds more before washing her hands and arms and coming to stand before me. "Norita," she said gently. "I invite Jesus to come into my heart back in 1932, after we go to Connecticut. He change me then. He take out bitterness. He show me a different way to live. It impossible for bitterness and love of Christ to share same space in your heart. God's love mean I have to forgive. And ... He give me power to do that."

/////

And so again nearly thirty years later, I cry out to my heavenly Father for the same sort of faith and hope and forgiving spirit that brought my people through harder times than these.

CHAPTER 22

"Time to Kill Her, My Son"

Those who want to kill me set their traps, those who would harm me talk of my ruin; all day long they scheme and lie.
Psalm 38:12

My personal notes continued …

Tall, dark, and handsome, Manny has asked if he could work with us out at Saray. Recently reunited with his older sister, his Abla Nina, he has heard so many stories of what Saray is like that he wants to come and work and help out. I agree and, before too many days, realize what a gift he is to the team and to the children in C Block. His tender attention to the boys who are desperate for an older male's unadulterated care has been noticed, and every time word gets around that Manny has come, a clamor for him rises from the Spastic Ward.

If any one of us had known him just six months earlier, we would have not said it was possible for This Manny to be That Manny …

/////

Every year, scores of young women in this region of the world are murdered by their relatives or "encouraged" to commit suicide. The reason: they are "tainted" and therefore need to be "cleaned." Their deaths restore lost honor.

Here, the tribe, clan, or extended family is still the primary social network. You know who you are because of your affiliation to the community. You are so-and-so from the XYZ family who has lived and worked and farmed or fought off enemies for thousands of years. The individual's value and worth is really only determined and measured by collective wealth, influence, power, and reputation. You're okay and I'm okay only if we're okay.

Reputation is as important, or in many cases more important, than material well-being. The family should be known as being pious, godly, and upright as opposed to being a band of scoundrels, immoral people, or unfaithful citizens.

One of the primary measures of "uprightness" in this communal culture is the virginity and demureness of the girls. Should a female in the clan come under suspicion of impropriety of any sort, or if she is the victim of rape and this becomes public knowledge, dishonor has sullied the reputation of the family. The only way to restore their good name is to remove the source of the shame. Hence, the girl is either imprisoned in a windowless room for the rest of her life, or executed. In some cases, the girl is pressured to kill herself by pouring gasoline over her body and lighting herself, by hanging herself, or by throwing herself off a cliff or the roof of high building.

In villages where honor killing is considered a necessary tradition, many end up immigrating to larger cities looking for work. More and more of these executions or forced suicides are taking place in Western countries or cities where these Easterners have gone to live and work.

Generally in these places, one of the elders (either living in the new country or directing family affairs from the old country) hears of one of their women or girls doing something shameful like going out with some man unchaperoned. Possibly she is under suspicion of living a shameful life, dressing in Western clothing, and going to parties where unrelated men and women socialize. In these cases, the father, the eldest brother, or oldest male cousin is then given the order to go and clean the shame from the family record by doing away with the girl.

Manny's sister Nina ran from home when she was fourteen. Her father, an alcoholic, became deeply disturbed after her mother died in the car crash that left Nina wheelchair-bound. He began to abuse her. (I do not know the intimate details since Nina cannot yet bring herself to talk about her ordeal, but her few hints make it clear that what happened to her is what happens to a majority of girls—and boys—in this nation. Some harsh cultural realities are too shameful to express publicly.)

Nina chose to leave when her father began physically abusing her six-year-old sister, Meryem. One day in a drunken rage, he knocked the little girl down and kicked her in the face, leaving her with some retinal injury. Another time, he pushed her down a steep flight of concrete steps, where she landed at Nina's feet.

Terrified but determined, two days later Nina and Meryem made their way to the local intercity bus terminal. After lying to a bus driver about their escape from terrorists, they got passage on a bus to Ankara. They walked and rolled several kilometers until they came to one of the large hospitals in the city center. Begging for bread and living on the street outside the busy hospital for several days, they were finally picked up by the local police who brought them to an orphanage. In this government facility (not Saray), they were fortunate enough to be placed in the care of a couple of employees who had compassion on them and treated them kindly.

When their father finally discovered that they were missing, he made no effort to go looking for them. "Good riddance!" he shouted to his other children who still lived with him. "I just hope they're dead."

Two months later, someone from the mayor's office showed up at the orphanage to interview the runaways. These people were making a television program and promised to raise money for the sisters and help them get an education and proper care. So, believing these "important people" would help them, Nina, resourceful as ever, concocted a story of homelessness and misery. Their parents had died, and with no one to care for them in the east, they'd come to the capital where the wonderful and generous government orphanage system would take responsibility for them. The telethon raised no less than thousands of Turkish liras.

Years later when Nina told me her story, she snorted. "The whole thing was a political propaganda program for the mayor. The politicians use their 'compassionate heart' line to get votes and money. One of the nicer caregivers at the orphanage where we were staying told me a few months later that thousands had been sent in, but that as far as she could tell, nothing was earmarked for us. It all went into somebody's account. Loads of questions surrounded where that money went. Of course, we never saw a penny of it personally."

This did not surprise me. Just how money was distributed to the needy in institutions remained a mystery. Nina was just one more victim of a flawed system and of insensitive opportunists.

"Norita Abla, I've learned hard lessons from my own experience as well as the experience of so many of my friends who struggle because of poverty and disability," Nina told me. "I don't care what they say. In this country when a TV station or a politician features the needy, it's usually to use them. We get promised lots of help, money, jobs, and what results? A program and not much else. I have no idea how much they made off us. But they never contacted us again."

Something else resulted, however. What the girls did not realize was that, even though they were living nearly a thousand miles away from their hometown, the television program brought their faces right into the living rooms of their relatives. Several people immediately recognized them. Phone calls were made, and their cover, as well as their father's, was blown. The family was embarrassed and enraged. The whole world now knew that "their women" were runaways, were liars, and had lived on the street. Tongues would have clicked and wagged: "What kind of family does not take care of its own and sends them to live as beggars? How else did they make their money?" Everyone would have surmised that the girls were no longer pure. The family was shamed. "Sin" had to be paid for. There would be blood, but because the girls were now under state protection, the action needed to rectify this great misdeed would have to wait. The family might have to bide their time for a number of years, but they could do that. The elders had come to a verdict and pronounced the death penalty. It would be carried out in due time …

/////

Winter 2002

Six years had passed, and the opportunity finally arrived. The family lost no time. Nina was out of the government fortress at last, so they prepared to act.

Nina had just moved into the Kardelen Association apartment in north Ankara. As soon as a phone was installed, she called a childhood neighbor friend. This girl lived next door to Nina's aunt, where it turned out that Meryem was living

Ecstatic, Nina began to dream of seeing her sisters and brothers again. To her amazement, she learned that Meryem, who had been given to a foster family in a southern city years earlier, had been able to return to their native city to finish high school. Her foster parents, an army officer and his wife, had agreed to accompany her back to her hometown, where they assured the uncles and father that she had been very carefully protected and was "unsullied."

Meryem had been so young when she left home, the elders (i.e., grandfather and uncles) reasoned that she could be pardoned. So the real shame-bringer was Nina. Their father, however, in an attempt to save face, would not allow Meryem back into his home. This in many ways was a relief, since Meryem had already decided she would live with an aunt rather than return to her father's unsafe home.

"Nina." Meryem had something important to tell her older sister. "I want to come out and see you as soon as I can, but they won't let me leave here without an escort. Guess who just came back home?"

Nina screamed with delight when she heard that the brother she had not seen for more than ten years had returned. She could hardly take it in. Manny was alive—and back!

/////

Manny's saga had begun eight years earlier. He had brought the clan honor. As the eldest son of this large extended family, he experienced the privilege of being given as a child recruit to an Islamic fundamentalist group for service and training. He had lived with this group throughout his primary and secondary school years. One theory posited that this organization, possibly numbering in the thousands, had secretly received financial and strategic support from the Turkish military. A secret group, and unofficial as an entity in this overtly secular state, they were to serve as counterinsurgents—trained to torture or indoctrinate those who were likely to have joined the "godless" mountain-based Communist rebels who were fighting government troops in the name of freedom for the largest ethnic minority group in Turkey.

Clearly a bright boy, Manny was groomed to be a *hodja* (teacher), and while others his age joined and lived much like child soldiers live in other camps around the world, he was allowed to spend more time reading and studying. While under their authority, he received special Qur'anic training. At the age of eighteen, he was sent to a state university in another nation. While there, he'd finally had enough of indoctrination and controlled movements. He ran away. He wanted to be free from what he now saw as a cult and showed up on his father's doorstep, begging to be reinstated there.

With this particular family, loyalty to the state or religious community never came before tribal ties and responsibilities, so his grandfather called the men in the family together for a council meeting. They decided they could use another hand with business dealings and planned to send him on various errands to cities in the west of the country.

One cold day in February 2002, Grandfather called Manny to his side: "It has fallen to you. Time to kill her, my son," his grandfather solemnly intoned. "You must go to Ankara, find that girl, Nina, and clean this filth from our name. She's not in the orphanage anymore. She is living a prostitute's life. As such, every day that she remains alive, the burden of shame grows heavier and heavier upon us. Before too long, news will travel here that she's still carrying on in Ankara. It will be even worse for the family name." He pulled a leather pouch from the top drawer of the coffee table. "Here. Take this dagger and cut her throat."

Prepared to follow orders, the young man bought a bus ticket the next morning, then phoned Nina. In a neutral but not unpleasant voice, he told her he was on his way to visit and would be there early the next morning, *insha'Allah*.

Nina bounced up and down in her wheelchair. She shouted out to her new friend, Elvina, Zeynep's mother: "My brother, my long-lost brother is coming here!" She explained to her new friend how at one time she had only had eyes for him. He was three years younger. She'd loved him in a special way and remembered crying hard for hours when he was first taken by their father from the house to join the secret Islamic group. She had been only eleven then but ever since had wondered and cared about what had happened to him.

Two nights later, the front doorbell rang. Nina, alone in the flat after Elvina had gone to her home, rolled her chair to the door and opened it. There, standing before her, was a tall, dark, and handsome young man. She gazed into his brown-black eyes and long dark lashes for a few seconds before bursting into tears. She drew him down in a hug as best she could from her chair. He looked shocked; their reunion awkward.

Manny had not realized that he'd find her sitting in a wheelchair. True, the last time they'd seen each other she had been walking with a bad limp. After all, childhood polio had struck Nina when she was five years old, but in the years before the traffic accident that had taken their mother, she'd been able to walk. Now before him sat a "disabled" woman. She was bareheaded, her long, wavy brown hair flowing down her shoulders and back. She wore close-fitting jeans; her bare feet with bright-red toenails peeped out of the cuffs as they rested on the footrests of her chair. Her faded yellow T-shirt fit snuggly too . She seemed comfortable and carried herself with an innocence, totally unaware of any impropriety in her attire. However, she had her hair unscarfed and, as far as he was concerned, was far too uncovered for a good Muslim girl.

"Welcome, welcome, welcome," she kept repeating. "I can't believe it's really you. You're here. Oh, I am so happy. Thank God, thank God."

She giggled with a mixture of joy and trepidation, pushing and pulling her wheels nervously back and forth. Abruptly she turned her chair and maneuvered her way back to the living room.

"Let me look at you," she said. "Oh my God, how you've grown. How strong you look. Gosh."

Leaving him no time to answer, she turned around and rolled into the kitchen to make some tea. She would make it for him and serve him the special lemon cake she'd baked that morning.

In the living room, Manny looked around at the sparsely furnished room. He began studying the two pictures Nina had hung high up on her wall. He stared first at the collage of photos of their sisters—besides Meryem—at their aunt's home. His interest sparked at a pen-and-ink drawing of a smiling man, a shepherd with curly dark hair, wearing a flowing cloak and nuzzling a tiny lamb he was carrying on his shoulder. In this drawing, the artist had colored the cloak red.

Manny took the jacket he'd been wearing and laid it on the sofa next to him. Back home, he'd replaced the dagger with a less ostentatious switchblade. Now he fingered it from the outside of the pocket.

Confusion set in. After a few moments, he made the decision to wait until he had absolute evidence that his "Abla" was living a life of sin and debauchery. She was certainly dressed like a prostitute, but her actions and words were so unlike someone who was a seasoned lowlife. True, she had run away and defamed his father and grandfather, but then again, the elders had never shown great loyalty and care for him as far as he could tell. They were the ones who'd sent him away from home and to grow up with fanatics. He shuddered when he remembered some of the things he'd witnessed during his training period. Unconsciously he pushed the jacket away.

"Who's that drawing of?" he asked when Nina returned, balancing a tray with tea glasses and a bowl with sugar cubes while rolling one wheel of her chair.

"Oh, that's a picture I got while I was living at Saray. That's the Lord Jesus. I love that picture. I'm His lamb, you see." She smiled broadly as though he'd already understood her story.

Uh-oh, Manny thought. *Not only is she living as an immoral hussy, but she's become a Christian—an infidel and unbeliever.* He grunted as if he acknowledged her belief, but continued to watch her closely for more signs of aberrancy.

With a deep breath, Nina decided to tell him her story. He heard all about the time she and Meryem left the east to when the sisters first were separated and Nina was sent to Saray. She described for him the horrible conditions there: the cruelty, the despair, and the darkness of her own heart.

"I tried to commit suicide countless times. But for some strange reason, I never died. Look, here are the scars from the times I slit my wrists. I was so bored and hopeless. It is endless imprisonment for people like me and my mates. Then one day in '97 or '98, some different kind of people—kinder and really caring—showed up at Saray and started doing REAL good. They chose to work with the very worst-off in that place.

"At first, my friends and I were skeptical. These visitors were not real. Year after year, we had seen the occasional do-gooder come, drop off some clothes or furniture, not even come into the wards but be escorted around Saray. No one ever stayed to just 'be' with us. Then these people came and STAYED. Day in and day out, they came and worked and were so kind to us. It was hard to see them as bad people.

"They prayed and sang at times, and the word got out that they were Christians. Frankly I never found that so strange, because all along, I believed that all foreigners were Christians. In fact, I was curious about what faith meant to them. However, I couldn't quite figure out the Turks among them. I believed like everyone else around here that if a Turk calls herself a Christian, then she is really a traitor or something worse. But these people were so kind. What's more, they were consistent. They had something that

I wanted.

"So after a couple of months of observing them, I started to talk to God. I said, 'If You really exist, then help me. I am going to ask Norita, the lady in charge of the Kardelen group, for a job with their team. If she says 'Yes,' then I will know You exist.'

"The next day, I went to the Kardelen playroom. Norita walked in a few moments later and seemed to head straight for me. Before she could take a chair to sit, however, I asked her for a job. Without even blinking, she said 'Yes.' She told me that she had been praying the night before about all us girls in A Block who sat around all day with nothing to do and that she had an idea. She wanted to give jobs to all the women in our dorm who would be willing to come and help the Kardelen workers feed the kids in Continuous Care Wards 1 and 2. I told her that I could cook. Right then and there, she made me the head of the kitchen. It was so fulfilling. Plus we got allowances so that we could buy phone cards or other stuff. Nearly every day of the week from then on, as a team we prepared afternoon snacks for the children in the cribs who were tied in. My team fed them too."

Some months later, Manny filled in details about his own inner struggle that night with Nina. As he listened to her story, he tried to imagine what she was talking about. *Saray? Wards with abandoned children? Everybody disabled? Not being able to leave when you wanted to? Americans, Christian Turks?*

Not by nature a hard-hearted or uncompassionate person, Manny slowly felt the wall of perceived affront and aggression—the one he'd been building in order to be able to carry out the execution order—start to crumble. Something like love for his sister began to take its place.

Several hours later, as the faint light of dawn peeped through the front window curtains, Nina finished off the story with her return to Ankara and the Kardelen apartment. By now, Manny not only loved his sister but felt a bit proud of her. She had faced giants and defeated evil. He thought she should have been honored instead of secretly sent away. What kind of cowardly government workers ran Turkey's social system?

"I should have died many times over these past ten years, but God saved me, Manny. Now He's my Father, and I will never be the same and can never thank Him enough. I don't want to kill myself anymore. He saved me at Hot Springs and gave me a reason to be there. I believe in Jesus. I think

He chose me.

"Now just look at this latest miracle. I am out of the institution, out of the system where I've been a prisoner for more than nine years. I have a roof over my head, friends, and enough food and clothing. But best of all, best of all that stuff, is this, my dear brother: the Lord has brought you back to me."

She started to cry. He joined her a few seconds later.

Later that night while lying in the spare bedroom, Manny stared at the ceiling.

"God? What is going on?" He was quiet for a moment, then made a decision. "I'm getting rid of the switchblade. No, I'm keeping it—my sister needs protection in this big city. I'm staying right here. This is where I belong now."

Within seconds, he drifted off to sleep, peaceful for the first time in a long time—and on the path to becoming the Manny who would soon serve alongside us at Saray.

/////

Nina came to church whenever she could get there. Sometimes she was either in too much pain or had a house full of her disabled friends staying over to enjoy her new "place of peace and joy"—no small victory given the opposition she and Elaina experienced.

As she sat in the front row of the church one day, arms raised and eyes closed, I began to think about all the changes that had been taking place in her. She had landed in a hospital bed for six weeks of therapy not too many weeks before and found herself again in a place where God has used her.

She had become cautious when talking about her life and sharing that she was a Christian, but another handicapped friend who was visiting her for some reason had felt it was important to announce to her ward that Nina was a Christ-follower, so she felt released to share her faith. The Holy Spirit led the way.

She believes that one day a miracle is going to take place and that she will walk. I truly hope so and don't doubt that this could happen, but I shared with her the truth that as a result of her weakened, dependent condition, many people are hearing Good News in a way they would never have before.

After a moment during that church service, she prayed a beautiful prayer: "Daddy, I am thankful for You and what You have done in my life. If I never walk here on earth again, I am willing to do whatever You want me to." There was a pause. "But ..." She giggled. "... my Lord, You have told me I would walk!"

After church, Nina told me the story of Faroush, a young woman brought into the same hospital with severe paralysis due to an accident. Faroush came from the poorest, most backwater region in Turkey, where the people speak another language and where women are treated as chattel. Her brother reported that she "fell from the roof," a commonly cited cause for death and paralysis in the southern and eastern parts of Turkey. During the hot summers, people often go up on the flat roofs to sleep or dry fruit and herbs there. Sleepwalking, drunkenness, and brawls might result in someone falling off the roof and onto the unforgiving rocky ground below.

Faroush had not been washed in weeks, and the odors permeated the large six-person hospital room where Nina was. After a female doctor visited this patient for the first time, she said that before any treatment could begin, a thorough bathing would be required, but even a good long bath didn't completely eradicate the smell.

"Oh my goodness, Norita," Nina recounted. "My stomach lurched every time she entered the room from therapy, and quite frankly, even though I speak a dialect of her language and probably could communicate with her, I didn't want to get too close to the girl."

Before too long, however, Nina felt a "softening in her heart." Compassion began to override revulsion, and she introduced herself to the girl. Faroush revealed that in fact, she had tried to commit suicide, but it hadn't worked and all she longed for now was death.

Nina went out that afternoon and bought some sweet-smelling body lotion to share with her. She spoke kind and encouraging words to Faroush, who then revealed that she couldn't read or write or even speak the Turkish language. I sat with Nina that morning at church, and after praying for Faroush, we discussed some informal ways to teach her the majority language.

Nina also told me about a young man named Bunyamin, who was paralyzed from the waist down due to a car crash. Usually he was deeply depressed. Nina had first met him when she took her two visiting paraplegic girlfriends (Ela and Betsy) on a tour of the wards. This trio of young ladies had gone from ward to ward introducing themselves to the patients and smiling and saying in Turkish "May this pass," something you say when people are sick.

Nina shared the message of Jesus's life and love, about His death and resurrection, with Bunyamin and his older brother who was there to look after him. Nina's brother, Harry, brought Bunyamin a New Testament after Nina had challenged them to read the Qur'an *Injil* in order to compare the two for themselves.

A couple of weeks later, Bunyamin was released to go live in a small apartment on the outskirts of town. After Nina's course of treatment was completed, she and Harry decided to go out and visit him. They brought Meryem with them, and she prepared food while they talked about their lives. That evening, Bunyamin prayed out loud: "Great God, I know I need You. I'm not a good person and have made many, many mistakes. Please come into my heart and soul and make me a good person. Thank You for what Jesus did on the cross, dying in my place, for my sins. I want Him to be my Lord. Amen."

"Amen," the others chimed in, all taking their hands and wiping them down their faces in traditional Islamic prayer fashion.

CHAPTER 23

What's Wrong with This Picture?

Say to those with fearful hearts,
"Be strong, do not fear; your God will come."
Isaiah 35:4

My personal notes continued ...

March 2003

Tuesday, the guards at the front gate stop me. Usually they wave back or nod when I greet them on my way to the main buildings.

Looking truly menacing in his black guard's uniform and holding his large gun, Ernie barks out, "You are not allowed to go in! Go see Mr. Hal. He's the new man in charge of public relations."

I drop my hand and stick it in my coat pocket before hurrying past them to the administration building and Mr. Hal's office.

Hal's a friend of mine. He has always been a proactive and inventive advocate for the children in his ward in B Block. We work well together. Last year, I was able to get funding to build special high chairs as well as to install new flooring for the large dayroom of Unit 12. He was so pleased and had even come out with me to the carpenter's workshop to give advice on the tables.

Evidently Hal has been "promoted" to a desk job where he's going to be responsible for volunteers and visitors. This is the first I have heard of his now having an official desk job.

When I knock on the closed door to his small office, he calls out "Enter," and I walk in to greet him sitting there half-hidden behind a desk, his computer monitor, and a pile of papers.

"Hey, Hal, my pal. How's it going? Congratulations on your promotion."

"Good morning," he replies tersely, unable to make eye contact.

Uncharacteristically he does not rise to shake my hand or offer me a seat. When I ask him what the deal is with the guards at the front gate, he coughs, clears his throat, and says that new regulations have been passed by the Department of Social Services and that I need to apply for permission again to get a visitor's card that would authorize me to come onto the grounds. He searches around in a drawer, produces an application form, and hands it to me without a word.

"You okay?" I ask. "You seem upset. Have I done something wrong?"

"I'm fine!" he snaps, turning to stare at his computer screen while I sit down on a folding chair in the corner and begin to fill out the form.

Confused by his attitude but determined not to let the chilly atmosphere affect me, I hand the finished petition back and politely ask if he has any idea how long it will be before I get official approval, adding, "I'm working on at least two renovation projects and I really do need to bring some donors onto the campus."

At that, he mumbles, "I don't know. I suppose in a few weeks you should hear. Ask again then. Excuse me, but I have a meeting."

With that, he accompanies me out of his office and to the front gate.

I walk back across the highway to catch the bus from the stop I got off at not fifteen minutes ago. I do not relish the thought of another ninety-minute trip back home. We do not own a car, which would cut the trip time in half, so I always gear myself up for a lot of time on the road in order to be able to spend quality time with the team and in the clinic and wards. Today was going to be a day full of activities and conversations, but alas ...

Saray is not located anywhere within the city but out on the open plateau farmland, so I need to flag down an intercity bus coming in from Golden Oaks. After arriving downtown, I catch the 413. This crowded bus climbs to my neighborhood, the southern hill dense with high-rises and apartment buildings. In a daze, I walk from the bus stop several hundred meters and slowly make my way up the staircase to our third-floor apartment. Something is wrong at Saray.

Week after week, I phone but cannot get any response from the Office of Public Relations. Hal is never at his desk. I realize, sadly, that I am, for some reason or another, being stonewalled.

Meanwhile Becky works tirelessly to try to break through the impediments to her visits. She phones all the Turkish consulates in the USA to try to get somebody on that end to advocate for her scheduled teams. They tell her it is not up to them to grant entrance to an orphanage in their country, which is in the hands of the Ankara officials. She will have to wait for a response from them. That response, of course, never comes. She is forced to cancel two scheduled teams.

After a month and a half, I decide to try my luck and implement a new technique for gaining entrance. Although I am no longer allowed to come onto the campus every day, I have to get on as often as I can. So I call the director's secretary and make an appointment first to see him. Never able to refuse a polite meeting, he offers tea and we have a fairly innocuous discussion about one or another problem he is dealing with in running this vast unwieldy institution. I talk about past or potential donation projects or about current Kardelen activities. He nods and says that he always wants to hear what the group is doing, and that I am welcome to come by for a chat anytime. He wants the on-site group leader, Aisha, to come in and give him a report of all their activities as well.

I take my leave of his opulent office, walk down the stairs, and from there slip unnoticed into one or the other living units on the vast campus where few administrators ever bother to go. Because I maintain the relationship with the director, I continue to be greeted politely every time I come on the campus. No one stops me from visiting the wards where Kardelen people are working.

Officially, however, something is not clear and I never receive the now-coveted "Visitor's Pass."

After three months of receiving the official cold shoulder, we face a new level of hostility. Stella, the Turkish woman who had worked with us during earthquake relief and who had taken over Annelies's job as on-site manager at Saray, finds out that she has been blacklisted by the national security police. One day, with no warning or explanation, she is confronted by a guard and summarily escorted off the campus and told she cannot return for any visits. She is required to turn in her volunteer pass that she has used for three years coming and going to Saray. She phones her friend, a secretary for the director, to ask for her help. The woman tells her that there is nothing she can do but that Stella is under investigation by the national security police and to be refused entrance onto the grounds.

"I'm so humiliated." Stella sobs into the receiver. "They treated me as if I was some sort of criminal. What is going on, Norita? Somebody is jealous of me. I saw Mr. Metin smirking when they walked me to the gate today." For Stella, the blacklisting is not nearly as devastating as the put-down she has received at the hands of uneducated guards. For a Turk, public humiliation is far worse than a private beating.

A cloud begins to descend on my spirit as she speaks. Confusion swirls like thick fog in my mind. I cry with her and confess that I am at a total loss as to what is taking place at Saray. Crushing, despairing thoughts begin to form: *What a fool you are to have ever attempted to take on the entire sick orphanage system of Turkey. The work of the Kardelen is nothing—means nothing in the larger scale of things. The bureaucrats will not change nor allow change. Give up now and go home to America. You are a foreigner, an outsider, an interloper. You know that deep down inside. Just get honest with yourself. The tender first flower of spring is in danger.*

CHAPTER 24

Shaken

You have shaken the land and torn it open; mend its fractures, for it is quaking.... But for those who fear you, you have raised a banner to be unfurled against the bow. Save us and help us with your right hand, that those you love may be delivered.

Psalm 60:2, 4-5

No.6 Apt. 2 Bartin Street, Ankara: September 10, 2002

At 11:00 p.m., there was a knock on the door of the Kardelen apartment. When Nina'a visiting sister, Terri, went to answer it, she was pushed aside by several men who came barging in with guns drawn and cameras flashing in her face.

"We're from the security police. We've come to investigate the people living here. You are storing weapons and involved in illegal terrorist activity," one of the men barked, pointing his gun at Terri.

She fainted dead away.

Nina's eight-year-old younger sister, Jessie, also a visitor, had arrived at the door a few seconds after Terri. When she saw the guns, she started screaming.

From the bedrooms at the back, Nina and her younger brother, Manny, yelled at the same time, "What's wrong?" Followed by Manny and their brother Harry and sister Meryem, who were also there visiting, Nina rolled into the hallway in her wheelchair and stopped abruptly as a wall of dark suited men stood mutely, staring at her.

Then one of the men carrying a walkie-talkie spoke: "We're here because of a complaint by a neighbor. You are storing weapons here, we understand."

"What?" Nina said. "That's crazy. Who would say such a thing? I'm here with my family. This is a nightmare." Her voice started shaking, and then she saw Terri lying on the floor. "Terri! Terri! What have you done to my sister? How dare you come in and terrify us all. She's only fifteen! Jessie! Come here. It's okay. It's okay."

"You are doing Christian propaganda here, and there's been a complaint. So we are investigating," one of the men said, apparently trying to appear more reasonable.

"We're not doing anything illegal here. Nothing at all!" Nina said.

Manny, Harry, and Meryem moved forward to confront the officials together. "What do you think you are doing?" Manny said, angry now too.

"We have a search warrant and are going to need to look around," another man answered.

"Well go ahead!" Manny said, incensed. "We have nothing to hide. But we're not animals. How can you treat us like this?"

"What are these books you have on your desk?" one of the men asked Manny.

"They are my books. It's a free country. Can't I read what I want?" Manny picked up his New Testament and two of his other Christian books.

"I'll take those." The officer grabbed them out his hand.

Harry took hold of his brother's arm, trying to prevent a bigger fight and worse problem.

"Show us your storage room," the leader of the team ordered.

While Harry and Manny were facing off some of the other men, Nina quickly got out her cell phone and phoned Annelies, the Dutch volunteer who was helping to run Kardelen while I was on sabbatical in the States.

"Annelies! Annelies, come here and help us. The police are here and charging us with all kinds of horrible crimes."

"Nina, what can I do? I am a foreigner. I don't know anybody who can help you. They would probably arrest me if I showed up. I'm sorry, but I have no idea what to do for you," she said before hanging up. Annelies was afraid. Friends of hers who worked in another mission had been deported after distributing some Bibles, and the same fate could easily have been hers.

In the meantime, the men searched the small storage room. All they found were some parallel bars used for physical therapy and some other orthopedic equipment. Believers had set up a small emergency clinic in Yalova just after the 1999 earthquake, and then later donated the equipment to the Kardelen team in Ankara. We were storing the equipment in a storage space on the ground floor of the building.

After looking in all the boxes stored there and searching all the cupboards and closets in the apartment, the man with the walkie-talkie turned to Nina and said, "We understand that you live here. You are under arrest."

Little Jessie started crying again, and Meryem tried to calm her down. Terri was lying down in another room, so she didn't see the officers handcuff her paralytic sister. Another of the officers rolled the wheelchair out and then carried her down the front stairs to the waiting police van.

Now the plainclothesmen had a problem. How were they going to get this girl into the van when she could not walk, and her hands were cuffed together? It took two of them to lift and sit her down in the backseat. After taking several minutes to try to figure out how to collapse her chair and not being able to do it, they stored the opened chair in the rear of the van, slammed the doors shut, and drove off, lights flashing.

Several people in the neighborhood stood at their apartment windows and stared. No one made a sound. No one came to ask the brother and sisters what had happened. Fear and suspicion took over that evening.

The next day in the late afternoon, Nina rolled up to the door of her apartment and knocked. When Terri opened the door this time, her cry was one of relief and joy. No one had slept the night before.

"Well, here I am, safe and sound," Nina said with a grin. "But what a crazy night!"

They gathered around her to hear what had happened.

"The men brought me to the office where they interrogate terrorists. It's in the basement of that big building on the Konya highway. It was cold, and they had pity on me and brought me some tea, but made me sit in a room all night until this morning. Then they rolled me in to see the department chief. He took one look at me and started shouting at the police officers who were with me.

"'What are you idiots doing with this poor girl? Take off her handcuffs immediately. What do you think she is going to do? Run away?'" Nina started laughing. "Just picture this. The big guy, the one who has all the power, was cursing his own men! They jumped like frightened cowards and did what he said.

"'Well, young lady, what exactly have you done?' he asked me.

"'Nothing, absolutely nothing,' I told him. 'These men came to our apartment last night, barged in, frightened us all half to death, and then charged us with crimes we have not committed.' I was sooo tired and more angry than scared at that moment."

The siblings looked at each other and grinned knowingly. Their older sister was a fighter who had managed to survive and help them regroup as scattered orphans. She was passionate and strong-willed. They had also experienced her anger—one of her survival weapons—and knew she could read anyone the riot act.

"'Is that true?' The chief had turned to the officer in charge of the arrest.

"'Well, sir, we received a tip that she was storing weapons and involved in terrorist propaganda,' he told his boss.

"'Did you find anything?' You should have heard his boss. It was like he was talking to a little boy." She laughed again.

"'Not weapons, but some propaganda,' the guy answered, as if he'd discovered some really bad things. He held out the New Testament and books he'd taken from Manny."

At this, her brother's eyes flashed in indignation.

She went on: "The chief didn't even look at the books, but instead asked me if I'd had anything to eat.

"When I told him that I was hungry, he ordered one of the men to bring me a roll and some fresh tea. He asked me what I did and where I came from and about you all. He wrote some things down, but after a long while, he turned to his men and ordered them to bring me back home. 'She hasn't done anything wrong,' he told them. To me, he said that somebody in our building wanted to make trouble for us.

"I'm sure it's the inspector in apartment 9. What is his problem? He has been against us from the first week I was here. Remember when he threw Ken Abi and Harry Abi out of the front entrance when they were putting up the portable ramp? Same guy. He's the head of the apartment owners association of this building, but he's so mean.

"I don't think that I will ever get over being handcuffed and taken away in front of the whole neighborhood, and all because this man is dead set against us being here, for some reason. It makes absolutely no sense."

/////

Three months later, a similar incident happened. This time, Nina and Harry had gone out for a stroll in the neighborhood. Her brother had brought her to sit on a park bench in a small corner of the local park. While she was sitting there, another young woman came to sit next to her. And they started chatting.

Somehow the conversation got around to spiritual things.

"I'm not satisfied with Islam," the girl said. "I think I need something else in my life. What about you, are you Muslim?"

"Well, actually not anymore," Nina answered. "I believe in Jesus."

"Oh, He's the one who wrote the *Injil* [New Testament]. I am curious. Do you have one? I'd like to read it."

"Why, yes, I can give you mine and get another one from church. Harry, go home and get this girl my *Injil*," Nina, ever the general, ordered her younger brother. After all, they were doing the King's work and there was no time to waste.

Harry, who'd come to faith in Christ just two months before, was happy to comply.

That evening, the police were at the door.

"We're taking you in for spreading Christian propaganda."

"But I haven't done anything illegal. It's not illegal to read the *Injil* or to talk about my faith. You must be joking."

"We have a complaint that you forced someone to take an *Injil* and Christian books. Don't you know that this is a Muslim country? What kind of a traitor are you to Turkish values and morals? You must have sold yourself to foreigners. How much did they pay you to become a traitor? This Kardelen Association—just what is it? A cover for covert missionary activity? Our records show that they own this apartment. Just what is your arrangement with them? Are you a secret agent for them?"

"More likely prostituting for them," another of the men said, then smirked as they were wheeling Nina out into the corridor of the building.

Manny heard the slur and jumped up, ready to attack the accuser. (You do not accuse someone's sister of immoral behavior and expect to get away with it lightly in Turkey. Stories of crimes of passion fill the newspapers daily.)

The neighbors in the adjoining apartments were all standing at their doors watching. Two of the onlookers grabbed Manny before he was able to touch the officer. Holding him still, they watched as the police escorted his sister to their van and drove her off—again.

This time, they took her to the local police station. After interviewing her and writing up a report, they brought her back to the house in the middle of the night.

CHAPTER 25

No Compassion, No Justice, No Mercy

Do you rulers indeed speak justly? Do you judge people with equity? No, in your heart you devise injustice, and your hands mete out violence on the earth. Even from birth the wicked go astray; from the womb they are wayward, spreading lies. Their venom is like the venom of a snake, like that of a cobra that has stopped its ears, that will not heed the tune of the charmer, however skillful the enchanter may be.

Psalm 58:1-5

A story from Nina in her own words …

"Nina, my sister, Nina," Ahmet's cry over the phone at 7:00 a.m. jerked me suddenly out of the deep sleep I crave and need. "We need your help! Please come quickly."

I cried with him when he told me what had happened: "They're holding Hakime at the police station by the state park. They found her naked in the snow earlier this morning. She's been beaten up. Something's wrong with her arm and I think whoever did what they did to her left her for dead. Somebody or some people picked her up and raped her and left her to die! Aaaahhhh!" He broke down completely and hung up.

I called out to Harry to help me get down the six front stairs in my wheelchair. I was off. This time I, on my own, as fast as I could, drove to the police station. Thank God for the Opel station wagon that had been donated by Friends of Kardelen. With it, I can go everywhere.

I thought about that poor girl Hakime and all she'd been through. Mentally disabled, she'd been brought to the Saray orphanage when her mother died. Her father, left with three small children, has no work. They live off of the occasional kindness of neighbors. He sent Hakime to Saray. How else was he going to take care of her? I was happy when last year he got my phone number from someone and called sometimes to tell me about his or her situation. Things had taken a turn for the better in his life and he'd gotten a janitorial job. Now he needed her to come back home to take care of the other little ones. He asked if I'd come over and teach her how to cook and clean the house and do the laundry.

I'm so glad that Norita helped me to find a used washing machine for them. It turned out they were living in the tenement housing not far from my place. Some friends of mine gave me some pots and pans. We started out trying to learn together. She was willing, but pretty slow, and I'd never taught someone like her these kinds of things. I've just been doing them for as long as I can remember.

I'd first gotten to know her when we lived at Saray together. She is so pretty, and a lot of people didn't recognize at first that she was disabled. She was quiet and sweet and wanted to join the team who did the afternoon snack for the kids in the D Block. She even joined our Kardelen Project sometimes. She was so homesick, though, I remember.

I learned how to teach her to do simple things in the kitchen. The way to do that was to do the same thing over and over and over with her. Pretty soon she got it. Now, instead of throwing spaghetti noodles in cold water—oh, we had a few laughs along the way—she remembers to let the water boil and cook the noodles until they are done. She can load and unload the washing machine, too.

I'd heard that the city government was offering a few jobs to people who had mental handicaps and took her down to the city hall to apply. She was accepted and even got a job working as a janitor at the same school where her father was working.

I visited them a lot at home, and we'd had lots of fun evenings talking and trying out some new recipes. I'd tried to guide her and warn her off of guys who would use her. She really didn't have the mental skills to see when she was being manipulated. When they sweet-talked her, she was putty in their hands, so she was always falling in love with creeps. So I wondered about last night's nightmare and her "boyfriends."

When I got to headquarters, I saw her on a chair in the front room. She was all dressed up in a man's shirt and trousers, lying crumpled up. But when she saw me, she collapsed onto my lap, sobbing. It was all I could do to keep from falling apart myself.

Her face was all swollen, and there were red and purplish marks all over her body. It looked like her shoulder was not in its right place—the police later said it was dislocated. She wouldn't speak. So none of us still know what actually happened or who did it. But the police said that she'd obviously been raped and beaten up and left for dead. They said there was nothing they could do until she told them some details.

They told us that we needed to get her to the hospital, so I bundled her up and brought her to the state hospital a couple of miles away and got her checked in. Then I went to talk to a psychiatrist there. She told me they needed to put Hakime on some strong medicine and that I had to go outside and buy it from a pharmacy. I used Kardelen money and did that. After I got back, I talked to the doctor again. This time, she said that it would be a long time before this girl would be able to talk, if ever. They were going to keep her in for a few days, but that I'd need to look after her and try to get her not to think about what had happened to her. The police had to stay away from her because questions would only make her stay all closed off for longer.

A week later, they called from the hospital to say that she was going to be released, for me to come and get her. "Is she able to take care of herself now?" I asked.

"No, not at all, but we need the bed. She'll be on the street if you don't get her today."

So I called her father to tell him to get ready to have his Hakime come home. This time, her young sister, Ayshe, answered the phone. "Oh, Daddy's gotten sick and he's in the hospital."

I couldn't believe it, but it turns out her dad was in a bed on another floor of the same state hospital. It sounded like he had some kind of lung infection, probably pneumonia.

Now two little kids were looking after themselves in their falling-apart tiny brick-and-mortar house.

I phoned Norita to tell her about this new problem and ask for prayer. "They have an aunt who lives in the neighborhood," I told her. "Her husband's a mean old guy, but maybe she'll be willing to look after the two little ones while their dad's in the hospital. Pray that the husband will say 'yes,' and then I'll bring Hakime to stay with us."

That night, I found the children hungry, in filthy clothes, and chilled. No one was there to light the gas-burning stove heater. I asked some neighbors to help, but they shook their heads and closed their doors. When I phoned the aunt to ask for mercy for her niece and nephew, she begged her husband and he did something right for once and agreed. After dropping off the two, I went and got Hakime.

She just sat and shook most of the time. She still said nothing, but would respond a bit when I asked her to come into the kitchen and sit with me while I made supper. Sometimes she'd just dissolve into tears and lie down with her face toward the wall.

Not even a week later, I got another desperate phone call, this time from my younger sister, Terri, in far off Daria to the east of the country. I was to come quickly; one of my aunts who was looking after my two youngest sisters was dying of breast cancer. Meryem, my sister who was home for winter school break, and I decided to take the bus. Harry needed to stay to work at the orphanage.

No way could a young girl like Hakime stay in a home where there was no chaperone, so now I had to find another place for her to stay for the weeks I would be gone.

I thought about my friend, Mrs. Fatma, with her two little spastic children living out in a brick-and-mortar slum dwelling on the outskirts of town. This woman was dirt poor and living off of handouts from the neighbors. But she was determined to look after her own children and not send them into the hell of the orphanage system. I wondered if she'd look after Hakime while I was gone. When I phoned Norita again and proposed that we ask Mrs. Fatma to care for Hakime and provide a small amount of cash, she agreed. We both felt that this was a good solution.

Mrs. Fatma said, "Yes, of course. The poor thing. I'll do what I can to make her comfortable. Maybe she'll be willing to help me out, and maybe that will help her not to think about things bad."

So that's where she is right now. I know she's in good hands, but she will need constant monitoring, given the heavy sedatives the state psychiatrist has given her. We must not give up praying for her. She's such a precious one.

CHAPTER 26

Fatma, Erol, and Ulash

He lifted me out of the slimy pit, out of the mud and mire; he set my feet on a rock and gave me a firm place to stand. He put a new song in my mouth, a hymn of praise to our God. Many will see and fear the Lord and put their trust in him. Blessed is the one who trusts in the Lord, who does not look to the proud, to those who turn aside to false gods.

Psalm 40:2-4

From my personal notes ...

Fatma had two sons. Both were born with several disabilities. Both could not speak.

After Ulash, the second son's birth, Fatma's husband left home. Why? It's hard to say. Maybe he was ashamed he hadn't been able to produce a normal child. Maybe he was unable to bear the load of bringing in the money to provide for these two children. In any case, he left Fatma to fend for herself: no income, no home, and no relatives who would come and help her out.

They were living on the outskirts of Ankara in a broken-down *gecekondu* (built-in-a-night brick-and-mortar building with an outhouse). She went to the mayor of that suburb to beg for charity; the mayor's office started to provide a little money for food. Their neighbors took pity on them and would occasionally send used clothes and extra food.

Fatma loved her kids and did all she could to provide for their necessities. If they were sick, she'd carry them on her back to the bus and bring them into town where the hospitals and clinics were.

One day when Erol was six and Ulash three, they all came into Ankara for a medical checkup. In the waiting room of the hospital, she struck up a conversation with a young woman in a wheelchair who was smiling at her and the kids. And that was the day that Nina told me about them over the phone.

"Believe me, Norita, they have nearly nothing. Harry and I took them back home from the hospital. I'm going to see how we can help them in some practical way."

She phoned me some months later with a proposal: "There's a government-sponsored one-month course in Istanbul. They help mothers learn how to communicate through sign language and other techniques with their handicapped children who can't speak. Fatma told me about it. She so wants to go with Erol but can't manage to take both the children.

"What would you say if Kardelen donated money to send Harry to be Erol's caregiver for the course? Then both Harry as well as Erol can learn a new skill. They'll show Fatma and Ulash when they get back to Ankara."

So, last year, Harry and Erol took off for a suburban school in Istanbul. When they got back, they were so happy. While there, Harry in his quiet way shared about his faith in Jesus with Erol. Something happened with Erol, and even though he couldn't speak, his eyes shone with hope and joy whenever Harry prayed for him. He joined in by bringing his hands together to indicate "prayer."

After that, whenever Nina and Harry visited the family, Erol would make the sign for "pray" and wouldn't allow them to leave before they'd prayed for the family.

A couple of months later, we got another phone call from Nina: "Please pray for Fatma and the boys. They are being evicted from their slum dwelling and have nowhere to go."

We prayed, and God opened a door. Some relatives of Nina who live in a neighboring city agreed to find Fatma a place to live and look in after her to make sure she was okay. They then moved to a new town an hour's drive from Ankara.

Five months after that, I received another phone call from Nina that sent us to our knees. She was crying. "My uncle just contacted me and said I needed to go out right away and take care of Fatma. Erol passed away this morning after being sick for some time. She is paralyzed with grief, and little seven-year-old Ulash is very sick too and cannot keep any food down."

When Nina got there, she took over the household: cooking, cleaning, organizing help from the neighbors, and trying to get suicidal Fatma back onto her feet. It was extremely exhausting work for Nina, and by the end of the week, she was in need of a break. She spoke seriously and sternly to the depressed Fatma, who kept repeating, "It's my fault he's dead. Now

Ulash is going to die and that's that."

"That's enough, Fatma!" Nina said. "Get up and take care of Ulash. It is not your fault that Erol died. You have to get a hold of yourself. I cannot stay here and take care of him. That is your responsibility. Now do it!"

Fatma seemed to respond and went into the kitchen to prepare a meal. Nina returned to Ankara.

One week later, however, another emergency phone call—another appeal for prayer from Nina: "Fatma slit her wrists and is lying in the hospital. Ulash is so sick and vomits everything he eats. He needs to go to the hospital too. I just got the phone call and I'm on my way. Tell people to pray."

I sent around an urgent prayer request to a few of the people who know Nina and this ministry, and we began praying.

Every day, I waited to hear what had happened. One week later, she called.

"How are you?" I asked Nina.

"Good, but sooo tired. My whole body aches and I need to lie down for a long time with my legs up. I've just had no time to do what the physical therapist ordered. It's been too intense here."

"Well, tell me what happened."

"We've had a breakthrough! As soon as I got here, I could see that Ulash was near death. I rushed him to the hospital where Fatma was. The doctor said he was in critical condition from malnutrition and dehydration. They immediately put him on a drip and intravenous feeding. This special food cost another $1,000! Thank God for the money you put in my account for ministry. Plus I had some cash I could help out with too. However, the rest of the hospital bills were in the thousands of dollars. When I heard the amount, I began to panic."

I knew Nina. Her first response to huge financial hurdles often mirrors my own. In her case, she phones me and begs me to find the money. Pretty soon, both of us are nearly hysterical with worry.

She continued: "But this time, something kept me from calling you. Instead I decided to seek the Lord for help. As I was praying, I sensed that He wanted me to go to this local mayor's office and ask for their help. When I told my cousin what I was going to do, he laughed. 'No way are they going to help you. They are so corrupt; they won't do a thing and it's a waste of your time.'

"Still I knew what the Lord had said and went anyway. I spent the day driving around town from office to office, getting out in my wheelchair, and getting people to carry me up and down stairs. But at the end of the day, I was rejoicing.

"You know that election time is coming up in three weeks. Maybe that's why they promised to cover all the basic hospital bills. They also promised to come and fix Fatma's roof, which was leaking like a sieve after the rains we had this week. AND they now have promised to move her and Ulash to a cleaner place and all for free! Only this time, they're going out to a village about an hour and half's drive from Ankara where there were these empty brick houses.

"Norita, can you imagine? They sent a truckload of workmen who fixed the roof. and I was able to bring drugged-up Fatma home. The psychiatrist said that unless Fatma kept taking these strong sedatives, she'd try to commit suicide again. He also said that she was incapable of taking care of her son while in this condition.

"After looking after her for a couple of days, I knew that the situation was, humanly speaking, hopeless. I couldn't stay and care for her and Ulash. There were too many responsibilities in Ankara which were going unmet because of this situation. But what was I to do?

"That night, I sat Fatma down and spoke honestly and seriously with her. 'This isn't going to work,' I told her. 'Only God's power can solve this problem. You need Jesus.' Then I told her whatever the Holy Spirit told me to say to her about the Lord Jesus, about His miracles, about His death, about His resurrection, and about Him being God. We talked until the early morning when I fell exhausted into bed.

"Fatma woke me excitedly this morning. She had something urgent to tell me.

"'Last night, I saw Jesus in my dream. Standing next to Him, smiling and strong, was Erol. He was so happy. Jesus spoke to me. He said that I must look after Ulash but that I must trust Him, and He would always be with me and help me.'

"'Oh, Nina, throw away those pills. I don't need them; I just need Jesus. I know it. I want to trust Him and I want to be baptized.'"

As I listened to Nina's happy voice, I began to shout out "Hallelujah" in Turkish.

"Ulash came home yesterday, and Fatma took seriously the doctor's command to carefully look after this son with his special diet. The Lord provided a pharmacist friend of mine here to secure the food at cost price, and what was going to cost over $2,000 for a three months' supply now is only going to cost $400. Can Kardelen cover this?"

After hearing this story, I had no doubt that we would find the funds, one way or another.

That was a year and a half ago. A little over six months after this incident, Nina, Fatma, and Ulash were all diagnosed with TB. They began serious medical treatments, and Nina and Ulash have fully recovered. Fatma, however, continued to remain quite weak. Then, after some examinations at the local hospital, it was determined that she had also contracted stomach cancer.

None of us were willing for Ulash to be sent away to a local orphanage for care, since it was highly likely that he would not survive that experience. Nor were we able to care for him in Ankara. A neighbor in the village agreed to take him in, in exchange for a salary that also helped her look after her aging ill parents. Fatma continues to go in and out of hospital for her treatments, and more than once we felt that she wasn't going to live more than a month, but ongoing prayer on her behalf as well as continued carefully treatment at the local clinic have kept her alive.

We now call this endeavor the Kirikkale Village Project. As time has progressed, the Lord continues to show mercy to Fatma and Ulash. Several times, she should have died but continues to care enough to stay with us. They are a sign and a testimony to the message of God's relentless love for the least of the least.

Chapter 27

Saturday Night Live

Sing to God, sing in praise of his name, extol him who rides on the clouds; rejoice before him—his name is the Lord.
Psalm 68:4

Nina tells another story in her own words …

After three weeks, I came back and had Hakime come stay again with me. She smiled for the first time in weeks! She even said, "Thank you," and started saying a few words. All of us obeyed the doctor and didn't ask her any questions that would stir up any bad feelings. But still, there were a couple of times when she'd begin crying and curl up on the bed to rock back and forth.

She'd gone into the bedroom one night to cry when we all were startled by a loud insistent knocking. "Who is it?" I called from behind the front door.

"Open up, it's the police."

"What is the meaning of this?" I demanded when local policemen entered the house without a word of explanation.

"There's been a complaint that there is a ring of Christians who live here and who take unsuspecting handicapped people and brainwash them to become part of Christian cell groups," one of the men responded harshly.

"Well, I'm a Christian, but there's no brainwashing going on here, and whoever made such a complaint is crazy. Who did this?"

"Sorry, ma'am, but I can't tell you. It's just our job to investigate every complaint. Who's living here?" another officer said.

"Just me and my brother Harry. We have a friend staying here with us, that's all. How many times am I going to have to put up with narrow-minded neighbors and mean, cruel, suspicious people?" I was furious. "Do you know that I have asked the city for my constitutional right to put a concrete ramp next to those six front stairs? The apartment holder's committee chairman physically threatened the guy who came to do that last week.

So he ran away. Mr. Chairman said he'll never allow a handicap ramp to be built here. Why don't you go and investigate him?"

"Well, you've got to file an official complaint, but you should know that there was a public protest against you two days ago, following Friday prayers. The imam denounced you and your Christian friends and proselytizing activities," a third officer said.

I started shaking. We'd had our small group over for Bible study and worship two weeks ago. I guessed that everyone in the neighborhood had heard our singing. *Is there no place where I can be left alone to practice my faith? Will life always be insufferably difficult for me as a believer in Jesus? I'm so tired of all this harassment, Lord.*

The next day, I went outside to find the rear window of my car smashed and a tire slashed. I had to call Harry to come back from work to help me get them fixed because I needed to go to my exercise class. If I don't get to swimming class every couple of days, my leg swells up and the pain in my hip gets excruciating.

When I got home in the early afternoon, no one was at home, and it had begun to lightly snow again. Generally, in the past, I'd call out to a passer-by to help me get my wheelchair out of the trunk and over to my door so that I could get in it and then that person would help me up the steep front stairs to my front door.

Today when I called out and asked for help, the people looked the other way and deliberately ignored me. I watched as people went in and out of the apartment building, but nobody would give me a hand. These were people who for the past two years had said ,"Hello, how are you?" and been so willing to help. Now they were clearly set on ostracizing me.

Before too long, I was desperate to get out and get to the bathroom. Still no one responded. I ultimately had to have an "accident." Sobs of anger and frustration and hurt filled my car, and I sat there with my forehead pressed against the steering wheel until what seemed like hours later when Harry came home and got me safely into the apartment.

"That's it," I told myself. "We're outta here. Unless I'm on my feet, I can't get in or out of this building on my own. My disabled friends are going to be treated like dirt, even the ones who aren't Christians. There's no point in hanging around here. I'll find somewhere else to live."

I phoned Norita to ask for her advice. She said she'd prayed that day and that the Lord had spoken a scripture to her about "shaking the dust off my feet and moving someplace where people were willing to hear the message." While I didn't understand the "dust" part of the verse, the "moving" part made lots of sense, and I began to feel a peace about leaving this home for another new location.

We're looking and praying and seeking and wondering. I'm just holding on by a thread, however. Sometimes the evil around me gets too much to handle.

/////

From my personal notes ...

It's 2:00 a.m. and I've just gotten off the phone. Nina is reeling from another visitation; this time from a completely different person. I got the first call about two hours ago.

"Noritaaaaaa, what am I supposed to do?" Her voice broke with a sob. Only after a few moments was she able to continue: "I am completely lost here. What do I do?"

"Whoa, Nina. You've got to calm down. I can't help you unless you slow down and tell me clearly what the problem is."

"Okay, okay." She tried hard to control her emotions. "Someone just rang my doorbell. I was afraid to open it at this time of night. And especially when I called out and asked who was there and no one answered. Actually I was so scared that I phoned Selin to go outside and look. You know, Selin, the woman who lives down the hall and who has shown me the only friendship in this whole building. Well, she was up watching TV and went out into the hall to check before phoning me back to say that no one was there and I could open the door: that it looked like there was a package on the mat.

"And just like she said, there was a shoebox sitting there. It wasn't covered and there was something in it, wrapped up in what looks like a dish towel. Then, as I reached down to pick up the box, the towel moved."

She started crying again.

"Norita. It's a baby. It's still covered in blood. It's alive. It's a tiny little girl. Oh my God, what am I supposed to do? I know nothing about this."

I gave her a few moments, and she continued: "I looked back into the dark hall, but of course, no one was there. I called out to the doorman who lives in the flat next door. He came to the door and looked at the 'package' and said that he had just let someone in who had rung the front door bell a moment ago, but that when no one came to his inside door, he'd looked out the window to see a woman getting into a taxi and driving away.

"So now Selin, the doorman, and I are staring at this child wondering what to do when Selin sees an envelope in the bottom of the box. She hands it to me, but I asked her to read it to me. Here's what it says:

"'I cannot take care of this baby. It's not possible. But I have heard about you and the way you are so compassionate and caring for people, so I think you should look after her.'

"Noooooowwwww what?" Nina was completely baffled. " I have absolutely no knowledge of what to do with babies, and I can barely take care of the ones I've got under my care now."

We stopped to pray together again over the phone. Both she and I "heard" the instructions: "Call in the police." And she promised to phone me as soon as they came.

Just a few minutes ago, they left with little Nura. The police asked Nina to name her and then took her into care with Social Services after assuring Nina that this newborn would not be going to Saray but to a local home much closer to where Nina could visit her anytime. When years before Nina first was picked up with Meryem, they lived at this place, and Nina testifies that it is a much better organized and compassionate place than the other institutions she was forced to live in. The fact that the first doctor's examination showed no observable disability in Nura was a mercy. Only the people with obvious disabilities were sent to Saray.

Tomorrow Nina is going to go out and buy clothes and diapers for her new "niece."

CHAPTER 28

"Tell Her Not to Be Afraid"

When you pass through the waters, I will be with you; and when you pass through the rivers, they will not sweep over you. When you walk through the fire, you will not be burned; the flames will not set you ablaze. For I am the Lord your God, the Holy One of Israel, your Savior....

Isaiah 42:2-3

Nina's incredible save in her own words ...

"Why, Why, WHY?" I cried out for the thousandth time. "Why does my life have to be so difficult? Why does our family have so many difficulties? There is a curse over us, for sure, or we wouldn't be experiencing so much trouble."

Norita tried to calm me down from the other end of the phone, but I couldn't hear anything she was saying. It felt like my life was nothing but pain and sorrow and disappointment. I wanted God to answer me. "I'm sick and tired. Stop giving me problems."

I'd just gotten a phone call from my cousin Alice. Terri, my eighteen-year-old sister who lives with our cancer-stricken aunt, had fallen down some stairs and broken her foot. I wasn't supposed to worry, but Alice said that it'd be good if I could come back there to help.

The way Alice told me the news (she giggles nervously when she's not telling the truth), I knew she was hiding something more serious, and I got really upset. I needed to get back there right away and try to help. My car was in the shop for repairs, but I was determined to pick it up as soon as it was ready and drive the thousand-kilometer road to get to the hospital.

"Nina," Norita said to me, "I know that you've driven hundreds of miles in that Ford. It's been a great blessing. You've driven in some tricky weather, and the Lord has been with you the whole time to sustain you and protect you despite the extra problems that stem from your paralysis. But that's too far away. You aren't physically strong enough to take nonstop driving. Road stops will be difficult. Who will get your wheelchair out of the back and help you? Take the bus. It's safer."

"I have to go," I told her. "If I have the car, I'll be able to get around the city easier, and if she needs me to bring her things, then I need a car. I have that handicapped friend, Murat. He said he'd be willing to come with me on this trip and that he could share in the driving. He's come with me to Samsun when we visit Mediha and Ozgur and the others there. He's willing to come. We've got to go."

While Murat has never had much time for my faith and at times called me "ridiculous," he's always had a positive attitude about helping others like ourselves who are physically or mentally disabled. He's not a practicing Muslim, more an atheist. Not so unusual among many of my educated handicapped friends who are probably pretty angry at Allah for "cursing" them with their disabilities.

"Well, if the Lord has not said 'No,' then go," Norita said. "We'll be praying in small group tonight, and I'll let people know by email to be praying."

The next afternoon, I phoned Norita to say that we were leaving for the "Wild East" in a half hour. I was feeling pretty stressed and poured out my frustration, questions, and anxiety over the phone again. Norita listened and then prayed again for us.

After driving all night, we arrived around six o'clock in the evening. I drove straight to the large university hospital where my sister Terri was. When I saw her yellow face and eyes through the window where she lay in the intensive care ward, it was all I could do from passing out from fear. She hadn't fallen and broken her leg. She was in a coma brought on by hepatitis, the disease she'd first contracted two years before. This time, shock and stress had brought it on.

The week before, I'd spoken with Terri and our younger sister, Jessie, on the phone. They were crying and telling me that outside their door a huge fight was raging between the police and protesters. They were scared and felt caught. Just that morning, a group of hooded men had come into Jessie's middle school and tried to intimidate the kids to join them in their antigovernment protest: "We're ready to give our lives for the Kurds, for you. Leave these classrooms now and join us if you have any courage or love for justice and our people." After hiding in the school, they ran home and shut the doors and curtains. Now the promised confrontation was happening on their very street.

After they hung up the phone, Terri had peeked outside when she heard shouting. To her absolute horror, she saw a six-year-old boy throw a rock at one of the security policemen who were marching behind their shields down the street. One moment later, the impact of a police bullet shattered his head; his body was thrown against the wall across the street.

The next day, she went to school, her skin a yellowish-gray, and she was silent all day. When she stood up to leave the room, she collapsed—unconscious. Now less than a week later, Terri's liver was dangerously enlarged to the point of bursting, and the doctor in charge emphasized that her critical condition could only be changed by an immediate blood transfusion.

I said I was ready to give my blood, but they refused me when I told them what medications I was on at the moment. No one else in our immediate family there was available to give blood, and Terri has a blood type that is difficult to find ready matches for in the under-supplied blood bank. I drove off to the local Red Crescent in search of blood, but no luck there. Then my cousin suggested another cousin who lives in a village not far from the city. When I phoned him and asked if he'd be willing to come to the hospital to donate, he said he would but needed transportation. The doctor also told us that soldiers at a nearby military camp were required by law to give blood. So after picking my cousins up at 10:00 p.m., we all set off to find the military camp.

It was dark, there were no streetlights, and the road had turned into a winding two-lane highway bordered by steep inclines and sharp embankments. Slow-moving vans and trucks often make this stretch of road a crowded thoroughfare, and it was busy that night.

About midnight, we were coming down the hill at about 50km per hour. As we turned a corner, we heard the explosion of a tire, and I lost control of the car. We were flying over the side of the road, the car flipping over three or four times in the air.

The next thing I knew, I was lying on my back next to the car, which had come to rest in a tree with its motor running and gasoline spewing out underneath onto the ground. When I looked around, people were descending the slope and crying. I looked to my right, and there was Murat lying next to me, then my seven-year old cousin, Jamal, and older cousin,

Mehmet. The four of us lay parallel flat out on a little grassy knoll. Jamal sat up, grinned, and made a turning motion with his hand and said, "Wheee, let's do that again! That was fun!"

After some moments of stunned silence, someone cried out, "They're alright; EVERYONE is lying here around the car on the ground, but it looks like they're all okay. But look at that car. It's totaled. How did they get out? It's a miracle. They should be dead. It's a miracle!"

When the gendarme (local military police) came to investigate the crash, they asked me what I was doing out driving at that time of night. When I told them that we were on the way to the hospital to give blood for my sister, they immediately put out an all-points bulletin over the radio calling for a blood donor with Terri's blood type. Another policeman in the city heard this and offered to give his blood. He arrived about the same time we did in an ambulance. They wheeled us in to lie down and rest while he went directly to the lab.

The following morning, I text-messaged Norita from the hospital with the news. When she phoned and I told her what had happened, she prayed over the phone and said she'd be calling others to pray. "Yes, please," I pleaded. "But WHY did this happen now? But it is a miracle." I was in shock, crying, trying to put all the pieces of this puzzle together and not succeeding. After hanging up, I asked for another sedative and lay there, still stunned.

The next day, Murat said he needed to get back to Ankara, so I took him by taxi to the bus station to get him on the overnight bus. While we were waiting in the tearoom, he told me what had happened the night before.

"I've got to tell you what I saw when the car went off the road," he said. "As soon as we were airborne, you screamed out 'Lord Jesus, come. Help me. I can't do anything. Where are You? Help!' At that moment, you hit your head on the steering wheel and went unconscious. I never lost consciousness, however.

"Right after you cried out, a large Man with a beard and long white robes appeared. The car was heading for a huge rocky wall. The Man put out His hand and moved the car so that it hit several trees instead and finally came to rest on one of them. He broke the windows of the car and, starting with you, lifted us each out one by one and laid us on the grass next to the tree. He spoke to me and said, 'Tell her not to be afraid. I will never leave her.'

"I spoke to him and asked Him if He was Jesus, and He nodded, then disappeared."

Murat looked me in the face, fear and wonder in his expression. "I'm afraid. Something very strange happened to us. I want to get home and try to figure out just what happened. I'm thankful to be alive, for sure, but ..."

When Murat finished telling me this story, I wept and wept tears of wonder and thanksgiving. I told him that he'd had a special blessing to be able to see the Lord Jesus and that this was a grace from God. He kept shaking his head and saying he just wanted to get home.

/////

Email from Norita to prayer support group around the world:
May 1, 2006 ...

Please continue praying: for Terri to be healed and back on her feet, for the finances to complete her present hospital treatment; for her to know the presence of the Lord there, particularly since her hopes for taking the college entrance exam this year have been dashed; a new car for Nina; for Murat to know Jesus personally; for Nina's cousins and uncles and aunts to hear and respond to the Good News of the God who is with us; for that hate-torn city and region in the southeast of Turkey; for this country and for those here who are His Light-bearers.

/////

Nina phones Murat: May 11, 2006 ...

"Hey, Murat, it's been two weeks and I need to give you an update on everything. Since Terri doesn't have insurance, we've had to come up with thousands of dollars to cover her treatment. Norita has sent us money which came in from friends in the States to help cover costs; I was owed some money which we used. Every time I thought that there was no way to carry on, that she might be sent home without getting the needed treatment, money came in. She needs to stay here longer, so I'm having to trust God for each dollar, each day.

"The insurance man, even though we had bought insurance, is coming up with all kinds of weird excuses not to pay the full value of the car. This has upset me more than you can know. I can't do my job without my car. It's my legs and means of ministry. Harry came out from Istanbul and has been helping with this. He's phoned Ken Abi, who is also phoning insurance people to learn what the facts are and how to get our money. I hope we don't have to open a court case, but that's one possible scenario at this point. It's all very tiring.

"But … I'm smiling. And more than grateful today. Ecstatic, you could say. Last night, Terri spoke to me for the first time since I'd gotten here. Today they are going to put her on some real food. For two and a half weeks, she's been in a semi-coma, at times crying out, at times staring and not responding.

"'Abla, don't worry,' she whispered to me last night as I wheeled over to her side. 'Just keep praying. I'll be okay.'

"I started crying both from happiness as well as exhaustion.

"'Listen, listen,' she made an effort to speak up, but it was obvious that she was very weak. 'I think I died and then came back,' she went on. 'When I came to in this hospital bed, I couldn't move; I was too weak. But there was an old man standing at my bedside and he put his hand on my shoulder, and he talked to me. He didn't move his lips, but I could understand what he was saying. I talked to him too without moving my lips. It was like our hearts were speaking to each other.'

"'Then, all of a sudden, I found myself in the most beautiful peaceful place imaginable, green and lush and clean. There I saw Jesus and He smiled at me and touched me, but at some point, He said that people still needed me and that my work wasn't done and I was to go back. "Don't worry," He said, "You have a future that is good. Tell your sister and all the many people who are praying for you not to worry. You will recover."'

"'The next thing I knew I was waking up here.'

"Like I said, through streaming eyes, I'm smiling in a BIG WAY."

CHAPTER 29

Ann

My adversaries pursue me all day long; in their pride many are attacking me.... All day long they twist my words; all their schemes are for my ruin. They conspire, they lurk, they watch my steps, hoping to take my life.

Psalm 56:2, 5-6

The distress in Bill's was obvious: "You need to go up to her town and see Ann. We just got back from visiting her and Nathan. At first, I wondered if she'd talk to me. I'd only been able to talk to Nathan on the phone, but when we got to their house, she came out of the back room and sat with us for a few minutes. Then she got restless and slipped into their back bedroom. There's something really wrong with her. Nathan seems okay but has become very protective. Go and see them, Norita."

Ann and I had last spoken face-to-face a year and a half earlier. I had been preparing to travel to the States. On her way to Istanbul to visit her daughter, she'd dropped in to show me some tablecloths she'd picked up from some handicapped women in a village near her home. We had discussed plans for making and selling bedding and tablecloths. Typically whenever we'd spend any time together, one or the other would begin brainstorming. We shared a heart of compassion and wanted to help really poor families. One obvious way was to help them sell homemade goods. So even though we lived a full thirteen-hour bus ride apart, we worked well together.

During one of our get-togethers, Ann had said to me, "If we can get some of your American friends to give the money, let's buy several hundred yards of this locally produced cotton material, have the village women embroider them, and we'll sell them."

"Yes!" I said, getting excited about the possibilities of not only bringing in funds to buy wheelchairs and orthopedic equipment, but also of including the families in the income-generating process. "Then I'll contact my friends in Europe or the US who could possibly market them. I've already been in email contact with one. She wants to be involved. These designs are uniquely Turkish and very attractive."

"That's fantastic," Ann said. "I'll get on it just as soon as I get home. With those sewing machines Kardelen bought us and some space in the basement of my apartment building, we can become self-sufficient. None of us want to become dependent on donations if we can help it. Besides, people get suspicious and start false rumors in our small town. My neighbors don't know that I visit the people in the villages."

That same year, Ann had led a short-term team from the USA, taking a volunteer physical therapist up into the tiny hamlets scattered over the large mountainous area of the region. There, they'd treated and advised families with disabled children who were essentially bound to their wooden huts due to lack of available transportation and finances to get them into the larger towns for treatment.

It was hard to believe that such a self-sacrificing woman would say that she was sometimes opposed: "Some are jealous of my foreign friends and have begun smear campaigns, saying that I'm a disreputable person. I don't care what they say. They're petty and could care less for the really needy. I think this passion is from God. I just can't sleep when I know about children who can't get to the hospital or doctors, or who don't have money for medicines or wheelchairs.

"You remember Chernobyl? This part of Turkey was severely affected. Our tea fields, our rivers, they were polluted with radiated dust. That's one reason that the percentage of children born her with disabilities is significantly higher than in any other area of Turkey."

I nodded. "That and close relative intermarriage are two of the main reasons why the percentage of disability in relation to the entire population is close to 17 percent. In Europe, it's much less. Put that figure together with the economic and educational situation of these special families, and you can't help but feel that this is a social need that far surpasses the abilities of government and state to handle."

"Well," Ann said, "it makes me feel so good and privileged that I can help some of these local families. The wheelchairs are so great. But more than that, you should see the joy and response in the faces of the mothers and the children. All we've done is show a little interest. They are praying for us, you know."

Before she left, we'd prayed together, asking the Father to bless our work and touch those for whom we cared about, thanking Him for all that we'd received and for our friendship.

Out of the blue, six months later, she phoned me from a pay phone in Ankara. She'd been summoned to the capital to sit before a committee of police commissioners who questioned her about her relationship with me and Kardelen. Both of us were surprised and confused as to the reason for this. She phoned her cousin who held a higher-up position in the security police. She said he, too, did not know what this was about, but had shown signs of concern about her friendships with Christians and foreigners.

That evening, she'd phoned me again. She said that she had answered their questions about Kardelen and me without too much stress. After all, a clear conscience is the best stress-reliever. Having a cousin in the police did help increase her credibility, though.

Three months later, however, she phoned again. This time her voice quivered over the line: "I need to hire a lawyer," she began. "I've been accused of propagandizing a minor here in town."

She related how, some months before, she'd agreed to help pay the room and board for two teenagers who were living as wards of the state in an orphanage several hours away. They were fifteen and had been given the chance to work as apprentices in town. In order to be able to do this, they needed some adult who would pledge to make sure that their housing expenses would be taken care of. Ann had met them and agreed to send them some support. At one point, they had all talked about faith. The boys had asked for Bibles, so she'd given them New Testaments, signing them and writing little encouraging notes inside the front covers. If the boys had been eighteen, there would have been no problem, but someone had informed the police, who threatened and then beat the boys until they gave up the books. Now Ann was being taken in for questioning.

This was such a strange scenario. Who had wanted Ann questioned? It had to be someone who claimed to be a friend or colleague. Or were the boys just "plants," set up to get at her? Why did they decide to make a big case out of something rather insignificant in the political realm of the Black Sea? Knowing that political rivalry in this country often caused conspiracies to defame reputation, I thought that a rival of

Ann's husband, Nathan, wanted his port aauthority job.

Ann was released to await trial, and I urged her to come back to Ankara, promising we'd go to talk to lawyers or officials to straighten out what was surely an error. The day after she arrived, I took her to see a former ssupreme court judge who lived in my neighborhood and was a friend of a friend. His office was full of students and friends and journalists. That day, he was launching out into the political arena and was preparing to hold a press conference in front of one of the government buildings. In spite of all the busy activity surrounding him, he called us into his office.

"I don't have much time," he began, "but how can I help you?"

Normally confident, Ann tried to clear her throat, then began mumbling about how she was being prosecuted for giving some kids a Bible.

"Nonsense," he interrupted. "There's absolutely no prohibition against giving minors or anyone else a book. Why, everyone should read all the books about religion and philosophy that they can. People should be educated not kept in ignorance. The Bible, the Qur'an, the Torah ... all the books. Don't worry; they can't do anything to you."

With that, he walked out of his office, put on the coat proffered by his secretary, and rushed out the front door with a crowd of supporters in tail.

Even though I was glad to have heard this news, Ann was not satisfied: "He may be a former supreme court judge, but he doesn't live in my town. The head of the gendarme at home gave me the name of a military lawyer whose office is in Ankara. This man is supposed to be quite powerful and would be the most likely person to get a successful verdict on this case. I have his phone number and am going to talk to him."

According to Ann, the lawyer listened carefully, spent some time on the phone talking to someone in her hometown, and said that for a fee he thought this whole thing might be resolved without loss of reputation or public embarrassment. "This is a serious charge, however, Ann," he continued. "The people in this region do not take lightly to religious proselytizing by Christians."

Ann explained more to me that evening: "Norita, you know how small our town is. This scandal will cost my husband his job. We'll not be able to do any more Kardelen projects there. This is serious. I need $5,000 as soon as possible. I know it's expensive for Turkey, but believe me, for this type of situation, it's necessary."

That night, I prayed about what to do for her. Deciding to give her the money from my account, I made the decision to share this need with a few other friends in the States, particularly for prayer. One couple later donated this amount. Ann was so anxious, however, that she did not want me to meet the lawyer or have the money transaction done through the normal bank transfer route. The lawyer didn't want to receipt his services. At the time, we figured it was because he didn't want to pay income taxes on it, but today I have a strong feeling that it was more of a situation in which Ann was being set up to be the pawn in a blackmailing conspiracy.

Supposedly the trial was postponed for a few months, and then the venue changed to another eastern city. During this time, anxiety made Ann quite ill with asthma and heart problems. I tried to get hold of her, phoning several times until finally her husband gave me the hospital number where she was in intensive care. She told me over the phone, all the while hacking and coughing, that her lawyer was able to get permission for her to stay at home while he defended her on the day of the first hearing. Nathan would go and sit in the courtroom while deliberations proceeded. Another postponement was announced. The lawyer was confident that all charges would be dropped at the next hearing.

Then, for nearly eleven months, I did not hear from her. I phoned from the States, where we'd gone for a sabbatical. I phoned from Turkey after we returned. Whenever I phoned, her husband would answer and promise that he'd pass on the message. She never phoned back. I phoned her daughter to ask for news, but her daughter, too, was unable to facilitate any communication between us.

Some local friends told me that her behavior was suspicious, and that more than likely, she'd set me up to get money, and that I should just strike her off my list of friends and just figure the whole thing was a relationship fiasco. I never could accept that explanation, but still was sad that neither she nor eventually her husband responded to my phone calls, messages, or emails.

Perplexed, I prayed daily for some word from them. I knew they were scared, so I prayed for their safety too. The board of directors of the foundation in the States, which had oversight of this project, needed to hear from me and know what was going on. The new Kardelen Brotherly Love Association was holding money in a bank account, which had been given for the orphanage work. The apartment where Nina was living with her brother and sister was still the official property of the Turkish association, but of course, the stateside organization shared a responsibility for the property too since they'd brokered the arrangement with the donor in England a few years before.

We had the threat hanging over our heads that we'd lose the apartment. It was absolutely necessary that we legally change the ownership papers into the name of a private individual, or the law demanded that a defunct association would lose all assets into the hands of the government. We had no way of knowing if the Kardelen Brotherly Love Association of the Black Sea was defunct or not.

Not only that, but Ann and I had bought land on which to build our own facility not far from Saray. Through public auction and a series of "coincidences," I had found myself walking into the city auction hall with Ann and buying land for $12,000 two years prior to her silence. Taxes had to be paid on this land or it, too, would revert to state ownership. I did research to see if she'd paid the taxes or if she'd possibly sold it, and found that no attempts to do anything with the property had been made since we first bought it. But since her name was on the deed, it was imperative that we contact her and make decisions regarding the future.

Now, Will's urgings, coupled with prayer, convinced me I should fly to Trabzon and take the 2.5-hour bus ride to their town. I needed to see her and talk to her myself. The only flights to Trabzon were evening ones, so I sat in the half-empty plane lost in my own thoughts with some anxiety.

"What if she won't see you?" my husband had asked. "Maybe you won't be able to find her."

"If she refuses to see me, then I'll at least know that our friendship is over and stop living in this fog of wondering. I can't stand this anymore. I know somehow that God is going to lead me on this trip."

After staying the night in a hotel close to the highway that ran along the shore of the tempestuous Black Sea, I boarded one of the numerous minibuses that drove up and down the coast, stopping at all the fishing villages and towns along the way.

What should I say, Father? I prayed. *How will they respond to me? They didn't reply to my letter telling them I was coming. What should I do?*

In the stillness of my heart as I peered out the dripping window onto the choppy gray sea, I heard Him whisper, "Don't say anything. Just hug her."

I arrived two hours later and motioned to the bus driver that I was to be let off on the side of the main road that runs through town. I looked up and down the highway trying to recognize a familiar landmark or address number on the buildings. Everything looked strange to me—it had been four years since we'd come as a family for a few days' vacation here. I knew I would never forget the beautiful, lush mountain meadows and streams found less than an hour away from the coast, but the town seemed a totally strange place to me this time. My memory for landmarks was not serving me well.

I walked about a quarter of a mile in one direction, showing shopkeepers the address of her apartment. At the first three places I asked, the men (there were only men visible in the shops) shrugged their shoulders and turned away from me. I was obviously a suspicious foreigner, an infidel—not one they wanted to be seen talking with. This kind of inhospitable behavior was so different from that of those I'd come to love who lived in the western regions of the nation. They seemed like they came from another country.

I looked for other women and noticed that farther up the road, women in scarves and colorful, baggy pajamas were standing at the side of the highway. It was market day, and they'd come in from a village to buy and sell. Two of them were struggling with an unruly, nervous cow along the dirt path that ran parallel to the asphalt highway. The people, noise, cars, and occasional minibuses kept unnerving the animal; the women were alternately pulling and being pulled by her.

Frustrated with the unhelpful shopkeepers, I spotted a taxi stand farther up the road a few yards. After thinking about my question for some seconds and then asking the attendant, he answered: "Well, I don't know where that place is, but it's got to be back the way you came.

There's a small bed-and-breakfast near the entrance of town. Ask there; they'll help you."

I hitched my shoulder bag back up and started traipsing back the way I'd just come. Although it had begun to drizzle slightly, the exertion of the walk kept me comfortable. I finally arrived at the small hotel. The desk clerk told me the apartment was directly behind them.

Marching up a dark stairwell, my stomach felt tense. I rang the doorbell, bracing myself for only God knew what.

No one answered. I could picture them standing right inside the front door, hiding, keeping silent. I rang again. Nothing.

Oh, Lord, did I miss Your leading? Did I make this trip for nothing?

At that moment, someone else came up the stairs and stood in front of the flat. He, too, rang the bell. I meekly told him that I'd gotten no response. He said that he'd come to ask about the "For Rent" sign in the window outside. Two doors down the corridor, a door opened and a scarfed woman in her very thick Black Sea accent said, "They moved out three days ago. No one's there. I don't know where they are, but try asking the lady who lives on the first floor, Mrs. Fatima. She might know. Try her."

"The place has already been rented, I think," Fatima soon told us. "You come in," she said, pointing to me. "I'll tell you what I know."

I removed my shoes outside the door and followed her inside.

"Nathan and Ann have left here and moved their stuff," Fatima said. "They've fixed up a place in a village not too far from here. It was just a couple of days ago. I've been phoning her all morning telling her there's fresh tea brewing and plenty of time to chat now that the move is over. All morning, the phone was busy until about a half an hour ago. I got through, but she told me she was too busy. Here, let me phone her for you." She got through again. "She's called Nathan to come pick you up from here. He's been out at the house and is returning to Segur where his office is. He'll be here in a few minutes."

Nathan arrived soon enough, dressed in a neatly pressed dark-blue suit, the smart active uniform of a public employee. He greeted me warmly enough but was obviously in a hurry to leave. After a quick glass of tea—his one concession to Fatima's insistent invitation to stay and visit—he stood up abruptly and said we needed to be on our way.

He drove me back into town to a modern-looking glass-and-brick teashop, just a few yards away from the taxi driver I'd spoken to earlier that morning.

Gaunt and wan, Ann sat at a small, Formica-covered café table—hair covered and tied up in a scarf, wearing thin-cotton denim-colored trousers and a worn reddish-brown pullover sweater. When she stood, I hugged her and kept on hugging her tightly. She said nothing, but eventually her eyes grew moist with tears. She didn't or couldn't speak for several minutes. Nathan kept trying to make small talk and obviously was embarrassed by my public show of affection. (There were two waiters standing in the corner watching us.)

After a few minutes, she suggested that we get out of there and go into Segur (twenty minutes' drive away), where she'd feel safer and would be able to speak more freely. Sammy, a colleague of Nathan, drove us to a waterfront restaurant where we sat outside until it started to drizzle again. With a lit cigarette in her hand, she began by telling me what had happened to her that very morning.

She'd gone outside to work in the garden of the village home they were temporarily staying in. After some moments, two bearded men drove up and parked a few yards from the house. Uncomfortable by their presence and the fact that she was alone, she went back into the house to phone her husband—only to find that the phone was dead. She didn't know that after phoning her for over an hour and getting a busy signal, Nathan had grown worried that she'd had an accident in the house and he had decided to drive the half hour from his office to find her. He and Sammy drove up to the house; the men in the car drove off. A few minutes later, the phone began to work again. She was sure that these strange men were following her. So she had one more reason why she and Nathan were going to move back to the anonymity of big-city Istanbul. Although neither her voice nor her facial expressions were those of someone who was paranoid schizophrenic, she did say that she was on some sort of medication—later I learned that she was being given heavy psychotropic drugs.

We sat and ate lunch, and she kept talking about those men and the events of that morning. She was sure they were sent to keep tabs on her; perhaps during the time the phone was dead, a tap was activated.

Who knew? Earlier that day when I was at Fatima's with Nathan, he had talked about the problem of the phone but thought it was probably a result of storm damage. When I mentioned this to Ann, she shook her head, saying the storm had taken place the evening before, and then the phone had worked fine. More than that, who were those men and what were they doing there outside her doorway in the village?

We sat on the patio while the wind alternately blew the cloud cover away, allowing a little sunshine or later bringing light droplets and dark clouds. We weren't bothered by the weather since our privacy was secured by it. She was not anxious to go back to her place, and as more time passed, she seemed to be ready to talk about the previous summer.

"They came from the special police force this time—just after I gotten back from Ankara while you were in the States. I'd gone to Ankara to finalize the paperwork issues on that apartment Kardelen bought. I was told that there were some mistakes in the paperwork and I had to come back to Segur to get the notary to rewrite the documents and then return again to the capital. The day I returned I received word that the police had seized the bank account and the official documents notebooks for the organization. We were under investigation.

"I couldn't believe it at first. What had we done wrong? What did helping the poor people and families who had disabled children have to do with crime? Someone from Ankara—someone who knows all about us and wanted us closed down, and wanted to make an example of me—did this. That's what my lawyer said, the one who helped me with the propaganda charge. But then it started …

"Bearded men in suits, dirty, unkempt, took me somewhere for several days. Where? I don't know. Why? I didn't understand a single thing. I forgot … but now it's coming back; some things are coming back, I mean. I remember things, but I am not sure if they happened. I think that I am losing my mind."

She went on to say that the Ministry of the Interior had accused the association of criminal treacherous misdeeds. Her newly appointed board members immediately resigned so as not to be implicated; Ann, as board president, was.

"I am on trial for taking money from the halfway house for the disabled in Ankara and not reporting it; for taking money from foreigners to get children with disabilities out of Saray orphanage to the States on false pretenses and not having the those two children brought back after an agreed-upon year's permission time was over. Do you understand that I'm being charged with being an accomplice to kidnapping? I don't even know these children or what they are talking about."

I knew that Becky's daughter, Amy, along with another of their friends, had been given permission to take two of the little orphans from Saray to the States. These kids were rescued from sure death in Saray. We hoped that they were being given the opportunity to live happy, productive lives in loving homes. Ann, however, never had met the children nor their benefactors.

"Then they tell me that we used that apartment in Ankara to secretly indoctrinate poor, incapable handicapped people into Christianity. I supposedly bribed Nina to become a Christian by giving her the right to live in that house.

"But those men, those men put me on unofficial trial for every known or made-up work of the Christians in the country. Can you imagine, the organization is responsible for passing out thousands of New Testaments in the southeast and being a front for antigovernment rebels?"

She grew restless and asked that we move. We drove to another place in town where students gathered to drink tea. Intermittently the sky cleared; the sun shone briefly through again. As we sat in this place for four hours, the sky continued to change. Later in the afternoon when I finally boarded a bus to go back to Ankara, it was pouring rain. The lush fields of tea almost ready to harvest and the majestic forested coastal mountains were shrouded in mist and rain, and I was left with my thoughts of the day's conversation:

"I have no idea where they took me, but it was not in the city" Ann had said. "Somewhere in the countryside; I saw no one else, just my interrogators. Men who were not clean shaven or well dressed, but who obviously wanted to scare and intimidate me.

"From the early morning to the middle of the night, they interrogated me. They'd change places, speaking horrid, coarse things; accusing me, accusing me, accusing me. I was evil, filthy, and treacherous. They mentioned a few names over and over. Yours, for one, Heinrich,

Schuler. Agents all, they said, co-conspirators intent on destroying the Turkish state. They ordered me to tell them all about my connection with the biggie leader who was born in this area and is supposed to be in charge of the operations in Ankara. I can't remember his name, had never heard of him. Borax, Border? Harun Bordex, maybe. I don't remember. Have you heard of him?"

She had stopped speaking for several minutes. Her eyes again teared up.

"My psychiatrists say I should not think about the past. They say I'm probably imagining things. Nathan doesn't want me to speak these thoughts out. I don't trust him, Norita. Maybe he's working with them too? Or could they be right? Am I imagining it? If I am, then I am truly deranged. This is too hard ..."

Her voice trailed off, as did her gaze.

After some time, she continued: "I don't know how much time we were there, but it felt like months. Every day, a new interrogation; every day, a new horrible interrogator ... They talked about how heinous and treacherous Christians were and then how stupid I was for having any dealings with them. Jesus was a bastard Jew, they said, no great man, a nobody, not worthy of losing life or reputation for."

As I'd listened, I fought the desire to stop her. I felt like I was being pulled into a black vortex of mental anguish. I remembered how OP, our musician friend, had been dragged into prison fifteen years previously on charges of terrorism—his only "crime" was being an outspoken believer in Jesus the Messiah. We knew that the police arrived at his door on the evening of his marriage. He, his new wife, all the celebrating guests, and a number of believers from a Muslim background, were all taken to the downtown dungeon for three weeks of questioning. He told us that as they were taken into the special "anti-terrorist" interrogation cells, he caught a glimpse of words block-printed above the door entrance: "There is no God, and Mohammed is away on vacation."

My thoughts went back to Ann, as she continued her story in her soft voice: "They kept putting my nose in a notebook, a forty-page document. Every missionary's name, every Christian's name they knew about, was listed there as people intent on destroying Turkey.

"'These are your so-called friends,' they said over and over.

'*&^%$# bastards.'" She was mumbling, staring at the table. "They've told me that you used me like a whore. They screamed and shouted over and over. 'You $%&*! You who claimed to love your country so much! You are an embarrassment, a fool. Who do you think you are, and how did you think you'd get away with playing your %$#@-ing games? You are the worst kind of traitor, pure #@*$, making money off of the disabled, selling your soul to the enemies of Turkey. Your husband, your daughters, your son. They're all ashamed of you. You whoring $^*&#.'"

Although the words came out in an unemotional monotone, she had begun to shake. In the distance, the muezzin had called the faithful to prayer, and Turkish pop music blared from the speaker in the corner of the tea shop. Someone on the street outside was hawking sesame bread rolls.

I sat there holding her hand, silent.

Several minutes later, she said, "Ohhhhh, the pain. I do not want to remember. I will not remember. I must forget. Do you think my children know what happened? I hope they don't. Please, am I crazy? Did I imagine this? I can't stop the pictures forming in my mind now, or the words ringing in my ears. The memories—nonstop nightmares."

Across the table, I gripped her hand again and told her that she was not crazy. She'd been the victim of unspeakable psychological and probably physical torture (she'd not mentioned any of that yet, but I'd spent time with enough other victims to know what happened in those secret cells).

"You didn't deserve that, sweet Ann, but evil swooped in to attack you." A pause, and then I couldn't keep from asking: "What about God? What was your experience of Him during this time?"

"He was there. In a strange way, I sensed His presence," she immediately responded. "But I must tell you—He is the only One I can trust. I can trust no one else now. Not my husband, not my children, not ..."

I knew she meant me as well.

I told her that hundreds of people had been praying for her and even reminded her of a dream she'd told me about after her first "mild" interrogation over a year before. At that time, her voice over the phone had been strong. There, she'd seen hundreds of people on their knees for her. She couldn't remember that but seemed to revive momentarily and whispered, "Well, I wasn't alone."

She lit yet another cigarette. "My psychiatrist said I should keep smoking, that they soothe me."

"Go ahead and smoke," I said. "What about other medications?"

"Oh, in the hospital, they drugged me up so badly that I got really bad. I couldn't really sleep, but at the same time couldn't open my eyes. I tried to get up off the bed, but couldn't do it, couldn't walk. I could hear the sounds of moaning and screaming from the other patients in the ward; the screaming of patients being hit by the male nurses, and all I could do was lie there and do nothing."

"When was this?" I asked.

"In the psychiatric hospital. They sent me from the place where they were questioning me to a psychiatric hospital, a place worse than any place on earth. Those men who had questioned me had wanted me to denounce all the people whose names were in the notebook. Although I didn't know most of them, honestly I had reached my limit and was ready to say and do anything to stop the nightmare.

"Then, suddenly, I lost the ability to speak coherently and started to babble. I couldn't speak an understandable syllable. Something snapped, I guess. I don't remember. Because the next thing I know, I'm lying strapped to a bed in some insane asylum.

"Nathan, at first, couldn't get in touch with me, then they wouldn't release me from the hospital. I don't know what he did, what he signed, what he had to pay, but after some weeks—I don't really know how many—he got me released out of there to a private clinic in Istanbul."

I wondered then if that wasn't the reason that their house had been put up for rent. Nathan told me earlier that day that he had sold their car in order to try to pay off the local police chief, an extortionist who'd said that more money, 100 billion Turkish lira (US$60,000), was needed to get the worst of Ankara's charges dropped. After getting his payoff, he returned to extort more: "You people are loaded with your foreigner friend contacts," he'd hissed. That had all happened over a year before, when the military had first begun the harassment procedures—before the association-related charges had begun in earnest.

I forced my attention back on Ann, who continued speaking in a soft, dull-sounding voice: "That's where my psychiatrists are from. They saw that the dosage of sedatives was way too strong and changed my medication immediately. After that, I began to feel slightly better. They said the drugs had caused me to retain water in my head and in my inner ear, so that I suffered constant vertigo. I've lost lots of my memory of people and events."

"Did you know who I was when I called today?"

"Yes, and I knew Bill, but, for instance, I don't remember who Brianna is [Bill's wife]. She phoned to come for a visit and I didn't want to see her—I don't know who she is. It makes me very, very nervous to have to see people I don't remember."

"Do you remember Ken?"

"No, who is he?"

"My husband. He makes the wheelchairs you bought. You drove us around Trabzon, and we stayed with you and went on picnics with you in the village."

"Like I said, I don't remember these people. I don't remember any such picnic ... but I am starting to remember what those men said and did ... and I don't want to remember that. I want to forget. I want to die...."

Again her voice trailed off, and she stared blankly out the window of the second-story café we were sitting in. Then she turned her head and focused.

"They know everything about us, about you," she said. "No place is safe. We are living a lie here. Nathan tries his hardest not to let on to any of our old friends what has happened to me. At work, he's no longer the director, and they tried to get him to resign from the job all together but after forced 'sick leave,' he's back and has opened a case against the government for full pension privileges when he retires next year. They're trying to steal that from us as well." She paused and sighed. "Who knows, though, what he's really up to or what he's agreed to.

"The government is closing the local port authority [Nathan's post] and moving all operations to Istanbul. We'll go there and move in with our daughters. There, I will try to forget. There, I will do what I want to do—which is NOTHING. No more people, no more helping people, no more nothing. My life is over and I pray daily to die."

I tried to get her attention again. "Whether you trust me or not isn't really important, Ann. You have gone through hell. But try to think about the ways that your husband has stuck by you. You and I know of other women who've been accused and abused, whose husbands would not bother to let them back into the house, who would be so unloving that they'd run from their wives as if they had the plague."

I detected a flicker of assent in her eyes; she slowly nodded and said, "Yes, that's true."

More silence, another cigarette, another glass of tea.

"You know, Norita, I used to read about how the secret police would torture political prisoners after the military coup during the '80s—about the thousands who have disappeared over the years. You know, the stories of sexual abuse and electric prods to the body ..." She paused to look me straight in the eye. "It's all true. I KNOW that's true."

/////

I could not sleep for several days, or at best, my nighttime hours were spent restlessly tossing. My friend had suffered so much.

"Oh, Father, have mercy and bring her back from the land of the walking dead and to life, in Jesus's name."

CHAPTER 30

The Eviction Notice

For in the day of trouble he will keep me safe in his dwelling; he will hide me in the shelter of his sacred tent and set me high upon a rock.
Psalm 27:5

May 12, 2004

Meryem and Nina were eating breakfast when the doorbell rang. This time, there were two people standing there, a woman and a man. The woman in a brown-and-white striped suit held a large envelope.

"You are now living in government property and must vacate the premises by the end of the month," her partner spoke out with introduction or greeting.

Stunned, Meryem took the envelope and opened it to find a court order evicting the current residents of the apartment. She looked up to see the couple of messengers walking down the hall to the front gate.

"Wait, wait!" Meryem called. "What is this about? This is our home. We don't have another home. What are you talking about?" She started to cry.

"Phone the treasury office and they'll give you the details. Our job is just to pass on documents. Good-bye. Sorry." And they left as quickly as they could.

They phoned me, and Nina and I went to see a lawyer. Mr. Hemet told us what his fees were, and after we agreed we needed his services, he went down to the Department of the Treasury and managed to get a stay-of-eviction for a couple months.

"The apartment will go up for public auction in a few months," Mr. Hemet said. "If you want to stay there, you are going to need to buy it through the auction. I'll help you get it at a reasonable price. I have my connections."

"But what happened?" I asked. "How could a place we spent $40,000 on suddenly be taken by the Department of the Treasury?" I thought I knew but still wanted him to explain it again. It was still very confusing and complicated, and Nina wasn't really able to take in the details.

"Well, you and your board of directors here bought the place in the name of your organization. Too bad you did that. It would have been much better if you'd bought the place in Nina's name, since she was going to live there. Didn't you ask for advice about this before buying it?"

"Yes," I answered in frustration. "But the donors were foreign and would not agree to buying property in the name of an individual. It was given with the requirement that it be bought in an association's name."

"Well, the Turkish law says quite clearly that when an association is disbanded, all assets are to be considered government property—so, anything in the association bank account or any property. Your board of directors would have known that. Were you a member of the board then?"

"No, all the administration of the association had been transferred to a woman who lives up in the Black Sea region, and to expedite matters, she formed a new board of directors from acquaintances of hers there. They disbanded everything last spring, and I've not heard from her since March, when I went up to see her. She was not well psychologically, and I think the others did the paperwork and wanted this whole organization thing out of their hair as quickly as possible. They didn't think about how that would affect Nina and those of us here in Ankara, however."

He was confident that we'd be able to buy the flat back and be secure in no time. He spoke to me in a sort of code talk, making it quite clear he thought that since I was an American running this charity, then I had plenty of money in my back pocket. He figured this would be no problem. In this country, anyone who runs a charitable organization generally does so as a volunteer and tends to come from a very well-heeled family. The idea of a nonprofit organization as it is currently understood in Europe or the US is one only now being introduced in expectation of European Union participation.

Mr. Hemet said, "You will need at least $15,000 to enter the auction. It's the starting price the office has set."

Nina, as well, was unaware of my financial situation. "Well, are we going to be able to do this? To buy the place back? Where else can I go? Where will my sister go? Or Harry? Or Manny, for that matter? Maybe I should never have left the rest home system?" She was in turmoil and speaking out her anxious confused thoughts.

"I don't know how we're going to solve this problem, Nina, but God has not brought us this far to let us be thrown out into the street. He has a solution. You know that. We will pray and trust Him.

"I will write everyone I know. You tell everyone you know, and God will place this on somebody's heart as a need and help us—just like He did the first time when Kardelen was able to buy the place. I don't even know who donated the money three years ago. Remember, my friend Helen, who'd visited us several months before, had phoned out of the blue to say she knew someone who wanted to give us money, and voila, we were able to buy this place for you to stay—and just when you needed to get out of that hellhole in Hot Springs." I spoke confidently, sensing my shaky faith building again. I recalled the marvelous way an anonymous donor had supplied the $40,000 practically overnight. God would have to do it again.

Soon money from donors like Cindy from Dallas came in when they heard about the emergency need. Cindy had come with her kids and mother-in-law the year before and visited with Nina and her family in the home. She'd been impressed with their love and faith.

In the end, enough was collected to be able to enter the auction. Nina phoned Mr. Hemet to tell him to enter her name with the official paperwork.

But Mr. Hemet was nowhere to be found. He did not return her phone calls or mine. Meryem phoned around until she could learn when the auction would be taking place. She discovered that the sale would take place in less than two weeks!

Aware that neither of us was savvy when it came to government affairs, Nina phoned Anthony, a businessman friend who had considerable experience in real estate and public auctions. She asked him to help her get to the correct office and navigate the auction procedure.

"Nina," Anthony said. "You enter the auction at $15,000, but you can expect that you will need to offer considerably more than that to win. Figure at least $30,000 is what it will take to finish the deal."

Anthony agreed to send two of his assistants to meet her in front of the office on the morning of the auction. She phoned me with the news. When I looked into the bank account, I realized that we had just enough to enter the auction, so I gave her the go-ahead to try and bid.

The morning of the auction, we all arrived at the parking lot in front of the city office in time to send Nina off in her wheelchair into the auction. Anthony himself had shown up in his black Mercedes-Benz, along with his personal assistant, Terence. They lifted her up the stairwell to the second-floor office where the auction was to take place. Meryem would wait outside the room and do the necessary administrative running from office to office should the need arise. None of the rest of us were allowed into the actual room where the bids were being verbally offered.

I spent those minutes in prayer standing in a corner outside at the bottom of the entryway stairs.

A half an hour later, they all emerged, smiling.

"We've made the sale," Anthony said, but I could see that Nina was jittery—her nerves shot from the morning's activities. "But only by a narrow thread and the goodwill of the auctioneer."

"We got there at the office," Nina said, "and who should we see there wanting to buy the apartment? My upstairs neighbor. That really awful man from apartment 9—our accuser."

"No, you've got to be kidding," I said. "Not the one who physically roughed up Chris? Gee, that was three years ago when he threw the ramp they'd made out into the street."

"Yes, the very man," Nina said. "He'd come to bid on the apartment and obviously had a whole lot more money that we did." She could barely sit still in her chair.

"But these gentlemen …" She pointed to the men preparing to get into their sedan. "These guys whispered something in his ear, and he, for some reason, decided not to bid."

"What did they say?" I could see that these friends of hers were not the kind of people whom she would ever want to get on the bad side of—definitely distant cousins of Tony Soprano.

"I don't know, but probably something like, 'That flat is Nina's. Don't even think about trying to buy it.'" She was laughing now. "But there were other people who were there to bid for it too, and the official in charge, a sweet lady, heard my story, turned to the other bidders, and said, 'Who here is willing to have it on their conscience that they are going to deprive this disabled young woman and her sisters and brothers from having a home?'

"One by one, the people standing there all shook their heads and changed their minds. Finally she looked at me and Meryem and said, 'Congratulations. You are the winner. You now will own the home you live in.'"

As soon as Nina finished saying this, Meryem took off to sign the paperwork and get the money out of the bank to finalize the transaction. The Lord had provided a home for these, "His mighty little ones"—even using the ungodly to help secure the deal!

CHAPTER 31

By the Rivers of Babylon

Record my misery; list my tears on your scroll—are they not in your record? Then my enemies will turn back when I call for help.
Psalm 56:8-9

From my personal notes …

March 2009

The digital clock above the bus driver reads 4:30. A cobalt sky turns aqua as we travel up the steep highway on our way to the newly built international airport. We still have another ten miles to go when familiar landmarks cause my heart to beat faster.

We sail past the sign advertising Husain's Turkish Barbeque, and I can just catch a glimpse of the spanking new stone minaret and mosque next to the gas station and mini-market. Green neon lights encircle the parapet, where decades ago, the muezzin would call the faithful to prayer. I know that, not too many minutes before, the recorded wake-up call had sounded. Street lamps continue to light the way, one illuminating the yellow-and-black sign announcing the presence of "Saray: Rehabilitation and Care Center."

I sit up. I can just make out the walls and guardroom, the gate and parking lot where three buses are parked, and some of the buildings beyond. The next moment, we enter an underpass only to emerge about fifty yards past the campus. If you hadn't known it was there and what is was, you'd never have known that you'd just driven past an institution that housed several hundred children and young adults.

I sit back and let a tear fall. One after the other, memories flood my soul. Twelve years of relationship, incredible suffering, much disappointment, and, in contrast, amazing connections and joy, a new understanding of God and the meaning of the Incarnation, a deepened understanding of the meaning of faith and love. And countless after countless opportunities to exercise that faith and share that love.

How much has changed? What has changed? What has happened to the older ones I knew and loved? In danger of breaking into sobs, I quickly finger my passport and ticket and try to focus on the upcoming trip back to LA. I have to focus now on the future of the Kardelen outreach. But the past still calls me back to reflection and prayer. I remember Eric and Laurie.

/////

Five years earlier …

On a warm spring day, Kerri, our American volunteer, has come for a week of helping out. As she walks down the hall of D Block to CC1, she sees a blonde woman dressed in a navy-blue pantsuit. As they approach one another, the woman stops her.

"Do you speak English?" the woman asks Kerri in a distinct Brooklyn accent.

"Yes, I'm an American and volunteering here for a few days."

"Oh, wow, that is fantastic," the woman replied. "I'm Laurie. I work for a United Nations-connected group. My colleague and I have been visiting various institutions in this country. We were directed to Saray and have managed to be given the official tour today. I just slipped out of the beautiful physical therapy gym while the group was listening to a lecture by the director there. There weren't any children there, which, frankly, I find odd given the numbers of children housed here. But actually I wanted to try and see for myself what's going on behind these wooden doors."

Kerri pulled her aside and murmured into her ear, "Listen, I'm on my way to one of the wards where a group of local Turkish and foreign aid workers are involved. The realities of this place are beyond belief. Every time I come, it takes me days and days to get over what I've seen."

"I've been in some pretty horrific places in more than one country around the globe," Laurie answered. "Actually what we are seeking to do is investigate the real situations in places like this and then bring some official pressure to bear to get laws and policies to change. In fact, last month, we came out with a policy and proposal paper that has brought about some real positive change in the country of Paraguay."

"You need to talk to Norita, then, but first, let's see if we can slip into the Continuous Care Ward without causing anyone to send us away. We just have to say that we're Aisha's friends who've come to help out."

They managed to slip into CC1 for long enough for Laurie to take in the thirty-five kids lying there in their beds. Within fifteen minutes, she had been given the "alternate" tour and was able to slip back into the group at the administrator's office without anyone noticing that she'd made the rounds without one of their escorts.

That afternoon, I got a phone call from her, and we arranged to meet up at a restaurant downtown. She was with Eric, a human rights lawyer.

Although their successes were admirable, I got a bit uneasy. "Well, the exposé-type documentaries won't work here. At least three times since we've been working on this campus, some local journalist has smuggled himself in, taken photographs, then published a gut-wrenching story in the newspaper he could sell his story to. This is a country where the political parties love to make mileage by using the poor and the disabled for their own purposes and taking potshots at those in charge that hail from the opposing parties. It's always the same story with a different party in the driver's seat.

"The exposé usually runs like this: the article is published, and the story is featured on the news channel that backs up the current opposition party. There is an outcry. The fallout here is that some administrator gets chosen as the scapegoat and is transferred to another department and usually to another facility. Within a month, the whole incident is forgotten, except that we as volunteers are usually given stiff warnings about talking to journalists or taking pictures. It can get pretty disheartening."

"Hey, we get that," Eric replied. "This is not our plan for Turkey. We are partnering with a local charitable association. Their concern is for the care of psychiatric patients. Under their umbrella, we intend to meet with some of the higher-up government officials. One of the women on our board is a disability rights activist and politician in Michigan. She's been in the struggle for getting disabled kids into schools and access to basic care and training ever since the '60s. She is a mother with a profoundly developmentally disabled son. As a result of her tireless work, she effected law changes and opened court cases against her city to make sure that those laws were implemented. She is the expert on struggle and success. If everything goes as we plan, then she'll speak at a gathering of parents and officials. We want to involve as many people as we can in working toward change.

"With local input and our observations, we intend to publish a position paper and make concrete recommendations for needed policy and administrative changes.

"What we'd like to know from you is how you got involved and what you all do here and maybe interview some of your team members. Their insights could maybe give us direction in how we report things."

Over the next several days, Aisha, Nina, Laliye, and I told Laurie and Eric some of our stories. As I reflected on the differences between our first days at Saray to where we'd come, I was again reminded that the greatest changes that had occurred had taken place in our hearts.

"You know," I said to Eric and Laurie, "there are so many problems here, and the more training we got, the greater the burden to be change agents was, but at the same time, the more convinced we are that at the center of the problem is a worldview issue.

"When I first came face-to-face with these children, I was overwhelmed by the enormity of the neglect and abuse. First, I felt such pity and sadness, and the weight of those emotions paralyzed me. Then I felt anger; a certain energy came from that anger which at least motivated me to begin sharing the things I'd seen that first day.

"Those emotions motivated me to begin to act, but you will be left eventually in a desert of despair, growing numb to protect your vulnerable heart—just like the majority of staff here have become—unless you have God reach into your mind and heart to give you His perspective and the courage to persevere. Without the power of God changing her mentality, the most dedicated social worker can become burned out and then part of the problem rather than the solution.

"It is a massive social evil that can only be made truly right by deep personal change."

Five months later, Laurie and Eric returned to hold the special seminars. I listened with new understanding as they made the cogent point that people with disabilities in the USA began to be taken seriously and their rights and abilities honored as a direct result of the civil rights movement. Eric pointed out that the needs and rights of special children and adults were ignored and misunderstood, and that there was much institutional abuse in the USA up until the civil rights leaders not only pushing for the elimination of segregation but also challenging every infringement of previously ignored laws by going to court. With legal consequences potentially costing city and state governments millions of dollars, the new laws were implemented. So it was with disability rights, shared Dr. Elizabeth, speaking to a gathered group of parent associations as well as Department of Social Services officials.

Ironically the country of Turkey has an "Office of the Council on Disability," a department of the Office of the Prime Minister. My experience had been that one of the major purposes of this department was to create media events that would communicate the activities of the politicians in regards to the disabled. Government offices and ministries are all about the PR. They hosted this two-day event.

Although I was not officially invited, I showed up anyway. I detected a definite uneasiness when I greeted Mrs. Umra, who was representing the office in charge of orphanages and rehabilitation homes. We had not seen each other since we'd spoken over the treatment of the Hot Springs "exiles." Representing Saray were Mr. Mustapha and Mrs. Melissa. They nodded recognition when I waved at them from the other side of the large auditorium.

I was particularly thankful that I got to spend the afternoon talking to two mothers who had started their own charity to try to raise awareness about their children's conditions and about special education.

"People in this country see us as cursed, or if not that, then objects of pity. We love our children and want to see them get the best possible treatment and education possible, Mrs. Norita," Abide Ozkal told me. "I am afraid, though. What happens when I die and my daughter, Deniz, is left without someone to care or advocate for her? When I hear about the conditions out at Saray, I have nightmares. I don't want her to be sent there."

We talked all afternoon about what needed to happen and what steps needed to be taken to change public opinion and governmental policy. It only gave me more food for prayer.

That afternoon, I turned on the TV to CNN Turkey. There was Eric holding a press conference to outline the content of their newest report on the care of the mentally ill and mentally handicapped in Turkey.

With voice-over translation, he was speaking and holding up his hundred-page report. "My name is Eric Rosenthal. I am the director of the UN-affiliated organization, Mental Disability Rights International. In partnership with the local charity, Caring for Our Loved Ones, we have just concluded our yearlong research project where we have looked at the various patient care facilities in this country.

"We recognize that the challenge of providing quality care for so many patients is a daunting challenge, and so it is our sincere hope that our findings and recommendations will provide the necessary foundational support to administrators and policymakers for a better future for the weaker, dependent members of Turkey society. Thank you."

The next day—"SHAME—Saray Abuses Exposed"—was the first headline I saw when scanning the front page of *The Nationalist*. The second line read: "When is this type of abuse going to stop?"

Eric and Laurie's "Report on the Care Policies of the Turkish Republic" was filled with our testimony. The stories they heard, plus what Laurie had observed, had given more than enough material for this.

Once more, an official communiqué went out to make sure no foreign group would again have access to state institutions. Because I wasn't officially connected, I still managed from time to time to get onto the campus to talk to the directors. They would complain to me about how they had been embarrassed by the Americans who obviously didn't have a clue about the difficulties they were working with.

One unfortunate result of a knee-jerk uneducated response to the report affected the children and wards we worked in very specifically.

Back in 1999, Paula and Carol had facilitated the training seminars on the campus of Saray, and they had encouraged us to implement a technique to keep autistic children from auto-regurgitating (that behavior of self-stimulation of sticking one's hand or fist down one's throat whenever his/her hands were unbound). After we had begun untying the children who were bound in their beds all day long, we were horrified to see that many of them immediately stuck their hands down their throats and vomited whatever they'd just been fed. We could see that the overwhelmed staff had tied them up to keep them from doing this and other self-mutilating behavior.

What does one do when you have too many children to look after who are like this? While we prayed for more staff to come, we were stuck with this dilemma. Paula's solution, meant to be a temporary solution until there were enough caregivers to do more one-on-one caregiving, was to use water bottles to prevent this behavior. We'd cut off the tops, poke holes in the bottoms of them to give some air, and put little marbles or buttons in them to keep the child's fingers moving and aiding in distraction. We'd then use packing tape to affix the plastic bottles to their shirtsleeves.

When Laurie saw children with plastic bottles taped to their arms, essentially limiting their hand use, she was horrified. It looked so backward and barbaric. In her report, she particularly focused on what she'd seen in CC1.

Now months later, her written words were thrown back at us as if we had brought shame onto the ward by bringing in this barbaric practice. What they failed to mention was that, had we not done that, those children's hands would have been tied to the railings. And they would have spent their days flat on their backs in the cribs.

But the next thing we knew, a directive was sent from the main office: "We have prepared more humane and less offensive-looking hand constraints." Laliye couldn't believe what she was seeing. Rejab, one of the young boys who always managed to get his hands, socks, diapers, you name it, down his throat, now was sitting in his crib with two heavy, hard-plastic, mitten-shaped gloves taped to his pajama sleeves. He was obviously unhappy and kept hurting himself when he'd lift his hand, knocking and bruising himself with his plastic mitten. He was already sporting several black-and-blue spots on his forehead and cheek.

We were told in no uncertain terms that this directive was from the highest office and not to tamper with the children wearing the mittens. After that, whenever we could, we would try to take some of them outside and do as much one-on-one play time to distract them as much as possible. But there were too many kids like this; all the needy children in the beds were overwhelming us actually.

Then we heard that D Block was to be completely razed to the ground and give way to smaller living quarters for fifteen to eighteen children. We were thrilled that the large wards were going to be taken apart and the children be given a much higher caregiver/patient ratio.

The only problem was that while some wards were dismantled and children moved out, we witnessed the sad fact that these children were sent away to newly opened rest homes hundreds of miles from Ankara. We were left with questions. Would those kids be treated well? Who had trained these new caregivers in good practice? What could we do to ensure that abuse was not going to be carried on in these out-of-the-way institutions?

As the months went by, from time to time we would hear stories about the new places: some positive, but most negative. All of the children we had spent so many hours lovingly caring for and who had been transferred had died within one month of their transfers. Our hearts were broken again.

We turned our focus to the newly formed wards.

A college friend of mine, Jim, who had been working in Latin American for several years, recently got reconnected with Ken and me. He had some vital things to teach us about managing teams of social workers and ended up working with me and the board of Friends of Kardelen until we came up with a workable, effective program.

We changed our strategy, and instead of having our own room to which we could bring kids—after all, this program had been nixed by the administration in 2005—we decided to create "Happy Corners" in the larger wards. Here we worked with one or two kids at a time, playing, feeding, massaging. At certain times during the day, our team joined in the normal ward activities by helping the hired personnel with the changing and feeding. We received permission from the administrators to put up a couple of temporary walls and then carry on as before. In addition to a new program of providing afternoon fruit and yogurt snacks for all the wards our teams were working in, this made us desirable again. Dahlia, Sherifa's sister, set up her own little school room in a small room next to the SPASTIC ward and spent time with Hussein, Dilara, and John-Sue teaching them the basics of reading and number recognition. Zeynep and Sherifa had their corner built up in Continuous Care Two where they helped out during feeding times as well as taking the littlest ones onto their laps for special one-on-one times. They were especially able to provide time out of their beds for Mehmet, Emin, Eliza and Nagihan.

Our Kardelen Team was soon busy buying, preparing, and delivering the afternoon snacks, as well as organizing ward birthday parties. While not able to monitor every ward, we made the greatest difference in the places where we were allowed and where we could continue to model what love looks like when you serve the least of the least.

I was happily directing the team and spending time communicating with friends in the States and Europe in order to raise money for the on-site projects. We assumed a new level of normalcy, and day-to-day work proceeded without upset. Then something happened that shattered us all.

CHAPTER 32

Chaos, Mayhem, and Murder

... the world was not worthy of them....
Hebrews 11:38

It was the 17th of April, the year 2007.

I had been able to bring an American friend, twenty-eight-year-old Jennie, who was living in Ankara, out to Saray and introduce her to the team as well as some of the administrators. She was considering coming out regularly and needed to fill out an application form and be interviewed to qualify for "Volunteer Mother" status. After a busy day meeting people and going from office to office on the campus, we were returning into town in her car. Her mobile phone rang, and before thinking much about it, she answered it. Within seconds, Jennie cried out, "Nooooo! No, this can't be. Oh my God! ... No, I had no idea. Thank you for your thoughts. I'll phone you later when I learn more."

And she switched off her phone.

"Norita, something horrific has happened in Malatya. That was Imren, a girl I knew when I lived in Izmir. She knows I am a Christian and came with me a couple of times to Pastor Zekai's church. She says that she just heard on the news that our friends from the Malatya church have been murdered in their office. It's the latest, breaking news, like it happened only minutes ago."

"Oh no, oh no, oh no. I know so many of the people out there. They are our friends. Our church is supporting the work there."

I phoned Ken to tell him what we'd just heard. He phoned Pastor John, who was crying when he answered.

"Yes, they've murdered Necati and Uğur and Tilmann. Gokhan and Ozge would have been killed too but were spared. I am getting in my car as we speak and driving with Soner [another of the elders] to Malatya right now. This is unbelievably horrible and wrong."

Ken phoned me back to tell me, and we decided to call a prayer meeting at Liberation Church.

As soon as I got home, I turned on the TV. There, in "breaking news" fashion, were the photos of my sweet brothers with the photos of the men who had been apprehended as they tried to escape. It was surreal. Why would anyone want to kill these godly and gentle men? Why? Why?

When Ken got home a few minutes later, we held each other and wept for some time, remembering the last time we'd seen Necati, how he'd been such a fearless evangelist and how he loved to go to villages, gather a group around him, and share the stories of Jesus from the *Injil*. He'd told us a few months before that there are thousands of villages in the east that are full of people who are sick of religious hypocrisy and are hungry for the truth of Jesus. *Of all the people who had been cut down, why him, Lord? Oh poor Shemsa. How will she cope without her husband? What about her two small children? How will they survive?*

Tilmann was a soft-spoken theologian who loved music and to teach the Bible. Although he wasn't Turkish, he still was considered more at home in that eastern town than the majority of other believers who lived and worked out there. Now his wife and three children were without a dad.

We didn't know Uğur, but had heard about him. Those who knew him said that he was passionate and direct, that he loved Jesus and he loved Melosh, his fiancée. They had planned to marry the following summer.

That night as we held a vigil, worshipped, and asked each other what was going on, we were accosted by journalists outside the door clamoring for statements.

We soon learned more of the gruesome details. Five men who had been coming off and on to the Sunday afternoon church meetings, and who claimed to be interested in becoming Christians, had made an appointment that Tuesday morning to meet at the church bookstore and office to "learn more about the faith." Necati, Uğur, and Tilmann were there on time, but another staff couple, Gokhan and Ozge, were running late and had not arrived when the "seekers" showed up.

Immediately they grabbed the Christians and began shouting at them, threatening execution for leaving Islam.

Then they began to beat the prisoners. One of them noticed that the door was not locked, so he got up and bolted it shut. Then they took their knives and started stabbing Necati, moving on to the other two quickly.

Not two or three minutes later, Gokhan and Ozge arrived to find the front door of the office locked. They knocked, but when no one opened it and when they heard the sounds of crying and shouting inside, Gokhan phoned Uğur.

From within the room with the attackers, Uğur answered his phone abruptly: "The meeting is changed. It's at the Apricot Town Hotel on Ataturk Boulevard. Go there."

Again Gokhan heard what he thought was the sound of sobbing in the background. When he hung up, he immediately phoned the police.

Within ten minutes, they arrived and broke down the door. As they did, the attackers tried to flee through the balcony window. After a struggle, all but one were caught there. The fifth assassin fell three floors onto the concrete alleyway and was immobilized with a broken leg.

Gokhan followed the police into the office to the horrific sight of his three friends with their throats slit and covered in blood. Later he learned a couple of them had more than thirty knife wounds each. By answering Gokhan's call, then, Uğur had helped to save the lives of both Gokhan and Ozge.

He and Ozge collapsed into each other's arms and began sobbing. Some of the police thought that they had been part of the murder squad and wrongly rousted them at that point, and they, too, were taken into the police station. Only two hours later and after much interrogation were they released.

Gokhan and Ozge eventually moved back to Ankara to try to pick up their lives. Ken and I spent time talking and praying with them as they tried to come to terms with all the terrible losses. They were angry about the heinous way the wolves in sheep's clothing had devastated the lives of so many of their friends and were genuinely hoping the court and police system would in a speedy and fair manner bring the murderers to justice.

Some of our coworkers, neighbors, and friends showed incredible sensitivity and outrage at what had taken place to our fellow Christians.

For days, we were all getting emails or telephone calls from enlightened Turkish friends offering their condolences and expressing the shame they felt that Turks had done such a thing. Out at Saray, one or two of the administrators were embarrassed about the murders, particularly at the murder of Tilmann, who was a foreigner.

We were shocked again when, some months later, a dearly loved Catholic priest was shot dead in a small church in Trabzon, a city on the Black Sea. The perpetrator was a teenager who later was clearly identified as a member of an ultranationalist society. Their core beliefs were not so different from other significant segments of the population at large: "Turkey is a Muslim country. True Turks are Muslims. Death to Christians and missionaries and ethnic minorities. Death to anyone trying to destroy this wonderful Turkish republic of Mustafa Kemal from the inside out!"

Again our hearts were broken; again we and our staff and church group were traumatized. Pastor John, his wife, and their twelve- and eight-year-old daughters were living on the edge of terror. It was clear that Christians were being targeted.

Nina and Harry phoned me the next day and asked if we could meet in some quiet place to talk. They were terrified and confused, wondering how a powerful God could allow such horrors to come to His chosen ones.

"You should have seen the looks on our neighbors' faces this morning when we left to come here!" Nina's voice quivered. "It's as if they are plotting something against us too. They know we are part of the church. They think the guys in Malatya deserved it for deserting Islam. My neighbor upstairs said as much as he passed us in the hall."

Harry looked at me and his sister with a look I'd never seen before. Normally this young man was fearless. When he'd been detained on one of their trips to the Hot Springs rest home by local police and questioned about missionary activity, he'd come back calm and relatively unruffled in comparison to Nina's fearful crying. But here he was suddenly in a new place. Now all the threats and interrogations had taken on a new weight.

"This is horrible," he whispered.

"It is horrible," I said. "And it beggars belief. These men were the most peace-loving and friendliest men I have ever known. They wouldn't hurt anyone and they were not political—at all. So sad … so tragic."

I poured out my own questions too as we held hands. After several minutes, we began to cry out to God, giving Him our hearts' questions and feelings.

After a period of silence: "Oh Jesus, Jesus!" Nina's cry changed in tone. "I have just seen Him on the cross." She began to relate her vision: "Tears are flowing from His eyes and sprinkling on a meadow where they are turning into little lambs, skipping and frolicking as the new lambs of spring do. Three of these lambs have a blood mark on their backs, like you see the lamb sellers put paint markers on the backs of lambs to be sold for the Feast of Sacrifices. They are jumping, though, and as I watched, they skipped through a gate before the other lambs. It was beautiful, and there was no evil there in this picture; no fear left there." She smiled through her tears.

I bowed my head and thanked Jesus for this vision. Jesus knew. Jesus led the way. Jesus's suffering was so that many could enter into heavens spotless and without sin. Necati, Uğur, and Tilmann were with Him and were now free of all pain. The comfort from the Holy Spirit was strong and tangible there: "the world was not worthy of them."

CHAPTER 33

Season's End

There is a time for everything, and a season for every activity under the heavens: a time to be born and a time to die, a time to plant and a time to uproot ... a time to tear down and a time to build.

Ecclesiastes 3:1-3

Life eventually moved into another phase of "normal." We continued working with the children and adults living at Saray. I now spent the majority of my time facilitating the on-site workers by regularly meeting for prayer and to evaluate their projects. Every one of the Kardelen workers had begun to take on board the idea that their work was valuable enough to measure, so we now organized and managed projects.

Aisha and Gul and Songul had asked for permission to use the empty dark room we named the Sneuzel Room. The Dutch have developed a space to be used in special education for kids with developmental disabilities and autism, where all the various senses are stimulated separately. While Aysel Hanim, the education specialist at Saray, had heard about this, she'd never actually seen it in action.

Our team worked with three children to help them come out of their alienated emotional worlds and start to respond to stimuli. Aysel eventually saw the change in one ten-year-old girl who would never allow anyone to touch her without kicking and hitting and who regularly banged her head on the wall. This little one names Elif noticeably calmed down, paid attention to the mirror in the room and even allowed Guliya to hold her in her lap and play clapping games. Aysel, the professional, could only shake her head and say, "This is a miracle. What you have done with her is tremendous. If only everyone who worked here would have the same dedication and motivation to work with these kids in such a purposeful and effective way."

We were encouraged by this response but also saw that her level of frustration with the system increased. Now she had learned just what could be accomplished for and with the kids. Before this new understanding hit, it was easier to deal with a view that the children could never improve, and therefore they simply needed to be cared for, much like potted plants, rather than do the hard work of convincing and educating other staff.

We all knew that the real powers needed to see this kind of change and to understand what it takes to truly bring humane treatment and long-term changes in behavior and treatment. This is the case world over where government officials adopt policies on the basis of cost effectiveness and vague ideas of social reform and political correctness, rather than regularly listening, watching, and studying what is actually effective and sustainable.

By this time we had come to the conclusion that our calling was not to change the political structure or system. At times excruciating, we nonetheless tried to ignore the inherent systemic problems and instead told ourselves repeatedly, "We are here for Mehmet, Ahmet, Gulistan, Hasan, Behide, Elif, and Little Mohammed, for Ali-John, so help us God."

/////

November 28, 2008

I woke to the phone ringing off the hook.

"Did you have a chance to look at today's newspaper?" Karin's voice was shrill with alarm. "Some British journalists have made a film about Saray. It exposes everything. Your name's in the paper too."

An hour later, Aisha phoned. She was crying. I could hear other voices rising in the background. Zeynep's. Gul's, Sharifa's, Dahlia's. They were sobbing.

"We have been accused of bringing TV crews and journalists to Saray," Aisha said through her tears. "We have no idea what they are talking about, but everyone here is looking at us like we are the world's biggest traitors. We've been summoned one by one to the administration office." Aisha's voice sounded shrill with pain and outrage. "I just got back from Mrs. Melissa's and Mr. Mustapha's offices. They handed me signed letters from the Ministry of Social Services saying that I have repeatedly acted independently and in ways that have been in opposition to the policies of the Turkish Social Services Ministry; that I have brought people onto this campus without permission.

"You should have heard the assistant directors today. I couldn't believe my ears. They were accusing us of all kinds of stuff that made no sense, and they told us to make sure that our foreign 'friends' were clear that any television program broadcasted in the U.K. which showed scenes from Saray, would lead the way to serious international consequences between our nations. Norita, what ... what ... what are they talking about?"

Next Nina called to ask me to phone England and beg the TV journalists there to stop the program from going out, knowing that if it were released, her life would be in danger. "Norita, the police picked me up downtown, forced me into their car, drove me to Saray, and took me to a back room. There, they told me that I was a traitor to Turkey, and that if I really cared about my country, I would get on the news program and denounce you as someone who hates Turks and has been using me in order to bring shame on the government agencies. It was so awful, and I kept saying that this was not true, but they kept shouting at me. Finally I started crying so hard that I couldn't get my breath and sort of passed out. They wheeled me back to their car and took me back into town, and when they dropped me off on the side of the road, they told me that I'd better contact these TV people and get them to stop the program or I'd be in big trouble. Please, please, PLEASE phone the duchess and tell her to stop the program."

That evening on the seven o'clock news, I learned that I had inadvertently involved all the Kardelen workers in a scandal. On every news channel, people were being stopped on the street and asked what they thought about this recent "slandering" of the Turkish state for the sake of the disabled. Some replied that they were incensed that Turkey had been shamed like this; others, however, spoke openly that they were glad that the hidden "dirty laundry" of the state was being aired.

That morning's local newspapers were full of pictures of the journalists from Great Britain who had secretly filmed at the orphanage over the weekend two months ago. There were also pictures of children who were tied up to a bench and/or lying on the floor or in cribs. A cameraman had managed to get himself behind one of the doors where even we as Kardelen workers had never been. What was depicted in that footage taken with a concealed camera was terribly disturbing, but everyone seemed to be saying that the really terrible thing was that these horrors were now going to be broadcast on British TV and that this was an affront to the Turkish Republic.

I whispered to my open paper: "If only you had seen 'our' rooms twelve years ago."

Then I wrote Chris and Sarah emails telling them what had happened to us and asking if they could help some way. I told them that if I had known that the outcome of letting myself be interviewed for an ITV news program was going to result in our ejection from Saray, I never would have accepted in the first place ...

/////

One Month Earlier: October 2008

"Am I speaking with Norita Erickson?" the man on the other end asked in a refined British accent.

"Yes," I said.

"My name is Chris Rogers and I'm a journalist who has been working for the past four years on the treatment of children and young adults with disabilities who are housed in orphanages. I've been doing loads of work in Romania and have recently been told by some mutual friends of ours that you have a work in Turkey among this same special group. May we come out to Ankara to interview you and hear your story?"

I asked what the purpose of his program would be and told him frankly that Kardelen was a charity, that we worked in the state-run orphanage and as such had no official status there, nor official clout. I told him that we ran our program on the basis of donations from local as well foreign donations. "Do you think that such a program could help us generate support for the on-site programs we run?" I asked.

"Oh, well, we can't guarantee any financial support for your work, but I will have a celebrity person coming with me to interview you. She has a foundation, which helps programs in Romania. It would be great to see what emerges from this program."

"Let me pray about it, Chris. Would you give me a day or two to think about this?"

"Sure," he replied. "But actually we'd really like to be able to visit the place you are working in. Could you get us an invitation?"

"Actually, no," I answered quickly. "You must go through official channels to get permission to visit. I haven't been successful for the past four years in getting people from outside the country into Saray, but maybe that's because someone in the main office doesn't want anyone connected with me to come in, or maybe because the requests have been from Americans. I don't really know, but you must apply at the Office of the Social Services Ministry's 'Office of Public Relations and European Union Contacts.' You'll need to send in a request in English and Turkish and state your reasons for wanting to visit and the dates you want to come. But I can tell you right now that they do NOT let journalists, even local ones, come for visits—and it is definitely forbidden to take photos or film unless you are working WITH a government official.

"The only photographs or footage I've seen from there for the past five or more years are those taken by the present mayor of Ankara. He's actually come onto the campus when we were hosting a birthday party and had his cameramen film him hugging one of the children and saying on his television station that he'd sponsored the event."

"Yeah," Chris responded. "That's the kind of stuff politicians do the world over. It's disgusting and outright hypocritical. Great fodder for us journalists, though."

After we hung up, I asked the Lord what I should do with this request. A calm peace entered my heart, and I knew that I was to give this interview and perhaps be able to tell British audiences that God cares about the abandoned so much that He commissions us, His children, to go and make a difference. I wanted to tell the story of the beginnings of our work, and how much we had been changed, and how much quiet but sure change had been accomplished.

A couple of days later when Chris phoned again, I told him I would meet with him and his crew, but with the request that I be able to tell the "God part" of the story too. "It was a vision and the clear call of the Holy Spirit that propelled us into that place and this work, and it would be dishonoring to God to leave that out of the story," I stated.

"Fine, no problem. Please tell your story. We'll be there in one week, then," he hurried on. "I'll give you a call on Saturday or Sunday and tell you where we're to meet."

The following Sunday morning, he phoned again. "We're here, staying at the Sheraton Hotel. Can you come over around 11:00 a.m. and we'll interview you in the garden behind the building? Also, do you think any of your staff would be available to be interviewed?"

I told him that all of my staff at Saray were very careful about their work and worked long and hard AGAINST getting their names, faces, or stories out in the local news, and I was sure they would not agree to being interviewed—even though the program was going to be aired in the UK and not Turkey.

"Well, it would be so much more powerful if we could talk to someone who was Turkish about this."

After a moment, I mentioned that maybe Nina—who no longer lived in Saray but was now a fellow team member out in the community of Ankara—might be willing to share her story.

Nina agreed. She and her brother Harry said they would come to the hotel around noon and be interviewed separately.

The following Sunday, I walked into the lobby of the Sheraton where Chris, the show producer, Hannah, and the rest of the camera and sound crew were. After a few minutes, we walked outside to sit at a table while they set up the cameras and we waited for the "celebrity" who I had just learned was Sarah Ferguson, the Duchess of York. She was there with her two daughters, Beatrice and Eugenie.

"She's an amazingly compassion and good person, Norita," Chris said, obviously star struck. "You shouldn't form judgments about her from the British press. She's not like they portray her. Maybe she'll be willing to arrange for a donation once she's heard your story."

I refrained from telling him that although I knew who she was—who doesn't in this world of paparazzi and British royalty stories?—I had no opinions about her at all. As far as I was concerned, she was a person who apparently cared about the plight of poor and abandoned children and the disabled. That was enough of a recommendation for me.

Sarah rushed outside, with her long, red hair and polka-dotted flowing dress confirming the image I had of her from past TV appearances. We sat at the table and, after being wired for sound, began to chat like old friends. After a while, I ignored the crew, although I was always aware of four obvious Turkish "secret service-type" men and women who took up their positions on the perimeters of the film set. I didn't know if they worked for the hotel or for the TV station, but they were obviously there to protect or guard the celebrity.

After sharing the story of my first day at Saray, I talked about the process of crying out to God on behalf of the desperately suffering. After I told Chris and Sarah that the Lord had said, "You are weeping My tears," Sarah asked for the cameras to stop.

"So you believe that God weeps?" she whispered. When I nodded, she looked intensely into my face and continued quietly: "I do too."

When we resumed the interview, I was able to talk about all the various ways that we had been able to affect changes at Saray, small but effective changes meaning that the personnel were beginning to change in their attitudes, that the children were being honored through parties and through the one-on-one care we could give to kids in the hospital section as well as three of the four of the other wards.

"You are not going to edit out this stuff, are you, Chris?" I asked him at another filming break.

"No, of course not," he answered. "But we are going to need to get onto the campus some way. Is there nothing you can do to help us? We did what you said, applied for permission to enter for a visit. We told them that our contact would like to make some sort of donation and we hoped that they would facilitate a look-see. That was a week ago, but we haven't heard back from them."

"Not surprised," I said. "First of all, you are connecting with a bureaucratic monolith. Applications and petitions sometimes take months before they are dealt with. Second, you are asking to go in on a date that falls on a holiday. Nobody wants to show visitors around on a holiday. The director's probably gone anyway, so there will be substitute people in charge.

"Let me phone my assistant, Baybora, and ask if he can maybe make a personal call to the assistant director we have a good relationship with there. Maybe he'll be able to host something unofficial."

Twenty minutes later, I was able to tell Chris that he and Sarah were allowed to come onto the campus courtesy of our assistant director friend. He would be happy to meet them in his office and introduce them to the campus and probably also be able to give some suggestions of possible items that could be donated.

In the meantime, Nina and Harry had arrived and were preparing to be interviewed by the duchess and her beautiful eighteen-year-old daughter, Eugenie. I rushed over and served as translator for my friend. It turned out to be a bit of a difficult discussion. Old, painful memories resurfaced during the course of the interview, and more than once, Nina asked that she not have to talk about things she'd experienced. What she revealed about institution life for the disabled was pretty damaging, and it was clear that life in any institution was often fraught with danger, violence, and injustice. We were all in tears at points during the filming. The last section of the interview focused on Nina's current work with young people and children who are specially challenged and living in poverty in the backwater neighborhoods of the city of Ankara.

The night before their visit to Saray, the duchess and Chris met up with Baybora and Banu, Kardelen's administrator and bookkeeper, at the hotel they stayed at.

"She certainly looked different, actually quite silly," Baybora later told me about the duchess. "She'd put on a black wig and scarf. When we asked about this, Chris answered that the disguise was for her security. I accepted that and the fact that there was a third guy with them, a John something, whom I assumed was her bodyguard.

"We drove onto the campus in my little Fiat and told the guards at the front gate that Mr. Murat was expecting us. After they called through to confirm this, we were told to park our car and walk over to his office in C Block. We spent about fifteen minutes talking with him. They asked him questions about Saray. He asked them about their charity. We drank tea. After we asked for permission to tour a few of the wards, he stood up, shook our hands, and thanked them for their interest. He told me to tell the guards to let him know when we'd left the campus and bid us good-bye.

"We walked down through the 'Labyrinth' and into the Spastic Unit, and they were confronted with scenes of children lying on the ground or in a playpen, scenes of unattended children with severe special needs. It was extremely upsetting for the duchess and seemed to firm up her resolve to try to help bring more change into this arena. I explained that Kardelen had one worker in that ward who came every day during the week, took five of the children at a time, and worked with them in her special education room—a tiny room found in the back of the ward.

"'But one of your workers with all these thirty-five or so very needy children is not enough! There shouldn't be so many children living in these conditions. It's an outrage!' she said with passion. She was still quite upset when, a half an hour later, we drove out of the front gate.

"She said that she's going to get in touch with some of her friends doing some special education work among the poorest in Romania. She wants them to come here and talk to you, Norita. They might have some concrete suggestions about how to best serve these people."

Four days had not passed when I got an email from Becky, the director of a British/Romanian charity partially funded by Sarah Ferguson's foundation. She said that she'd heard from the duchess, and that Becky and her Romanian doctor colleague, Alex, would be in Ankara to meet up with me the following weekend.

We met up at a café, and I listened as they described the conditions of children with developmental disabilities, autism, and physical deformities who are housed in Romanian orphanages and how their charity had been given permission to start a family-based day-care center where special education training took place. Becky had adopted one of the boys who had been severely abused as a result of his autism. She showed me photos of him and a short video of their center.

They then listened as I told them about my experiences and our work's progress in the institution. They urged me to start a day-care/educational center and to get out of the institution.

"It's so overwhelming in such large places, Norita." Becky's clear, blue eyes bore into mine. "As long as the government houses large numbers of children in one place, there is never going to be the best type of care for them. They need family-type solutions and love. Consider starting your own place. Start small and keep it small, manageable with smaller numbers of children. The institution will swallow you up and drain you all of your energy before too long."

"Maybe, you can get some funding through the duchess's charity. I will most certainly put in a good word for you," Dr. Alex added.

This encouraging meeting was all too soon forgotten two weeks later when news of the actual TV program broke. John—the third person Baybora had thought was a bodyguard—turned out be a cameraman who had a concealed camera in his shoulder bag. Somehow he had gotten into rooms that even Baybora had not accompanied him to: rooms that showed children tied up to benches and workers sitting in the corner drinking tea, rooms that we as Kardelen had not been allowed into. John's footage featured prominently in the exposé, along with footage of the children on the floor or in playpens.

Chris and the producer, Hannah, had also invited the Turkish ambassador as well as the Romanian ambassador to the UK to view their program and then give their reactions to what they were seeing.

The Romanian ambassador's response was clear:

> "Romania is a nation undergoing change. Since its desire to be a fully contributing member of the European Community, Romania has begun dismantling institutions like orphanages where children have been housed for many years. We recognize that the scenes portrayed in this documentary indicate that we still have a long way to go in eradicating the kind of institutional abuse that has plagued our country for decades. We still have much work to do."

The Turkish ambassador was livid and immediately registered his outrage that foreigners had shown the audacity to come onto sovereign Turkish territory and film anything. He had nothing to say about the content of the show. He summoned to London the state minister in charge of social services in Ankara. She, in turn, put into motion an investigation about how such footage could have been taken and who was to blame for this public shaming. Someone smuggled out the news about the upcoming program along with some footage of kids being tied up, as well as the duchess in her disguise. Turkish officials now were in a race to try to create such a diplomatic uproar that the British government would put a stop to the showing of the program. Obviously the thinking was that the concept of freedom of speech was not applicable to the ruling powers and that the Brits would do what the Turkish official would do: squelch anything damning to government policies.

The program, without the interviews of Nina and myself—they honored my plea to remove our segments—was aired one week later. The Turkish ambassador held a press conference with the then British Prime Minister, Gordon Brown, in which they lodged a public complaint about their territorial sovereignty being impinged upon and that they were going to take the case up in the Hague and the international courts. The Turkish press secretary issued the following: "No country in the world recognizes such behavior as legal. These people have broken Turkish sovereign law by their audacious behavior. No comparable British institution would stand for such invasion of privacy. They will have to suffer the consequences. It is our opinion, as well, that this program is fraught with lies. They most likely spliced, edited, and fabricated scenes to vilify our great and compassionate nation."

Gordon Brown stated publicly that the television program was the work of independent journalists and that the Duchess of York was not representing the British people or government in her part. "It is our true hope that the European Community will fully embrace Turkey as a model of modernity, democracy, and economic stability in the Muslim world. It is our sincere wish that the relationship between our two countries will mean security and progress in the entire region."

Later that month, the Turkish government through Interpol issued a warrant for the arrest of Sarah, Chris, and John on charges of infringing on the privacy of children. Since the children were wards of the state and were dependents, their well-being was the responsibility of the government, and no one had asked the government officials if they could film. They formally lodged a request that Interpol hand these criminals over to Turkish authorities. This request was denied. Four years later as I write these words, the case is still open and every once in a while makes its way into the back pages of Turkish newspapers.

During the days of the scandal, Internet posts, as well as letters to the newspapers, revealed that there are many educated and thoughtful Turks who decried the barbarism inherent in the system and who are calling for immediate change and reform.

Saray became the hottest talk-show topic on Turkish television for a week. Internet posts and comments to the local newspapers pointed out how deeply ashamed the public felt. "Good for the Brits," one reader to *Radikal* wrote. "At least they are so courageous to say what our own officials are so quick to cover up. I am ashamed to be called a Turk when such terrible treatment of the weak is perpetuated day after day in institutions across the land. I can only hope that the people responsible for this so-called 'care' are thrashed within an inch of their lives."

Another wrote: "Injustice in Turkish orphanages? So what's new? Our newspapers have been exposing this kind of stuff for years. No one takes any notice. The people in charge get demoted, someone new comes to be the head, and then it's business as usual there. When people care more about money and their cushy government jobs than they do for serving the poor, then this is what you can expect. No one would have gotten so upset if it had been a Turkish TV program. A few heads would have rolled, true, but nothing new to report after that."

As days went by and the furor over this scandal died down and something new consumed the public's interest, the Kardelen Team hoped that gradually all the brouhaha at Saray would also blow over. In spite of an unofficial ban, the Kardelen workers kept taking the bus out to the orphanage and working in the wards. So far, no one at the front gate or the people responsible in their wards had stopped them, and all were continuing to benefit from the afternoon snacks and special education projects.

But two months later, this all changed.

/////

A new set of guards was installed, and when the 8:30 bus discharged the Kardelen Team at the front gate, all of our workers were told they had no permission to be on the grounds. With that, one of the black-capped security guards pointed to a poster on the wall. There for all to see were all our names in large black print with the following order:

THESE PEOPLE, BOTH FOREIGN AND NATIONAL, ARE BANNED FROM ENTERING THE PREMISES OF THIS INSTITUTION OR ANY OTHE GOVERNMENT-RUN REHABILITATION, REST HOME, OR EDUCATIONAL INSTITUTION. THIS BAN GOES INTO EFFECT MARCH 1, 2009.

Aisha could not believe her eyes when she read this and, pushing back the two armed guards who tried to block her, ran up into the director's office. When she asked him about this, he shook his head. "Your boss should have realized that she was causing you all so much harm by helping these foreign press people. There is absolutely nothing I can do. This directive has come from the highest office in the land. You have been truly and forever banned from working with us. Good-bye." And he got up and shut the door.

She was escorted to the gate, where she found the others from our team waiting, crying, in shock. Twelve years of blood, sweat, and tears, of bonding with so many children and young adults, with programs for feeding, bathing, partying—all dismissed in an instant.

Father, I cried. *How could I be so stupid? Was I so full of righteous anger that I effectively laid to waste all the years of work and "building"? Oh, have mercy on us. Full of ourselves, maybe even proud that "We're so more compassionate and merciful than the folk out there at Saray." Look what my muckraking soul created. If I'd been smarter and wiser, this never would have happened. I am responsible for this.*

Self-contempt and the accusations of friends as well as enemies left me in an emotional mess. I could hear my old friend Ann whispering in my ear: "You are the reason I've had my breakdown"—even though she'd never said it directly.

At the gate, Aisha and Derya gave me looks filled with pain and confusion. I had betrayed their trust. Maybe it was time to give this so-called call of God a rest and recognize that I was actually doing this to fulfill some need to be important and special.

What a miserable excuse for a human being you are. What a stupid woman.

/////

"Attention, attention, Turkish Airlines Flight 645 to New York is ready for boarding. Will all passengers kindly go to Gate 3B?"

Already seated in the waiting lounge, I automatically rechecked my boarding pass and passport in anticipation for the flight attendant's boarding announcement. In ten hours, I would be back in the USA, getting ready to go through the lengthy customs check and then waiting around for the connecting flight to LA. Our next Friends of Kardelen board meeting would take place the following day.

I glanced at the headlines of the newspaper thrown on the seat next to me: *CONSPIRACY TO OVERTHROW GOVERNMENT—'Retired generals, admirals, journalists and NGO heads' Caches of weapons unearthed. Shocking Allegations."*

On the flight, I read further, amazed at the scenario. The government had uncovered a long-standing group of nationalist military and journalists who had supposedly been creating a scare scenario in Turkey. Their primary target was the present Islamic-leaning government. According to the theory, if they made the Islamicists look like radical al-Qaeda-type Muslims, then the scene would be set for the secular nationalists to garner enough popular support to execute a coup in order to save the republic.

It looked like there was evidence that the murders of the Christians at the supposed hands of radical Muslims, as well as the vilifying of Christian missionaries, churches, and service organizations, had been part of a carefully planned conspiracy to foment an atmosphere of fear and one that would bring on a coup by the military to unseat the ruling party..

So EP's book, *In the Spider's Web*—his propaganda piece—was actually the brainchild of the conspirators. The security police were in on it. The judges were in on it. The military were in on it, and some of the press were in on it.

"That which was hidden will be shouted from the rooftops." I knew the Lord was bringing the truth out of the darkness. This was mercy. *What does it mean for Turkey's spiritual future?* I wondered.

I forced myself not to meditate on this at all but rather to think again about the conversations I'd had with Aisha, Nina, and Dahlia.

All three had been accused of treachery against the nation; had been interrogated as evil people before being taken home and told that they would be blackballed from other work. Both Aisha and Dahlia had applied to work as caregivers in a home for the elderly, a low-paying job often given to illegal immigrants from Moldavia. Both were rejected when their names came up as personae non grata in computer searches of the government files.

More than the inability to be hired at care facilities, their greatest heartache was missing those special children and the other staff with whom they'd made such deep and good relationships over the years. Twelve years of work over in a moment. Nina, too, while saved from imprisonment or worse, couldn't believe it was over. They all were heartbroken and grieving.

So was I.

I started to cry, my heart full of grief. As we winged our way over Greenland, my mind began to again reflect over the years at Saray and how much had actually changed. I remembered standing outside that place twelve years before and praying, "Lord, may every single one of these buildings be razed to the ground."

Just one month before my trip bulldozers had lumbered onto the campus and were in the process of destroying all the buildings there. The officials announced that they were going to build smaller, family-sized housing. Now, instead of forty children to a ward, there would be housing for twelve children, and each home would have a separate kitchen and laundry and bathing area. C Block, D Block, and all the former buildings—where so much suffering had been perpetrated behind closed wooden doors down labyrinthine corridors—were all going to be gone.

Perhaps the motivation was to destroy all evidence of the place so recently made a symbol of shame in the press. Perhaps administrators had been convinced that these children deserved better than cattle-like warehousing. Perhaps our example of setting up happy spaces in the wards and caring for children one on one or in small groups had been the reason for this new decision. Whatever the motivation, the outcome there would be better than it had before.

The personnel at the orphanage, the ones whom we worked next to when we were in the wards, were lamenting our absence. Gone were the birthday parties, the organized picnics, and the added help for bathing and changing the bedridden children. But I remembered just how very different it had been twelve years earlier when the personnel-to-child ratio had been even poorer.

We had cried out to God to have the government change their hiring policies and bring in more caregiver staff. Three years ago, this happened, with the numbers of caregivers increasing five times the numbers we had first come across. Granted, the new staff were untrained and junior-high graduates, but they were new and able to be influenced by staff that had been trained by our team. We still were getting phone calls asking for help in dealing with this or that child's situation.

The dietician had taken on board our suggestion for afternoon fruit and yogurt mini-meals and had implemented her own program for all the wards. We hoped that all the unit directors would follow through, and she assured us that she had clout and could enforce this program. Good news.

My greatest joy, however, during that flight home was being reminded of a prayer I had prayed more than once in the years of our service at Saray: "Lord, would You work in the hearts of mothers and fathers to do something that would mean that they wouldn't abandon their children to such an institution, but rather would have them keep them at home?" I knew that even if the people lived in a hovel of bricks and straw, a mother could be a better caregiver than someone who has no blood relation to the child.

Two years ago, I realized, the present political party had begun taking the numbers of disabled people and their families seriously. They realized that with 17 percent of the population being affected by some sort of physical or mental challenge, this was a huge constituency for their political ambitions. Here was a vast pool of voters whose families were ready to receive help in exchange for support. Undoubtedly there were those in the government who do care for the plight of the handicapped, as well. In any case, a new law and program was passed, which gave a small stipend to mothers of disabled kids or those caring for the disabled in their homes. In effect, what this meant was that those former "Cursed Ones" now could become a source of blessing, bringing income into the home just by being there.

Every time we cry out to the Lord, He hears and answers. Sometimes it takes days or months or years, but God is not deaf to our pleas nor is He slow or behind schedule. In the right time, he gives wisdom, or finance, or friends or new ideas to make a way forward and in so doing brings glory to himself and increase our faith.

As I thanked Him for all the help He'd given, all the protection and rescues He'd facilitated, I looked down on the white glacial fields of Greenland—vast and stunning testimonies to the power of a God whose creativity far exceeds our own. As I stood at the plane window gazing down from the sky, I heard a still small voice.

"Remember the three thousand families waiting to get their children into Saray?" the Lord whispered. "I want Kardelen to go to those families now. Find them; love them. They need to know that I am the Lord who loves and saves, the Lord who listens to the cries of His beloved. Cry out for the families now, and then share with them what you have seen. Your work is not finished here yet nor have I changed one bit. I am 'the One who was, who is and who is to come.' And I haven't gone away and left you."

I went back to my seat and wrote down my prayer of response.

"Dear Jesus, You are faithful and true. You know what it's like to be rejected, to be considered a blasphemer, a rabble-rouser, a false prophet. You gave up all your prerogatives as God to live in our skin, to know disability in a complete sense. They abused you on the cross. Your family totally didn't understand you. You were tested with psychological and emotional and physical torments but you never gave up. You, who for the joy that was set before you endured the cross (Hebrews 12:2) and you purchased for every tribe and tongue for every human being on the face of this planet the right to become your Beloved Son or Daughter. You have gone before and made a place for each of us in your Father's House.

You defeated Death and gave gifts and callings to men and women, boys and girls that you would be glorified and worshipped and that your glory could be shared. You are preparing one big, big party and feast, some day in the future at the end of all things. I am so glad my place is reserved, that Murat's place is reserved, that Gulistan is in the waiting room there with you.

So, where you lead me, I will follow and go with you, with you, all the way."

////

Since February 2009 the Kardelen Ministry has been serving those impacted by disabilities and their families in the Ankara province, in a village outside of Ankara, and in the residential facility near the Black Sea. While we as a team were ejected from Saray, we continue to raise the support for two care providers at the Black Sea institution. Our supported staff were threatened with ejection as well due to their relationship with us, but then the powers-that-be there realized they would be losing two highly motivated staff and reneged on their threats. Since our staff there have no official legal relationship with us, at this time their jobs are "secure." They have, however, in recent months been under tremendous pressure. Our one worker there, N. came upon an administrator beating a naked young man who has obviously severely disability. N. intervened to stop the abuse and that day was fired from her job. She phoned us and got the go-ahead to find a lawyer to appeal her case in court. The case continues to this day, but the residents of the home wrote and signed a secret petition testifying to N.'s stellar performance and caring heart. One of the staff smuggled it out to her lawyer who after presenting it to an incredulous judge was able to get N. re-instated at her job until the case is finally closed. It is the Lord's work, of this we are convinced. We continue to support her spiritually and materially, and through her those under her loving care.

We continue to cry out on behalf of our now large extended family across the nation of Turkey. Join with us in prayer. Every prayer spoken out in faith will produce fruit. Pray for us to not lose heart, nor to grow cold or deaf to the Holy Spirit. Pray for us to stay committed to standing with one another as we stand for the least of these in this nation.

We, as well, are aware that similar communities of those struggling with rejection as well as disability are found throughout the world. When Jesus calls us to cry out on their behalf, He starts to call out His Mercy Teams. Maybe He's calling you today. Say: "Yes, Lord, send me." And He will. And He won't leave you—ever.